Russia

1800-1914

PROBLEMS, ISSUES, SOURCES, SKILLS

PHILIP CUMMINS

A division of ...dline Australia

Hodder Education
A Division of Hodder Headline Australia
(a member of the Hodder Headline Group)
10-16 South St
Rydalmere   NSW   2116

First published by
Hodder Education in 1996
Reprinted 1998
©Philip Cummins 1996

National Library of Australia
Cataloguing-in-publication data

Cummins, Philip
Russia 1800 - 1914: Problems, Issues, Sources, Skills

ISBN 0 7336 0633 4

1. Russia - History - 1801 - 1917. 2. Russia - History -
1801 - 1917 - Sources. 3. Russia - History - 1801 - 1917 -
Problems, exercises, etc. I. Title.

947.07

Text and cover design by R. T. J. Klinkhamer
Edited by Brenda Pittard
Typeset in Sabon 10/12 Pt by Midland Typesetters, Victoria
Printed in Australia by Ligare Pty. Ltd. Riverwood, NSW

Contents

CHAPTER THREE

1855—1894 Reform and Repression

CHAPTER FOUR

1894—1914 Nicholas II—The Last of the Tsars

CHAPTER FIVE

Studying for the Exams

Preface

FOR THIS BOOK, I owe an enormous debt to three groups of people. My parents, Brian and Rohma Cummins, exposed me to historical tomes with wonderful pictures before I could read and have continued to indulge my passion for matters historical since then. My colleagues, Mark McAndrew, Greg Stone, David Thomas and Alan Jones, have taught me most of what I know about the practice of history and spelling, and have kept me honest. Finally, my wife Juliet, with whom all is possible. All three groups have put up with far more than they should have and far more than I can ever give in return.

This book has been designed to help Year 11 and 12 students learn effectively about the history of Russia from 1800-1914. The material has been tailored specifically to meet the requirements of the Preliminary Course and Higher School Certificate in Modern History in New South Wales.

History is fun, but only where the facts have a meaning to the reader. This book has been written so that students can enjoy the fabric of a remarkable period of history and go beyond the constraints of the syllabus to develop a genuine and personal passion for the people and past of a nation enormous in every aspect and sad in many.

There are five chapters in *Russia 1800-1914*. Chapter 1 defines and explains the nine problems and issues which are relevant to the course of nineteenth century European history. Chapter 2 deals with the nature of Russia at the start of the period and the reigns of Alexander I and Nicholas I . Chapter 3 covers the reigns of Alexander II and Alexander III with the program of brief reform followed by renewed repression. Chapter 4 shows Russia under the control of Nicholas II up to the start of the First World War and covers his attempts to hold back the forces of revolution in his country. Chapter 5 is concerned with preparing students for their examinations on this topic and concludes with a series of practice questions.

Each chapter has the following features:
- focal issues
- chronology of events
- comprehensive textual content designed to address the problems and issues
- mind map summaries of key content and the problems and issues
- a wide range of primary source extracts with accompanying exercises
- prominent historians' opinions
- maps, illustrations and statistical charts

- exercises and task questions
- glossaries of key terms and personalities
- guide to note-making on the content
- review questions
- reading list

In addition, 'how-to-do-it' sections have been included for the key skills of:
- answering questions
- paragraph answers
- note-taking
- formal essays
- three part structured responses
- researching and reading texts
- analysing sources
- document studies
- examination preparation and techniques

These skills have been built in progressively, and each chapter includes exercises to build on skills previously covered, as well as developing new skills. These skills and exercises have been included to make it easier for students to assess their performance in the areas necessary for preparing and sitting for the examinations.

One striking observation with respect to Russian history from 1800-1914 is that it was a period of enormous suffering for the vast majority of the people and simultaneous enjoyment of excessive opulence at their expense by a privileged few. With the benefit of hindsight, we can see that the attempts of the Romanov Tsars during this time to hold back change failed ultimately with the revolutions of 1917. Force alone propped up the regime until then. Thus the consistent policies of violence and autocratic repression, tempered with sporadic bursts of reform designed more to preserve the Tsars' control than relieve genuine social and economic misery, failed to achieve their purpose. Whatever the reader's opinion about the nature of the Communist regime put in place soon after the collapse of Tsarism, perhaps in the brief period of freedom in March 1917, we can observe something desirable in the state of human affairs — that eventually a system of oppression will be overcome by popular will.

ACKNOWLEDGEMENTS

To Juliet

The author and the publisher would like to thank the following sources for assistance with respect to copyright material:

L. Kochan and R. Abraham, *The Making of Modern Russia*, Penguin Books, London 1983 (pp 268), reproduced by permission of Penguin Books Ltd; A. Nove, *An Economic History of the USSR 1917 - 1991*, Penguin Books, London 1992 (pp 2, 7), reproduced by permission of Penguin Books Ltd; Richard E. Pipes, *Karamzin's Memoir on Ancient and Modern Russia: A Translation and Analysis*, Copyright © 1959 by the President and Fellows of Harvard College, reprinted by permission of Harvard University Press; The David King Collection, London for the cover photograph, 'Father and Son'.

Every effort has been made to trace and acknowledge copyright. The publishers apologise for any accidental infringement and welcome information that would rectify any error or omission in subsequent editions.

God, save the Tsar!
Mighty and strong reign for our glory;
Reign for the dread of our enemies,
O Tsar of the Orthodox Faith!
God, save the Tsar!

— *The Russian National Anthem, 1833-1917*

1

An Introduction to the Problems and Issues

Introduction

RUSSIA during the nineteenth century can be seen as the last bastion of European monarchic autocracy. For over 100 years, the Tsars battled against the tide of change with some limited success. Ultimately, they failed — the revolutions of 1917 put an end to the decayed remnants of centuries-old dynastic rule.

Thus the history of Russia in the nineteenth century needs to be viewed not only in the context of the events as they occurred, but also with regard to the fact that just 102 years after Alexander I reaffirmed the principles of his autocracy in the Holy Alliance, that autocracy was ended.

Russia also needs to be studied in the light of the general history of Europe in the nineteenth century, for it was the changes emerging in the west which the Tsars fought so hard to deny in their own country. In many ways, the history of Russia (and of Europe in general) in the nineteenth century can be seen as a continuing battle between the forces of change and the forces of conservatism.

When you study this history, you should study the events, people and institutions within the framework of nine problems and issues, which act as your points of focus on the ideas and themes you need to understand. The problems and issues are isolated in Fig. 1.1. Broadly speaking, they can be bracketed together as shown in Fig. 1.2.

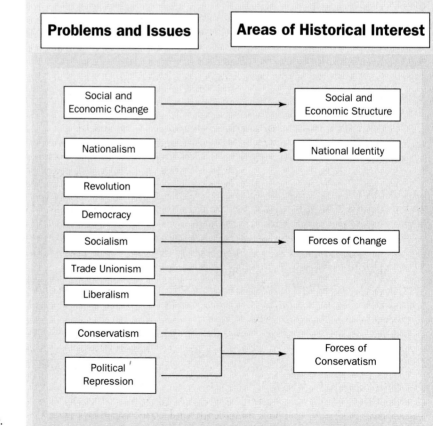

Fig 1.1 Problems and issues in nineteenth century Europe.

Fig: 1.2 Bracketing of problems and issues in nineteenth century Europe.

Definitions

In the sections that follow, definitions of the problems and issues shown in Fig. 1.2 are offered for your consideration. They are intended to be simple guides and are not exhaustive. The definitions incorporate the views of some historians.

They are complex issues and it is important to realise that while an attempt has been made to encapsulate the basic principles behind each problem or issue, they all meant different things to different people in different countries at different times. Do not make the mistake of assuming for example, that, a German liberal of 1825 came from the same class group and had exactly the same beliefs as a Russian liberal of 1880.

However, do not accept these definitions at face value—you should read widely to decide whether or not you agree with them. If you do not agree, then substitute your own definitions.

Social and Economic Change

This means a change in the social and economic systems of a nation and thus the living and working conditions of the people of that nation. It is a very broad concept, but the major social and economic changes observable in nineteenth century Europe were as follows:

- The spread of the Economic Revolution changed the underlying emphasis of the economies of Europe from agriculture to industry, commerce and trade.
- To accommodate this, major portions of populations changed:
  - their place of residence from the rural villages to the new cities
  - the nature of their occupations from predominantly rural labouring to such jobs as factory workers, domestic servants, miners and clerks.
- Industrialisation led to changes in class structure including:
  - the rise of a **bourgeoisie** (commercial and intellectual middle class) at the expense of the agricultural aristocracy
  - the development of a **proletariat** (industrial working class) and the idea that ordinary persons, not just the wealthy and noble, were important.
- Increases in nationalism in the late nineteenth century saw the promulgation of cultural and social institutions which idealised government-sponsored symbols of nationhood.
- Industrialisation led initially to shocking living and working conditions for workers in the cities. Depending on the degree of reactionary conservatism in governments and the nature and extent of agitation for change from liberals and working class representatives such as the socialist parties and the trade unions, these conditions were improved through government reforms in some nations during the late nineteenth and early twentieth centuries.

- Improvements in hygiene, medicine, transport, communications and access to education saw rising birth and education rates, decreases in premature mortality rates and led to increased social mobility and more leisure time for ordinary people, as well as greater exposure to the culture and ideas of other nations.

Fig: 1.3 Illustration from a Russian folk tale showing village inhabitants. By the end of the nineteenth century, despite the attempts of Sergei Witte, the fundamentally agricultural nature of Russian society had not changed substantially.

Nationalism

Nationalism is an ideology, developed in the nineteenth century, and concerned with the concept of the 'nation' in order to identify a political unit. There are several characteristics of a nation which set it apart from other attempts at identifying political units. According to the principle of nationalism, people in a nation are supposed see themselves as different and separate from people in surrounding areas. They may see themselves as having a common culture, language, ancestry, race, religion, territory, customs and laws, mythology, political or economic system, or any combination of these factors. Typically people in a nation allegedly share many of the same interests by virtue of their being citizens of the same nation.

Above all, nationalists do not simply limit their view of a nation to an area within physical boundaries. In each nineteenth century European nation, nationalists saw their nation as special and superior to all other nations. They felt that all the physical, social, economic, emotional and intellectual characteristics and institutions they wanted their nation to have, created this superiority. They believed that this gave their nation unity and a higher moral value.

In turn, nationalists in a nation used their ideology to justify all of these characteristics to their people and the rest of the world, to give it a legitimacy and elevate its image. Thus this powerful force became a source of unity for the people of a nation.

Nationalism could be — and was — taken to extremes. There were some cases in which it led to an almost blind belief in the superiority of one nation over other nations and of the priority of the state's interests over those of the individuals within the state. This led further to the practices of aggressive imperialism, suppression of individual liberties, repression of national minorities and economic, cultural and political imperialism.

Nationalism in the nineteenth century was an ideology that appealed to and was believed in by many different and otherwise opposite political groups, including conservatives, liberals and some socialists.

Revolution

At its broadest, revolution means a significant change in the nature of affairs.

- In the context of an **economy,** it means a dramatic change in the way goods and services are produced and distributed through society.
- In the context of **social change,** it means a marked difference in the ways people live their lives and relate to each other socially.
- In the context of **politics,** it means a dramatic overturning of an existing form of government and its replacement by a new politcal system.
- When a revolution covers all of these areas of society, McAndrew and Thomas identify four common features which usually also occur:
  - a transferral of power
  - an attempt at reconstructing the society
  - violence and rapid change
  - some popular participation.

Democracy

Democracy is a political ideal which is usually expressed in degrees. There have been many attempts at interpreting the notion of democracy, but all express a belief in **rights.** These in turn may be defined as a group of things to which people are entitled naturally and without reservation or restriction. Ultimately, democracy is a belief in the power of the ordinary people, and thus the right of these people to share in the government, the decision-making process of a country or state.

In a small community, it is possible for all members of the community to participate fully in the decision-making process. However, in larger groups this is too unwieldy and so the people elect representatives on a regular basis to govern for them. This is called **representative democracy.** These rep-

Fig: 1.4 Odessa
November 1905.
A street barricade
has been made
from overturned
trams and carts
during the 1905
Revolution.

resentatives are then accountable to the people for the quality of their decision making; they become responsible for their actions and this becomes **responsible government**.

The fundamental law setting out the political structure of a democracy is called a **constitution**. A constitution establishes the rules and restrictions under which a government must operate. Within this constitution, or sometimes in a separate document called a **bill of rights**, democratic nations can also protect what the people perceive to be their basic civil rights. Under this system, the people are guaranteed certain freedoms and are allowed to express their opinions, even if they oppose those of the government. In its ultimate form, opposition of this kind can mean **sanctions**, or the expression of opposition, against the government which can lead to the removal of the government, either by casting votes at regular elections, or by special procedures authorised by the constitution.

Socialism

Socialism is a political ideology that sees all the institutions of society as dependent on the economic system. Socialists believe that the system of **capitalism,** in which the means of production are owned and funded by private capital and the profits are returned to the owner, leads to political, social and economic exploitation and denial of rights to the people who work for the owners to produce the goods and services.

The **means of production** is a term which refers to the specific areas of society producing things used in the economy, such as factories, mines, shops, communications and transport systems, farms and financial institutions.

Socialists believe that the means of production should be owned by the state, which in turn will distribute the resulting goods and services to citizens, according to their needs. By creating an economic system based on needs, by eliminating the individual profit motive (and therefore the temptation to set up economic, political and social institutions favouring those who own the means of production), socialists aim to create a more equitable society, in which all people are guaranteed equal opportunities for fair living and employment. Socialism identifies three main class groupings in society:

- The **upper classes,** who include the landed aristocracy and the monarchy.
- The **middle classes,** or the bourgeoisie industrialists and professionals who promote the values and ethics of capitalism.
- The **lower classes,** or the agricultural and industrial labourers.

Fig. 1.5 Karl Marx and the title page of the second volume of the first Russian edition of Das Kapital *(co-authored by Marx and Frederick Engels). Despite the popularity of socialism in Russia from the 1870s onwards, Marx maintained that an agricultural nation such as Russia was not suitable for a socialist revolution.*

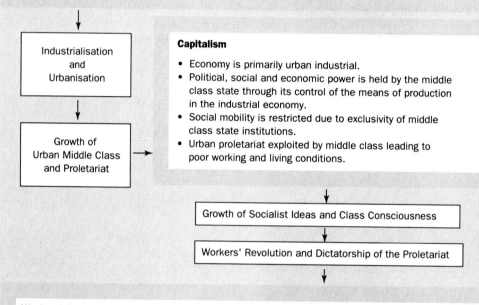

Feudalism

- Economy is primarily rural agriculture
- Political, social and economic power is held by the monarchy and the landed nobility through their control of the means of production in the agricultural economy.
- Church gives religious authority for the nobility.
- Society is rigidly structured with enserfed peasants working for the nobility at the bottom of the hierarchy leading to poor working and living conditions.

Industrialisation and Urbanisation

Growth of Urban Middle Class and Proletariat

Capitalism

- Economy is primarily urban industrial.
- Political, social and economic power is held by the middle class state through its control of the means of production in the industrial economy.
- Social mobility is restricted due to exclusivity of middle class state institutions.
- Urban proletariat exploited by middle class leading to poor working and living conditions.

Growth of Socialist Ideas and Class Consciousness

Workers' Revolution and Dictatorship of the Proletariat

Workers' State

- Economy is primarily urban industrial.
- Political, social and economic power is held by the workers through their control of the means of production in the industrial economy.
- The institutions of the state wither away, class structure is abolished and true social equity is achieved. Working and living conditions improved and goods and services distributed according to needs.

Fig. 1.6 A Marxist view of history.

There were three main branches of socialism in nineteenth century Europe, based on the different theories as to the best way to achieve the socialist state:

- **Socialism from above:** the aim was for an upper class elite to impose socialism on a politically inactive and deserving lower class. This was the form of socialism most prominent in the earlier parts of the nineteenth century, but it never really gained popular support, as it denied control to the workers.
- **Revolutionary socialism:** the aim was for the industrial working class to attain a high level of class consciousness and impose socialism on society from below through revolution.

- **Parliamentary socialism**: the aim was for democratically elected representatives of the people to introduce socialist reform gradually by passing laws in liberal parliaments. This was seen as the first step towards attaining socialist, social, political and economic goals.

The most prominent and influential socialist of the nineteenth century was Karl Marx (1818–1883), a German who advocated revolutionary socialism and justified it with a theory of the laws of historical materialism called dialectics. Marx believed in the economic progression of society from **feudalism**, dominated by the aristocracy, to **capitalism**, dominated by the bourgeoisie, until the lower classes could no longer tolerate their exploitation and misery, and would rise up in revolution, from which the **socialist state** would emerge.

Socialism came to represent a political ideology which claimed to champion agricultural workers and the proletariat (the industrial workers) against the practices of political systems favouring middle and upper class control of society and the economy through the sponsorship of private ownership. Socialism provided the theoretical basis for many other political ideologies, including **populism** and **communism**.

Trade Unionism

A trade union is an association of workers paid by wages or salary, who come together to take action against what they perceive to be unacceptable economic, social and sometimes political conditions. Trade unions achieve change in these conditions by solidarity and group agitation. The most common functions of early trade unions were:

Fig. 1.7
A Moscow
Workers' Union
demonstrating in
the early 1900s.

- improving working and living conditions
- raising wages
- decreasing the hours of work
- establishing mutual benefits funds to assist members unable to look after their own welfare fully.

Usually members elect officials who lobby and negotiate on their behalf with employers and politicians to achieve the desired improvements in the members' position. Trade unionism is thus a belief in:

- the validity and legitimacy of trade unions within a society
- the rights of members to form and belong to trade unions
- the sanctity of the rights and conditions won previously by officials for their members.

Trade unionism and socialism became closely associated as the nineteenth century progressed. However the conservative policies of some governments meant that trade unions were banned in many countries in Europe in the nineteenth century; therefore, although it remained a valid ideology, trade unionism did not achieve much in countries such as Germany, Russia and Austria.

Liberalism

Liberalism was a by-product of the Age of Enlightenment and the French Revolution and represented a belief in freedom, change and fundamental rights, including:

- the right to vote and to participate in government
- freedom of expression, religion, press and association
- equality before the law
- commercial freedom
- constitutional government.

There were two main branches of liberalism in nineteenth century Europe:

- **English laissez-faire liberalism:** this aimed mainly for commerce, trade and industry free from government regulation. The classic English liberal theorist was John Stuart Mill (1806–1873). Usually laissez-faire liberalism was strongest in nations where political reform had already been granted.
- **Continental liberalism:** this was mainly concerned with creating a state which provided for political freedom, usually in the form of constitutional reform.

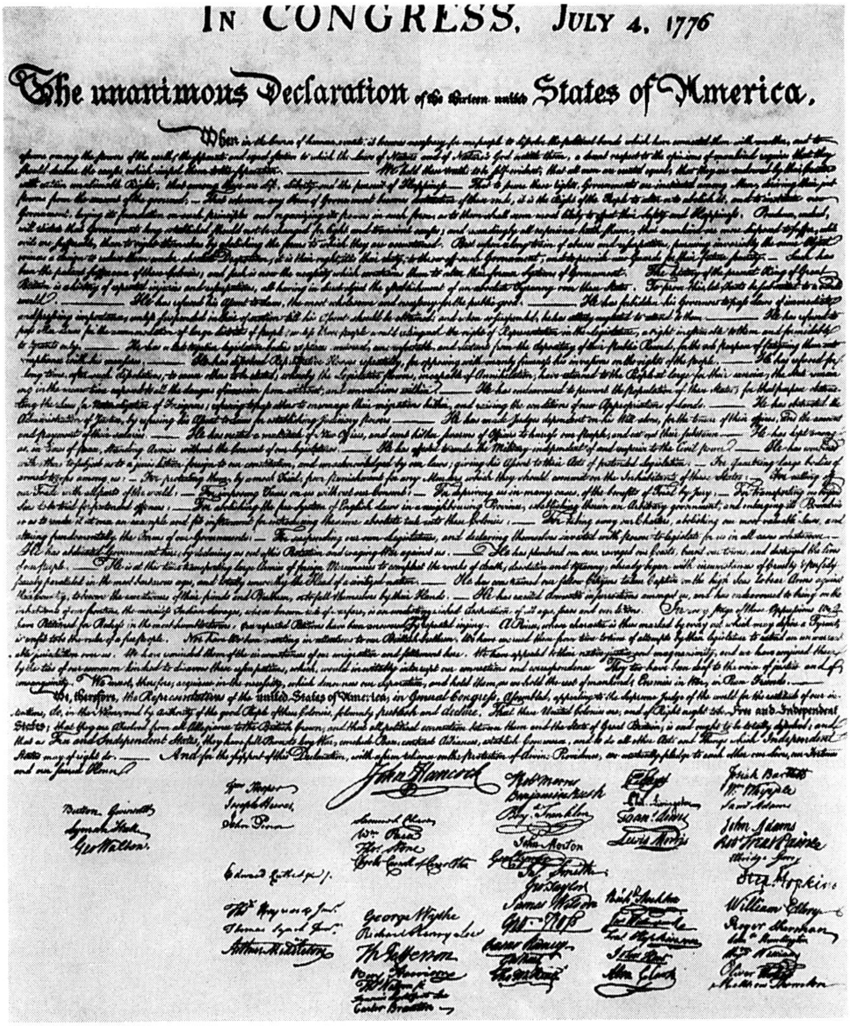
IN CONGRESS, JULY 4, 1776

The unanimous Declaration of the thirteen united States of America,

Fig. 1.8 *The American Declaration of Independence 1776. Profoundly influenced by the European Enlightenment thinkers, this document represented the first great statement of popular liberalism.*

Although the exact philosophies and beliefs of liberals changed from country to country and over time in nineteenth century Europe, in most countries it became associated with the aspirations of the middle classes. Socialists and workers in some nations saw liberalism as a stagnant force, not concerned with the interests of workers, but a means of support for the forces of conservatism in preserving the system of capitalism at the expense of the conditions and rights of the lower classes.

Fig. 1.9
Censorship. An
English
newspaper, The
Graphic, (dated
28 November
1891) after treat-
ment by Russian
government
censors.
Censorship was
commonly used
by conservative
governments to
prevent critical or
revolutionary
thought from
being
disseminated.

Conservatism

Conservatism is a movement which stands for the maintenance of the status quo. Conservatives usually are supporters of the traditional political, social and economic institutions of society and oppose any changes to these institutions. Generally speaking, the most hard line of conservatives will oppose the notion of change without even considering the substantive merits of the proposed changes. This extreme attitude is considered to be **reactionary**.

Overall, the desire of the conservatives to oppose the forces of change reflected the fact that the strongest supporters of conservatism in nineteenth century Europe came from the same upper classes who dominated the sources of power in Europe. Thus their conservatism can be seen as an attempt to maintain and control their own power.

Political Repression

Political repression is the way a government attempts to restrict or prevent change to the political structure and institutions of a nation and the rights and freedoms of its people. It arises from a desire to protect the political status quo and the power of those who hold government, and is thus linked to conservatism.

Political repression usually intensifies in reaction to the forces of change in a nation, and governments which oppose the forces of change are reactionary. Typical methods of political repression employed by governments in the nineteenth century included

- restrictive laws
- censorship
- suspension or denial of democratic reform, especially political and civil rights and the establishment of a constitution
- the use of force, in particular, secret police and the army, to enforce the rule of a regime
- regulation of the education system through conservative syllabuses, the appointment of teachers and the access of students to education
- arbitrary and undemocratic promotion of conservative values and ideals.

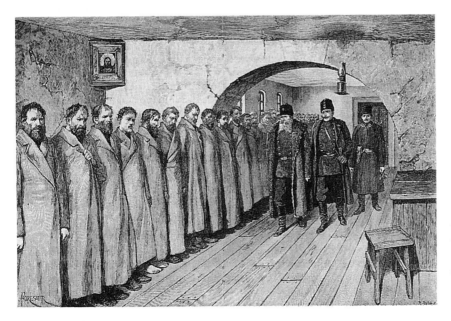

Fig. 1.10 Exiles in Siberia. Political prisoners in the men's gaol at Yeneseik.

Problems and Issues in Nineteenth Century Europe

Fig. 1.11 shows the conflict between the forces of change and the forces of conservatism in the social, economic and political institutions of nineteenth century Europe. The stronger the agitation for change, the harsher the reaction from those who already controlled the nation. The stronger their reaction, the more radical the forces of change became.

Eventually, be it in the nineteenth or twentieth century, the forces of change won and the political, social and economic face of Europe was altered. But the image of this change was determined by the level of social and economic change granted by the governments of Europe in nineteenth century Europe.

The more that real social and economic change was granted, the more likely it was for milder forces such as liberalism to succeed. The less change, the more likely it was that more radical forms such as revolution and socialism would triumph.

Underpinning all of this was the concept of **the nation**. Throughout Europe, people were questioning what it meant to be the citizen of a nation, and what it was that identified different nations as separate social organisations.

An appeal to nationalism was common to all political ideologies. What differed was their view of what the nation should be.

New Skills and Exercises

Answering Questions

There are generally two parts to a question:

ANALYSING THE DEMANDS OF A QUESTION.

- **the question on the material** asks you to reveal your knowledge of a particular area.
- **the instructions** inform you as to the particular format (how it is required to look on paper) which your answer should take, and therefore the particular writing skill to use.

FIVE STEPS TO UNDERSTAND-ING QUESTIONS

Follow these five steps in order to understand what a question requires of you.

- **Read the question.** This means that you read both the question on the material of the topic and the instructions for the format of your answer.
- **Identify the topic area.** Underline the broad topic area of the material that you have to cover.
- **Identify the focus of the question.** Underline the particular part of the topic the question requires you to concentrate or focus on.

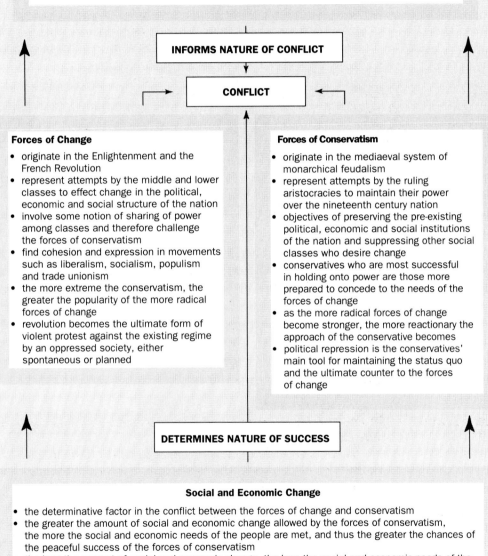

Nationalism

- a belief in and an appeal to the superiority of the nation and a political device used by both the forces of change and the forces of conservatism to increase their popular support and thus their overall power base, as well as furthering the cause of their nation

INFORMS NATURE OF CONFLICT

CONFLICT

Forces of Change

- originate in the Enlightenment and the French Revolution
- represent attempts by the middle and lower classes to effect change in the political, economic and social structure of the nation
- involve some notion of sharing of power among classes and therefore challenge the forces of conservatism
- find cohesion and expression in movements such as liberalism, socialism, populism and trade unionism
- the more extreme the conservatism, the greater the popularity of the more radical forces of change
- revolution becomes the ultimate form of violent protest against the existing regime by an oppressed society, either spontaneous or planned

Forces of Conservatism

- originate in the mediaeval system of monarchical feudalism
- represent attempts by the ruling aristocracies to maintain their power over the nineteenth century nation
- objectives of preserving the pre-existing political, economic and social institutions of the nation and suppressing other social classes who desire change
- conservatives who are most successful in holding onto power are those more prepared to concede to the needs of the forces of change
- as the more radical forces of change become stronger, the more reactionary the approach of the conservative becomes
- political repression is the conservatives' main tool for maintaining the status quo and the ultimate counter to the forces of change

DETERMINES NATURE OF SUCCESS

Social and Economic Change

- the determinative factor in the conflict between the forces of change and conservatism
- the greater the amount of social and economic change allowed by the forces of conservatism, the more the social and economic needs of the people are met, and thus the greater the chances of the peaceful success of the forces of conservatism
- the less the amount of social and economic change, the less the social and economic needs of the people are met, and the less likely that they will accept slow, peaceful solutions to their problems
- while the forces of change are new and weak, the denial of social and economic change leads to short-term success for the forces of conservatism, but in the long-term, for forces of change will develop strength and popular support and they will ultimately defeat the forces of conservatism
- eventually the forces of change succeed, but the level of social and economic change determines how this success is gained (progressively or suddenly) and the role that the forces of conservatism play in the emerging social order (as part of the new system or as victims of revolution)

Fig. 1.11 Relationship of Problems and Issues in Nineteenth Century Europe.

- **Identify the nature of the task.** Underline the key words that tell you:
  - the **thought processes** for dealing with the material of the topic: whether to state the reasons behind it, any methods involved, the results of it and so on.
  - the **written format** of the required answer: what this really means is that you have to identify the particular skill you need to use to answer the question.
- **Plan your response.** On a separate sheet of paper, plan the structure of your response, where you link together the requirements of the topic and also the format in which you have to write your answer.

SOME KEY WORDS IN QUESTIONS	

Compare:	are the aspects similar? are the aspects different? which is the best aspect? why?
Contrast:	how are the aspects of two or more factors/sources different?
Define:	what is the meaning of?
Describe:	write in enough detail so that someone without any knowledge of the topic will end up understanding it
Discuss:	what are the important aspects of a topic? can there be more than one answer to a question? what kinds of information can be used to explain the topic?
Evaluate:	make a judgement about the importance, success or failure
Explain:	make clear
Illustrate:	give examples to make the topic clear
Interpret:	explain the meaning in your own words
Justify:	present evidence to support an action or point of view
Outline:	present a simple explanation or description based upon the main points
Relate:	point out the connections between the main aspects of a topic
State:	briefly write about the main point
Summarise:	bring together the main points using your own words
Trace:	point out how something has developed from start to finish

Structuring a Paragraph Response

The structure of a paragraph response contains three logical and simple parts – the key sentence, the body and the conclusion:

- The first sentence in a paragraph is called the **key sentence**. It introduces the topic of the paragraph and answers the question immediately. The sentence is fairly short and to the point, and to answer the question by the most direct means possible, you may use the words of the question itself. However, this can often be boring for the reader and you should try to find a different way of referring directly to the issues of the question if possible. **KEY SENTENCE**

- The second part of a paragraph is called the **body**. It is a series of well-structured sentences explaining the factual detail and opinions relevant to the topic, providing direct support for the answer you gave in the key sentence. Use a logical order for these details wherever possible — chronological order is best. Do not include lists in either note or point form; the sentences follow each other without a break. Wherever possible, try to include some direct reference to either primary or secondary source material in the body of your paragraph. This can either be a direct quote, or by paraphrasing the source into your own words. **BODY**

- The **conclusion** is the third part of a paragraph. It summarises the evidence given in the body and relates it back to the question by explaining how and finishes off the topic. Do not use the same words as in the key sentence, but restate the central argument first revealed in the key sentence. You may also use a conclusion to point out any inconsistencies or doubtful areas relating to the evidence. A conclusion is not necessarily limited to one sentence. **CONCLUSION**

EXERCISES

Write a properly structured paragraph response for each of the following questions.

1. In your own words, explain what each of the following terms mean:
   a. Social and economic change
   b. Nationalism
   c. Revolution
   d. Democracy
   e. Political repression
   f. Socialism
   g. Trade unionism
   h. Liberalism
   i. Conservatism
2. What was the function of social and economic change in relation to the other problems and issues in nineteenth century Europe?
3. What were the forces of change and how did they relate to each other in nineteenth century Europe?
4. What were the forces of conservatism and how did they relate to each other in nineteenth century Europe?
5. What was the relationship of nationalism to the other problems and issues in nineteenth century Europe?

Note Making

Notes are useful in helping to understand a piece of work. By keeping notes you can identify the important points and create a shorter form which is easier for you to learn from and therefore helps in studying for exams. Notes are made up of

- headings — the main ideas
- sub-headings — the secondary ideas belonging with each main heading
- points to explain the headings
- source material and references

HOW TO TAKE NOTES There are six steps to follow in taking notes:

- determine the purpose
- skim read the material
- read closely
- list the headings
- make the notes
- review your work.

- **Determine the purpose.** What task have you been set? What you are using your notes for will decide the way you set them out and what you put into them:
  - if you have to write a set of notes simply to summarise a topic, you will include the most important points
  - if you are making notes for an essay, you will be looking for the points that suit the topic and are relevant to the question.
- **Skim read the material.** Quickly read all of the material that you have to note, but do not try to take it all in at once.
  - try to gain an overall idea of the content and relate it to the purpose of your notes
  - look for ideas and information relevant to your task.
- **List the headings.** The most important ideas and points in the material will become the headings in your notes. You can either use the headings in the material or make your own headings.
- **Read closely.** Read the whole passage again very closely, this time trying to collect information to group under the main headings. This time you are reading the passage to find the information to include under the headings you have made to meet your original purpose.
- **Make the notes.** The information you have gathered is now put together on the page. Write the notes in you own words as far as possible. One of the main reasons for making notes is to express the ideas in your own way, so there is little point in copying out great slabs of the text book. But you should also strengthen and support what you are saying with sufficient detail.
  - a neat clear layout is vital
  - the notes must be well-spaced and easy to read

- use a consistent way of setting them out so that it is easy to see the importance of different parts of your notes.
- **Review your work.** Read over your work and re-read the material. Compare the two. Do your notes include the most information you need to fulfil your original purpose? If they do not, then insert that information into your notes.

There are several different ways of setting out your notes. Experiment with these different forms, and do not be afraid to include different forms in the same set of notes. Remember, different forms of note taking suit different purposes. Here are three common forms of note taking:

HOW TO SET OUT YOUR NOTES

- **Linear notes.** In this form of note making the information for each point is in the margin and follows the lines on the page. Linear notes have the following features:
    - the notes move down the page and are lined up with the margin
    - the headings are distinct from the rest of the notes
    - a consistent numbering system is used in order to separate the main headings, sub-headings and notes: 1, 2, 3 etc for the main heading; A, B, C etc for the sub-headings, and i, ii, iii etc for the notes
    - the notes leave enough space to be clear and legible
    - short phrases are used to reduce the amount that has to be noted and learnt, but no important information is left out.

Linear notes are suitable for chronological and narrative descriptions, quotations and essay drafts. They allow you to record great amounts of detail and include all your ideas, as well as helping you to develop your vocabulary and writing. Be careful, however, not to give that narrative more attention than the analysis and make sure that important ideas are not hidden beneath the detail.

- **Charts and tables.** The information is shown in a table or chart of columns and rows with the following features:
    - the information is collected in categories within a chart or table
    - the major heading is at the top of the chart
    - the information is simplified into sub-sections within each category

When they are suitable	Advantages	Possible disadvantages
• for making summaries	• compact	• may lead to over-simplification
• analysis of topics	• can show relationships between events and ideas	• difficult to include all details
• for recording statistics	• easy to visualise, and therefore easy to recall	

Fig. 1.12
Advantages and disadvantages of charts and tables

– the notes are drawn up in such a way that it is easy to compare categories with each other.

Fig. 1.12 on page 19 is an example of a chart and shows the advantages and disadvantages of charts and tables.

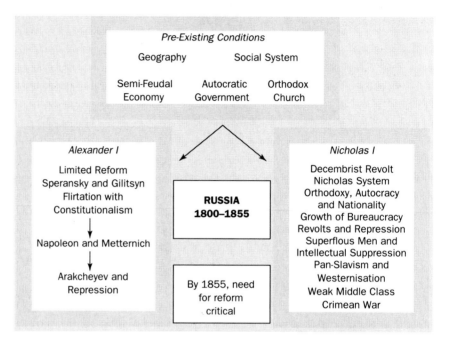

Fig. 1.13 Mind Map Russia 1800–1855

- **Mind maps.** The notes are arranged in a pattern on the page, with the central idea in the middle and all the ideas that relate to it are grouped around it. Fig. 1.13 provides an example of a mind map on Russia 1800-1855. These notes have the following features:
  - the major heading is in the middle of the page
  - the sub-headings are grouped in a circle around the main heading, starting from the top left hand corner—they may be joined to the central idea by arrows or lines
  - the notes that belong with each sub-heading are written neatly beneath the sub-heading—the notes are very compact

Mind maps are suitable for analysing topics and essay planning, because they look interesting and are creative. They are good for making full topic revision summaries because they make you analyse topics as well as structuring your thoughts. Because they are easy to visualise, they are easy to recall, and they present information in a compact and relevant way.

They are not intended for recording things in great detail, so use them appropriately.

EXERCISE

Chapter summary. Now that you have refined your knowledge of note-taking, re-read and take notes from this chapter. Your notes should incorporate a brief definition of each of the following problems and issues and an explanation of their general relationship to each other.

- Revolution
- Socialism
- Trade Unionism
- Liberation
- Democracy

- Political Repression
- Conservatism
- Nationalism
- Social and Economic Change

Russia before Emancipation

Introduction — Russia in 1800

A T THE BEGINNING of the nineteenth century, Russia was a country with about 40 million inhabitants, only 40 per cent of whom spoke Russian. Russia's vast size was an obstacle to efficient government and communications and the multi-racial nature of the population hindered a sense of national identity — only half the Tsar's subjects were Russian. In addition, the vast size of the country meant that there were very different climates and terrains, ranging from the steppes of the Asiatic provinces, to the mountains of the Urals, to the rich agricultural plains of the Ukraine, to the frozen wasteland of Siberia.

Social System

At the beginning of Alexander I's reign, most of the population were agricultural serfs, virtual slaves bound to the land and at the mercy of their aristocratic landlords. They were either privately owned by the landlords or they were state peasants and owned by the Tsar. They could not protest, had to work as directed and could be sold like slaves. Flogging was the usual punishment for minor transgressions of the rule of the landlords, but for more serious offences the serfs could be sent to Siberia or into the army. They bore most of the tax burden. They worked on and were legally attached to the land. They paid rent for this land as either **barschina** or **obrok**, or both.

- **Barschina** was a form of rent whereby peasants were required to provide free labour for the landlord in return for the privilege of farming a section of the landlord's estate.
- **Obrok** was a different form of taxation whereby peasants paid rent for the privilege of farming the landlord's land based on the composition and number in a peasant's family — in short, obrok was a form of poll tax paid to the landlord, in addition to a separate poll tax which peasants also had to pay to the Tsarist government.

During the nineteenth century, the peasants became increasingly frustrated by the increase in privileges for the upper class and in burdens for peasantry. Less than 10 per cent of the population were members of the

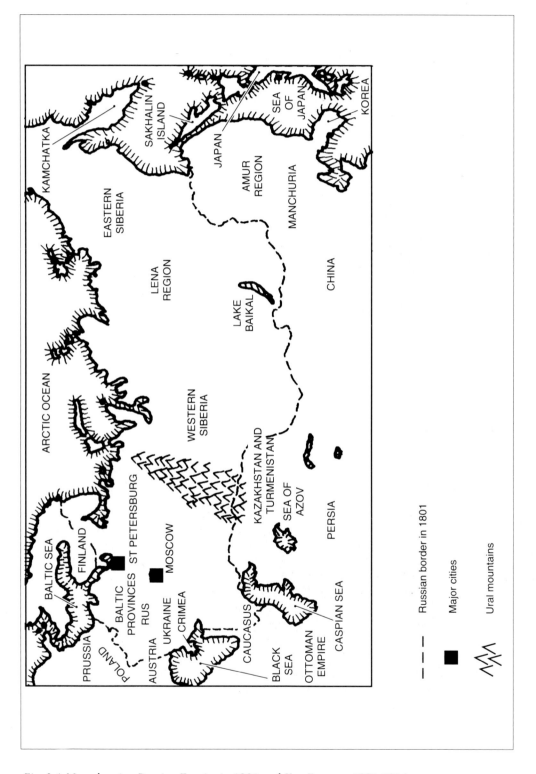

Fig. 2.1 Map showing Russian Empire in 1801 and Key Features 1801-1914

privileged classes and less than 2 per cent were members of the nobility and clergy. These two sectors bore the fewest taxes and by nature most were conservative and supported the Tsar. Very few of them saw the need for reform. Since only 4 per cent of the population lived in towns and the economy of the society was still a feudal agriculture, there was no commercial/industrial middle class to speak of.

Nature of Russian Government to 1800

The government of Russia centred around the autocracy of the Tsar, whose power was based on the theory of the **Divine Right of Kings**. This was a political theory which stated that a monarch gained the right to rule from God. Because the monarch's right to rule was divine and therefore enforced by the church as well as the state, to contradict it was an act of blasphemy as well as an act of political rebellion. There was no popular involvement in government because there were no elected assemblies or advisory bodies. The Tsar was an absolute ruler restricted only by the opinions of the upper classes, who dominated the clergy, bureaucracy and judiciary. The word of the nobility and gentry on the land was law.

The **Chinovniks** were a special caste of the nobility who acted primarily as the administrators of the empire, rather than as landowners; they controlled the administration of the empire and the Tsar, depending on their strength of character, could be very influenced by them.

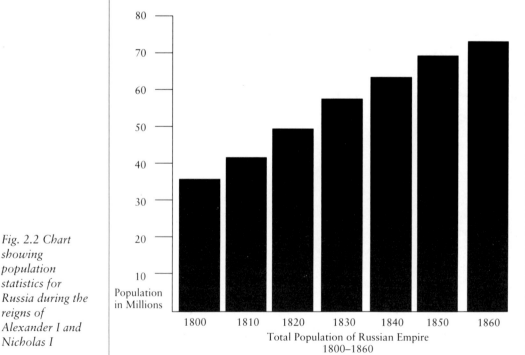

Fig. 2.2 Chart showing population statistics for Russia during the reigns of Alexander I and Nicholas I

Fig. 2.3 The interior of a Russian peasant's hut, 1798.

The 18th century policy of Westernisation introduced by Peter the Great (1672–1725; Tsar 1683–1725) was no longer followed but his policy of territorial expansion was continued. Russian tradition remained culturally paramount, with the two symbols of Mother Russia and the Little Father (the Tsar) as the predominant means for the promotion by the nobility and the clergy of a brand of Imperial Russian nationalism centred around the Tsarist autocracy.

Fig. 2.4 Family Tree of the Romanovs 1796-1855.

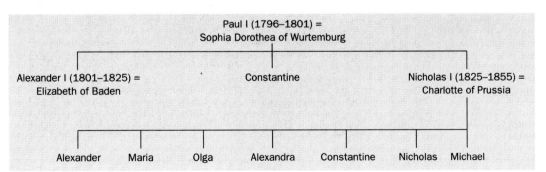

Paul I (1796–1801) =
Sophia Dorothea of Wurtemburg

Alexander I (1801–1825) =
Elizabeth of Baden

Constantine

Nicholas I (1825–1855) =
Charlotte of Prussia

Alexander   Maria   Olga   Alexandra   Constantine   Nicholas   Michael

Fig. 2.5
Alexander I and Nicholas I.

Prior to 1861, Russia was an empire of many different nationalities controlled by a Tsar and his government. Conservative policies dominated the politics, the economy and society of the country and the notion of change was flirted with only briefly and without much substance.

Overall, it was subject to the often extreme, autocratic methods of a government which strongly resisted the impact of more modern ideas from Western Europe.

The most important concepts for you to address concern this lack of change.

FOCAL ISSUES

- Why was there no significant change in the nature of politics, the economy and the society of Russia in the period 1800 to 1855?
- By 1855, what needs for change had become apparent?

Alexander I
- What were the major political, social and economic features of Russian life at the turn of the nineteenth century?
- In what ways did liberalism influence the government of Alexander I?
- Why had the forces of conservatism re-asserted control in Russia by 1825?

Nicholas I
- What was the Nicholas System?
- How did Nicholas I repress the forces of change in Russia in the period 1825 to 1855?

- What effects did the reign of Nicholas I have upon the political, social and economic institutions of Russia?

Fig. 2.6 shows the areas to concentrate on when you address these issues. Ask yourself how much each of them contributed to this general condition of stagnancy.

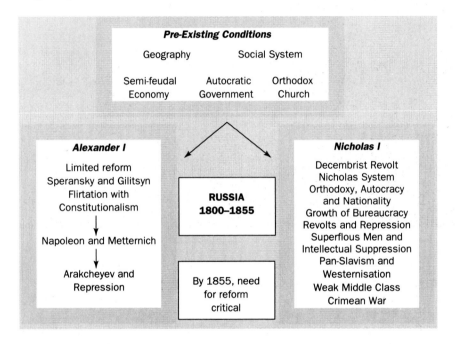

Fig. 2.6 Mind Map Russia 1800-1855.

Reading List

Listed below are some of the books you can use to find out more on this area:

D Christian, *Power and Privilege: Russia and the Soviet Union in the Nineteenth and Twentieth Centuries*, Pitman, 1987
D Christian, *Living Water, A Social History of Vodka*, OUP, 1992
R Cowie & L Wolfson, *Years of Nationalism — European History 1815-1890*, Edward Arnold, 1987
L Kochan & R Abraham, *The Making of Modern Russia*, Pelican, 1983
M McAndrew & D Thomas, *Century of Change*, Nelson, 1990
L Seaman, *From Vienna to Versailles*, Methuen, 1965
D Thomson, *Europe since Napoleon*, Pelican, 1987
J Westwood, *Endurance and Endeavour: Russian History, 1812-1992*, OUP, 1994

Guide to Note Making

For your notes on Russia between 1800 and 1855, you will need to consider both:

- a **chronological coverage** of the areas of concern — it is suggested that you use Fig. 2.4 as the source of your headings for a set of brief linear notes
- an **assessment** of the problems and issues.

Do not forget to include sources in all of these notes and do not forget the focus for this section of the course:

> **Why was there no significant change in the nature of politics, the economy and the society of Russia in the period 1800 to 1855?**
> **By 1855, what needs for change had become apparent?**

TIME LINE

1801	Assassination of Paul I
	Accession of Alexander I
1802	Creation of eight new government departments and strengthening of the bureaucracy
	Abolition of secret police
1803	Golitsyn appointed Over Procurator of Holy Synod
1804	Education Statute
1805	Russia declares war on Napoleonic France and loses Battle of Austerlitz
1807	Treaty of Tilsit and alliance with Napoleon
	Speransky appointed special advisor to Alexander
1808	Arakcheyev appointed Minister of War
	Re-establishment of secret police
1809	Draft constitution presented to and rejected by Alexander
	Formation of State Council
1810	Arakcheyev leaves War Ministry
1811	Formation of National Advisory Council
1812	War of 1812
	Dismissal of Speransky
1815	Defeat of Napoleon
	Formation of Holy Alliance
1816	Foundation of first revolutionary societies
1817	Arakcheyev appointed chief advisor to Alexander
	Golitsyn appointed Minister of Spiritual Affairs and Education
1819	Second draft constitution presented to and rejected by Alexander
1820	Rebellion among St Petersburg regiments
1822	Edict dissolving all secret societies
1823	Dismissal of Golitsyn
1825	Death of Alexander I
	Decembrist Revolt
	Accession of Nicholas I

The Reign of Alexander I

Domestic Policy

In his early years, Alexander I showed some tendency towards liberalism. Early in his reign he abolished the secret police, expanded the administration of Russia, permitted Russian nobles to travel abroad and the publication of foreign books in Russia. One of Alexander I's major liberal advisers was Count MM Speransky. As Minister of State, Speransky was responsible for proposing many, and instituting a few, liberal constitutional reforms before he lost his influence due to the intrigues of his conservative enemies. Later, during the reign of Nicholas I, he was responsible for many of the proceed-

LIBERALISM

Fig. 2.7 Map showing division of land in European Russia according to rents and taxes, c 1820.

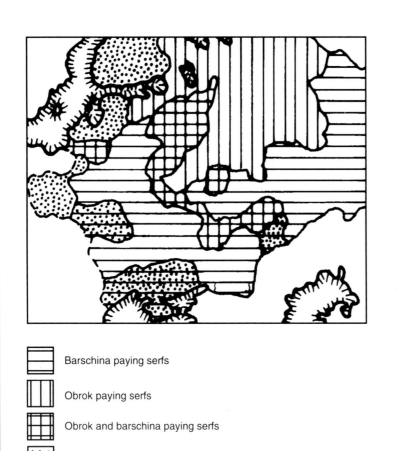

☰ Barschina paying serfs

▥ Obrok paying serfs

▦ Obrok and barschina paying serfs

⣿ Free peasants (Poles, Finns, Latvians, Lithuanians and Estonians)

⣿ Mixture of barschina paying Russian serfs and free German peasants

Fig. 2.8 Mikhail Speransky 1772–1839, leading statesman and administrator.

ings against the Decembrist conspirators and for codifying Russian law. Alexander I was greatly influenced by Mikhail Speransky and instituted Constitutional Commissions in 1807 and 1812 to investigate the possibility of introducing a liberal constitution. However, their final proposals of 1809 and 1819 were never accepted, although he did grant Poland a constitution in 1812.

Speransky did achieve the establishment of a national advisory council in 1811 but in pushing too hard for the introduction of a **duma** (parliament) and income tax, he upset the nobility, who in 1812 persuaded Alexander I to sack him. Just prior to this, the Tsar had permitted landowners to emancipate serfs if they wished, but few nobles supported this gesture and only 37 000 serfs were freed. Thus Alexander did not achieve much significant reform. Between 1810 and 1812, Alexander and Russia were preoccupied with resisting the threat of France and domestic policy was not really a major concern.

REPRESSION

After the defeat of Napoleon, Alexander followed the trend of other European monarchs by complying with the **Metternich system** and introducing political and press repression. He used the arch-conservative Count Arakcheyev to run his administration after 1816 and allowed him to institute reactionary conservative policies such as the repression of liberals, the dissolution and illegalisation of secret societies, censorship and the deposition of liberal ministers and advisors. In 1809 even before the defeat of Napoleon, Alexander re-instituted the secret police, reversing his decision of 1802 to abolish them.

In 1816 Alexander attempted to introduce a policy of **military colonies** – a system of self-sustaining villages whose produce was used to support the small military garrisons stationed in them, especially in western provinces such as Poland and the Ukraine. However the policy was stifled by the balance of

The Metternich System was a system of diplomatic agreements and alliances originating from the monarchies of Austria, France, Prussia and Russia at the Congress of Vienna in 1815. Also known as the Holy Alliance, it was designed to preserve the position of monarchies in Europe, to promote conservatism and oppose the forces of change where they arose. Its chief architect was the Austrian Foreign Minister, Prince Klemens von Metternich, who as the Austrian Chancellor from 1821-1848 ensured that the system remained effective until the revolutionary year of 1848.

General Count AA Arakcheyev: An ultra-conservative and devoted servant of Alexander, Arakcheyev was a strange personality who could be loyal, virtuous and cruel at the same time. He was responsible for the conduct of internal affairs from 1816 until the death of Alexander, and his chief achievement, apart from the repression of liberalism, was the establishment of the military colonies. He did not have the same degree of persuasiveness over Nicholas I, who dispensed with his services soon after taking power.

Fortunately this unbending tyrant is succeeded by a generous and high-minded prince, Alexander, who swiftly rouses his new subjects from the state of prostration in which they have been left by Paul.

But, perceiving with sorrow that baseness is ingrained in the Russian character, this high-minded prince sheds tears of warm-hearted contempt over his people.

Fortunately, however, he discovers in his huge empire several writers of a liberal persuasion whom he swiftly raises to the highest rank.

Alexander shows these simple-minded theorists, whose writings have been adopted to the letter by some people, that action is followed by reaction.

Even so, the stern measures that he is obliged to take, against his will, cause him great distress.

Fig. 2.9 The Reign of Alexander I. French illustrator and critic Gustave Doré gives his impression of Alexander's tendencies to flirt with liberalism but reaffirm autocracy.

power inherent in the Metternich system and Austria and Prussia in particular, fearful of the presence of Russian troops stationed permanently so close to their eastern borders, were able to force Alexander to tone down the extent of the scheme, which was eventually disfavoured by Nicholas I and abandoned in 1857.

BUREAUCRACY

With his reformation of the bureaucracy, Alexander I began the shift of power away from the decentralised feudal system, where the nobility held power in the name of the Tsar, to a more centralised system, with officials, appointed and paid by the Tsar, directly responsible for the administration of the Empire either in the ministries or the Tsar's personal Imperial Chancery.

Religion

BLACK AND WHITE CLERGY

There were two levels to the Russian Orthodox church — the 'black' clergy and the 'white' clergy, names based on the colour of the vestments. The higher-ranked black clergy (bishops and above) were the administrators and policy makers of the Orthodox Church. Financed by the government and

Fig. 2.10 Photographs showing Russian clergymen in the mid-nineteenth century. The man on the left is a black clergyman — his finely embroidered vestments are meant to represent his very strict vows of obedience, chastity and piety. These expensive robes also indicate the wealth of his order. The man on the right is a white clergyman — the condition of his vestments reveals his poverty.

appointed from the upper classes, the black clergy were reliant on the state payroll and thus in turn could be relied on by the government to support and authorise the Russian system of autocracy. They gave a spiritual legitimacy to the regime. The lower-ranked white clergy were the village priests, counsellors and, acting under the instructions of their black superiors, they were disseminators of the pro-Imperial social structure to the working classes.

Alexander, influenced by Golitsyn and increasingly fascinated by fringe religious and spiritual elements, began to turn away from Orthodoxy after 1815 and allowed more freedom for mystics, sects and freemasons. He also linked the church and education together by creating the Ministry of Spiritual Affairs and Education under Golitsyn in 1817. However, Golitsyn's influence was diminished by the politicking of Arakcheyev in 1823 which led to Golitsyn's sacking and the return to favour of the Holy Church. Nonetheless, education remained largely under the aegis of the church for the rest of the Tsarist period.

GOLITSYN

> **AN Golitsyn (1773–1844):** An old acquaintance of Alexander, he had introduced the monarch to bible-reading and as Over Procurator and also later Minister he showed great tolerance for fringe religious groups and attempted to spread bible-reading to the peasants through the Russian Bible Society and its first ever Russian translation of the bible and also through the new expanded education system. Never popular with the conservatives, he was dismissed in 1823 after the intrigues of Arakcheyev.

Education

Starting with the Education Statute of 1804 and throughout the next 15 years, Alexander established a new primary and secondary education system based on western models, in order to combat illiteracy. He also created three new universities which were supported by technical and professional institutions and colleges. The appointment of Golitsyn, in 1817, as Minister of Education encouraged the liberalisation process. By 1825, 265 000 Russians were attending school, 100 000 of these in military academies. The system of **gymnasia** (high schools) was quite successful in the larger towns, but less than 600 parish schools were established in rural districts and thus the benefits of these reforms did not really reach the agricultural peasantry.

REFORM

However, after 1823 and the sacking of Golitsyn, universities became more strictly controlled, usually under the directorship of retired generals, and the liberal culture of academia, which had been fostered so briefly, became discouraged and actively repressed.

REPRESSION

Fig. 2.11 Map showing Imperial Acquisitions 1809-1812 and Napoleonic Campaigns 1812.

Foreign Policy

EXPANSION

From 1805-1812, Alexander was preoccupied with defeating Napoleon and appeared to champion the cause of freedom in Europe. However, after 1812 he became more concerned with expanding the Russian Empire and to this end he conquered Finland, Bessarabia, Georgia and part of Persia. His liberal treatment of conquered Poles and Finns, such as granting Poland and Finland some degree of self-government and a constitution, and thus the emancipation of their peasants, seemed to indicate that he was prepared to extend his earlier interest in liberal ideas into his relations with other peoples.

However, it needs to be noted that in granting constitutions and emancipation to Poland and Finland, Alexander was effectively blocking the ambitions of the Polish and Finnish nobility to overcome Russian overlordship. This poses the question: were these genuine liberal reforms, or were they merely designed to strengthen Russian control in unruly new provinces?

After the defeat of Napoleon at the Battle of Waterloo in 1815, the triumphant monarchical nations of Europe met at the Congress of Vienna to decide Europe's fate. Alexander I, fearful of the physical and ideological threats posed to his nation since 1789 by the spirit of the French Revolution, became obsessed by the need to prevent the rise of a new revolutionary force in Europe. He was also consumed by a belief that God had given him a holy mission to restore order to the nations. He played into the hands of the Austrian Chancellor, Metternich, who used his domination of Austrian politics, Alexander's naivety and the weakness of the un-unified German states, to construct a series of agreements and treaties between the monarchs of Austria, Russia and Prussia (then the largest of the German states). Formalised first by the Holy Alliance (1815), and later confirmed by the Protocol of Troppau (1820), the treaties confirmed the dominance of absolute monarchy in Continental Europe. This system of international co-operation between the monarchs (which was really manipulated by the arch-conservative Metternich) is known as the Metternich System and dominated European politics until the revolutionary year of 1848.

By allowing Metternich to use him as the figure-head of the Holy Alliance, Alexander I established Russia's new status as defender of conser-

METTERNICH SYSTEM

Fig. 2.12 Contemporary illustration of the Vienna Conference of 1815.

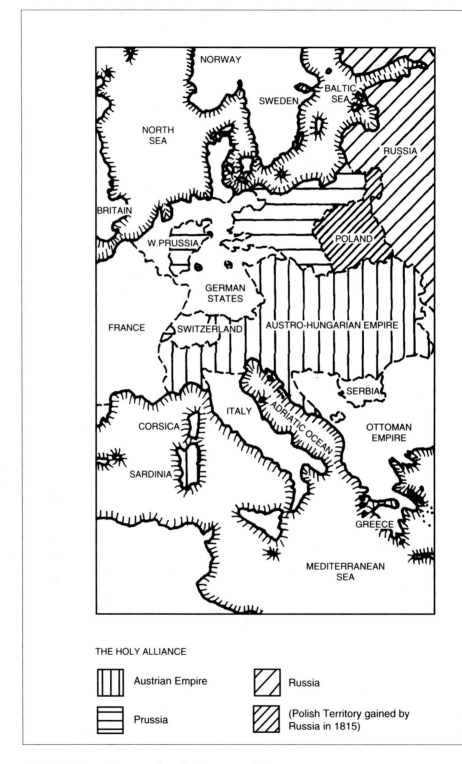

Fig. 2.13 Map of Europe after the Congress of Vienna.

vatism. By agreeing to intervene with force to suppress any revolutionary takeover of his fellow European monarchies, Alexander once again provided a contrast of ideologies in his policies, a contrast which seemed to indicate that his interest in the radical was more whim than deep-seated belief.

Primary Extracts and Questions — the Metternich System

In the name of the Most Holy and Indivisible Trinity.

Their Majesties, the Emperor of Austria, the King of Prussia, and the Emperor of Russia, having, in consequence of the great events which have marked the course of the last three years in Europe, and especially of the blessings which it has pleased Divine Providence to shower down upon those States which place their confidence and their hope on it alone, acquired the intimate conviction of the necessity of settling the steps to be observed by the Powers, in their reciprocal relations, upon the sublime truths which the Holy Religion of our Saviour teaches . . .

They solemnly declare that the present Act has no other object than to publish, in the face of the whole world, their fixed resolution, both in the administration of their respective States, and in their political relations with every other Government, to take for their sole guide the precepts of that Holy Religion, namely, the precepts of Justice, Christian Charity and Peace, which, far from being applicable only to private concerns, must have an immediate influence on the council of Princes, and guide all their steps, as being the only means of consolidating human institutions and remedying their imperfections.

FROM THE HOLY ALLIANCE — 1815

(a) What does this extract suggest was the basis of the power of the monarchs of Europe in 1815?
(b) According to this extract, what principles did the monarchs of Europe use to 'guide their steps'?
(c) How appropriate is the title 'Holy Alliance'?

[The Holy Alliance] is nothing more than a philanthropic aspiration, clad in a religious garb.

FROM METTERNICH'S PRIVATE OPINION ON THE HOLY ALLIANCE—1815

(d) How does this extract contradict the previous extract?
(e) How does this extract reveal the relationship of Metternich with Alexander I?

Europe thus presents itself to the impartial observer under an aspect at the same time deplorable and peculiar ...

The Governments, having lost their balance, are frightened, intimidated, and thrown into confusion by the cries of the intermediary class of society, which, placed between the Kings and their subjects, breaks the sceptre of the monarch, and usurps the cry of the people—that class so often disowned by the people, and nevertheless too much listened to, caressed and feared by those who could with one word reduce it again to nothingness . . .

We are convinced that society can no longer be saved without strong and vigorous resolutions on the part of the Governments still free in their opinions and actions . . . By this course the monarchs will fulfil the duties imposed upon them by Him who, by entrusting them with power, has charged them to watch over the maintenance of justice, and the rights of all, to avoid the paths of error, and tread firmly in the way of truth. Placed beyond the passions which

FROM METTERNICH'S SECRET MEMORANDUM PRIOR TO THE PROTOCOL OF TROPPAU — 1820 agitate society, it is days of trial chiefly that they are called upon to despoil real-ities of their false appearances, and to show themselves as they are, fathers invested with the authority belonging by right to the heads of families, to prove that, in days of mourning, they know how to be just, wise, and therefore strong, and that they will not abandon the people whom they ought to govern . . .

There is a rule of conduct common to individuals and to States, established by the experience of centuries as by that of everyday life. This rule declares 'that one must not dream of reformation while agitated by passion; wisdom directs that at such moments we should limit ourselves to maintaining'.

Let the monarchs vigorously adopt this principle; let all their resolutions bear the impression of it. Let their actions, their measures and even their words announce and prove to the world this determination—they will find allies everywhere . . .

(f) What does Metternich mean by the term 'the intermediary class'?
(g) What principles of autocracy does Metternich affirm in the third paragraph?
(h) Rewrite into your own words Metternich's 'rule' of the fourth paragraph.
(i) Given Metternich's statement on page 37, what reasons can you suggest for this memorandum?

FROM THE PROTOCOL OF
TROPPAU—1820

• States which have undergone a change of government . . . cease to be members of the European Alliance.

(j) How does this brief extract reflect the opinions of the previous extract?
(k) What do you see as the consequences of 'a change of government'?

Economic Policy

Before and during the reign of Alexander I the Russian economy was based almost entirely upon the agricultural system of serfdom.

AGRICULTURE

Agricultural techniques were primitive, relying on exhaustive strip farming, simple farm equipment and a reluctance to modernise. A revenue system largely based on a poll tax and the feudal dues of barschina and obrok emphasised landlord ownership of the countryside.

VODKA FARMING

However, it was the tax farming of vodka that provided most of the gov-ernment's revenues. Vodka is a clear spirit, distilled from potatoes or grains. The vodka farms produced varying qualities, depending on the number of times it was distilled. The fewer times it was distilled, the cheaper and rougher it was. It could be flavoured with aniseed, spices, citrus fruit or berries, but was generally drunk neat and in great quantities. It was a very important part of life for most Russians, in a culture where drinking was integral to all village festivities and where vodka was the only recreational outlet for working class men in the towns.

The production and distribution of vodka was structured to give financial benefit to the monarch and the upper classes. The process of distilling was a privilege reserved for the nobility, and sale of liquor was restricted by law to government-owned taverns and outlets, which were rented by peasant merchants from the government for a fee generally based on expected revenue. These merchants could then charge as much as possible to recoup their tax expenses and make a profit, usually a very healthy one. During the reign of Alexander I, vodka provided between 24% and 37% of all government revenue, more than the obrok and poll taxes in most years, and it paid for up to 75% of the total defence budget.

Russian industry and trade was very minor and much was foreign controlled — a system based on serfdom and alcohol impeded development of industrialisation and urbanisation, but ensured a stable social and economic system for most of the century. Certainly Alexander I saw no need to change the direction of his revenue-gaining activities and thus the economy as a whole. His one innovation was the use of military colonies to create economically self-sufficient standing army, but this ultimately proved to be a failure.

TRADE AND INDUSTRY

In 1825 the peasant Savva Morozov bought his freedom with the proceeds of his Moscow lace and silk factory and established Russia's first cotton mill, using English equipment. This was significant for several reasons. It was extremely rare for serfs to be able to afford to buy their freedom and to gain the landlord's permission to do so. It was the first time a peasant had been able to establish a sizeable business and it was still operating at the time of the Russian revolutions of 1917. It also showed that Russia itself could not yet produce the machinery necessary to operate a modern industrial plant. Finally, it remained an extremely isolated example in the period 1800 to 1890 of an industrial business set up by the private sector in Russia. Neither Alexander I nor his successor Nicholas I saw the long-term benefits of a strong local industrial economy.

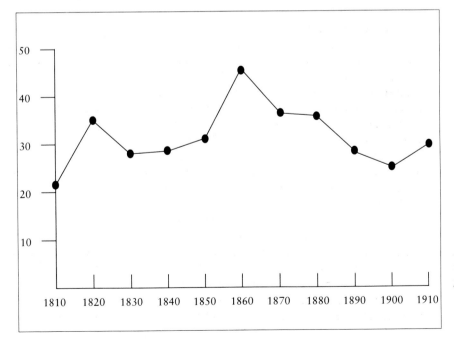

Fig. 2.14 Liquor revenues as a percentage of total government revenues 1810-1910.

Revolutionary Movements

The Napoleonic Wars brought many Russian soldiers into contact with French ideas of liberalism and revolution which they began to support. After 1815 and the Congress of Vienna, Alexander turned increasingly to the repressive Metternich System for inspiration for his domestic policies. This only served to encourage the development of revolutionary societies.

The most prominent of these was the **Society for Public Good** (SPG), largely made up of junior army officers and freemasons. The earliest manifestations of disaffection amongst the military came with the rebellion of the St Petersburg regiments in 1820, but this was quickly suppressed. Like most revolutionary movements, the SPG had factions: the Northern Group wanted a liberal constitutional monarchy, while the Southern Group, led by Pestel, a veteran of the Napoleonic Wars, wanted a revolutionary republic, freedom of serfs and land system based on peasant ownership.

DECEMBRIST CONSPIRACY

When Alexander I died in 1825 without an heir, some of the junior army officers in the SPG were inspired to attempt a coup. This **Decembrist Conspiracy**, led by Pestel, failed due to internal disagreements on policy, lack of preparation, the refusal to use popular discontent as a means for garnering further support and the members' lack of confidence in the likelihood of their actions being successful.

Fig. 2.15 The leaders of the Decembrist Conspiracy, hanged in 1826. This engraving is taken from Alexander Herzen's journal, The Polar Star, printed in London and smuggled into Russia.

Colonel PI Pestel (1799–1826): A veteran of the Napoleonic Wars, Pestel was prominent among the revolutionary societies from 1816 to 1822. Perhaps the leading Decembrist, he was also the most radical, believing in an authoritarian republic whose laws and values would be implemented as a police state. He wished to restructure military service so that all classes had to serve and to create equality before the law. He wanted to abolish serfdom and redistribute the land into both private and public sectors, with each family receiving land according to its needs. Hanged after the failure of the conspiracy, he remained an influence and inspiration for later revolutionary groups, including the socialists.

Historians' Opinions — Alexander I

- the backwardness of Russian industry was due to the absence of a banking system, a lack of capital and difficulty in obtaining labour   **COWIE AND WOLFSON**
- the most cultured and educated group and the source of reform were the higher nobility
- the dismissal of Speransky was due to Alexander I's instability and vacillation and meant that he lost the opportunity for reform — the loss of liberal ideals coincided with his religious conversion to more mystical beliefs
- in the Society for Public Good, differences in views and methods created weakness and a loss of wider support

- class distinction was accentuated more in Russia than anywhere else in Europe   **ALLSOPP AND COWIE**
- the Russian system of administration was feudal
- the Russian economy was wholly agricultural, commercial activity undeveloped and communications were rudimentary — 1825: there were only 200 000 industrial workers and most of industry was foreign owned
- Alexander I's program of liberal reform was cancelled because the liberals demanded too much
- during the Napoleonic Wars, the Russian army became familiar with the concept that rulers have a duty to society and should only rule with the consent of the people they govern

- the domestic policy of Alexander I was swayed by Metternich at the Congress of Vienna — their agreed aim was to keep the clock stopped at 1815 for 50 years   **SEAMAN**
- in agreeing to the Protocol of Troppau, Alexander I was not converted to being a diehard reactionary — instead the other states took advantage of his weakness and vacillation to persuade him to sign the agreement which made the primary aim of the Holy Alliance the repression of revolution in Europe — when later he wished to change his mind and support Greek revolutionaries, Alexander I was hamstrung by the Troppau principles

- by 1815, Alexander I was so distracted by foreign policy that he had little time for domestic policy   **CRAIG**

WESTWOOD

- the practice of serfdom, the tying of peasants to the land, arose in the 18th century when the Russian land was so plentiful and labour was scarce — later in the time of Alexander I there was much discontent among the peasants when this necessity no longer existed and the nobility's obligation to serve the state was relieved but the peasant's obligation to serve the landlord increased

- the character of Alexander I was greatly affected by his love of military spectacle — his inconsistencies were due to a conflict between a fear of disorder and his wish for the improvement of Russia — at the end of his reign he dropped most of his liberal pretensions but not his liberal friends — as he got older, more and more he believed in a worldwide conspiracy theory
- Arakcheyev was a virtuous, religious, honest, sadistic and uneducated man
- the military colonies arose from the economic crisis after the Napoleonic Wars — huge public debt meant that it was necessary for a system where the standing army could be economically self-sufficient
- before Alexander I died, Russia's reputation as the champion of the oppressed won during the first decade of the century had evaporated because the Tsar by his actions and foreign policy proved to be the champion of the oppressors

THOMSON

- the gentry were not opposed to the freedom of the serfs so long as they retained their land — the peasantry objected bitterly to this saying that 'We are yours; the land is ours'
- the Holy Alliance was a result of Alexander I's mystical sense of the dangers of revolution but few European rulers took it seriously
- the Protocol of Troppau was a result of Alexander I's fear of the possibility of revolution in other states

Problems and Issues — Alexander I

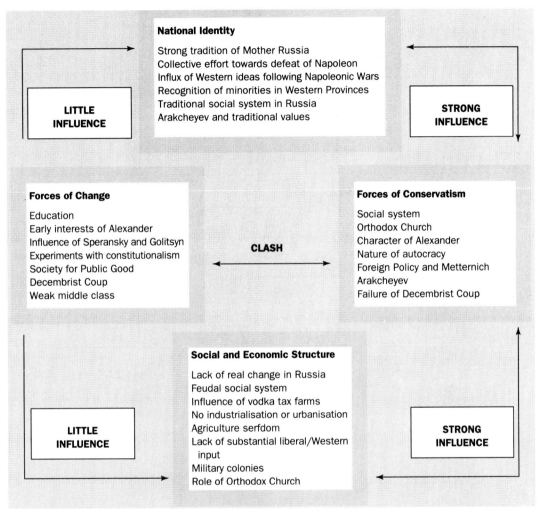

National Identity

Strong tradition of Mother Russia
Collective effort towards defeat of Napoleon
Influx of Western ideas following Napoleonic Wars
Recognition of minorities in Western Provinces
Traditional social system in Russia
Arakcheyev and traditional values

LITTLE INFLUENCE

STRONG INFLUENCE

Forces of Change

Education
Early interests of Alexander
Influence of Speransky and Golitsyn
Experiments with constitutionalism
Society for Public Good
Decembrist Coup
Weak middle class

CLASH

Forces of Conservatism

Social system
Orthodox Church
Character of Alexander
Nature of autocracy
Foreign Policy and Metternich
Arakcheyev
Failure of Decembrist Coup

Social and Economic Structure

Lack of real change in Russia
Feudal social system
Influence of vodka tax farms
No industrialisation or urbanisation
Agriculture serfdom
Lack of substantial liberal/Western
  input
Military colonies
Role of Orthodox Church

LITTLE INFLUENCE

STRONG INFLUENCE

*Fig. 2.16
Problems and
Issues—
Alexander I.*

EXERCISES AND SKILLS REVISION

1. For each of the following questions, write a properly structured paragraph
response:
a. What liberal reforms were introduced by Alexander I?
b. What were the living and working conditions of serfs and state peasants?
c. What was the role of the Orthodox Church in Russia during 1800-1825?
d. What influence did Arakcheyev have upon the reign of Alexander I?
e. What were the major trends in the foreign policy of Alexander I?
f. How and why did revolutionary movements develop among the military
during the reign of Alexander I?

2. Construct a Mind Map which addresses the following issues:
   a. What were the major political, social and economic features of Russian life at the turn of the nineteenth century?
   b. How did liberalism influence the government of Alexander I?
   c. Why had the forces of conservatism asserted their dominance in Russia by 1825?

Fig. 2.17 Map showing provinces and key towns/cities in European Russia

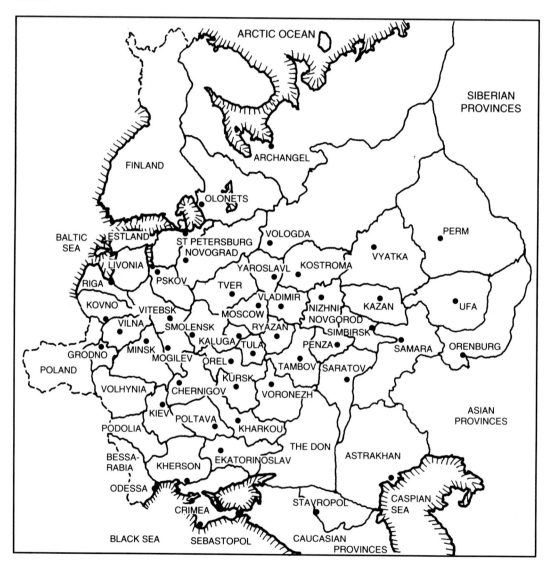

The Reign of Nicholas I

TIME LINE

1825	Death of Alexander I
	Decembrist Revolt
	Accession of Nicholas I
1826	War against Persia
	Acquisition of Kazakhstan and Turkistan
1827	Administrative system of the Imperial Chancery consolidated into the Five Sections
1830	War against Poland
	Russian expansion into the Caucasus
1833	Muchengratz Convention
1835	Education regulations introduced placing educational curators directly under the control of the Minister of Education
1836	Publication of Chaadayev's 'Philosophical Letter', thus beginning the Westernisation debate
1849	University Statute
	Hungarian campaign
	Trial of Petrashevsky Circle
1851	First Russian public train line (Moscow — St. Petersburg)
1853	Crimean War begins
1855	Death of Nicholas I
	Accession of Alexander II
1856	Crimean War ends in Russian defeat
1859	Vodka riots
1861	Emancipation Edict

Nicholas System

REPRESSION REINFORCED

The brother of Alexander I, Nicholas I was an enthusiastic and competent ruler. Terrified that the Decembrist Conspiracy might have led to disaster for him, he decided to adopt policies of repression to ensure that this threat would not materialise again. He set up a system of strict censorship, the dissolution of secret revolutionary or even simply radical organisations; close supervision of university lecturers and students under the regulations of 1835 and, via the University Statute of 1849, higher barriers to entry into all areas of university life.

This **Nicholas System** was an attempt to shift control away from the once feudal land-owning nobility whom Nicholas identified with the aristocratic Decembrists. It resulted in the formalisation of the central, executive power of the Tsar. This affirmation of the autocracy, begun by Peter the Great, was abandoned in the latter half of the eighteenth century due to the agitation of the landowners and culminated in the assassination of Paul I and the installation of Alexander I by this caste. However, in restructuring the bureaucracy in 1803, Alexander had begun the move back to the centralisation of power—this was completed by Nicholas. By reforming the

Imperial Chancery into five sections (see Fig. 2.18), each of which was responsible for a key portfolio of Russian Affairs, Nicholas clearly identified and administered directly those areas he considered vital.

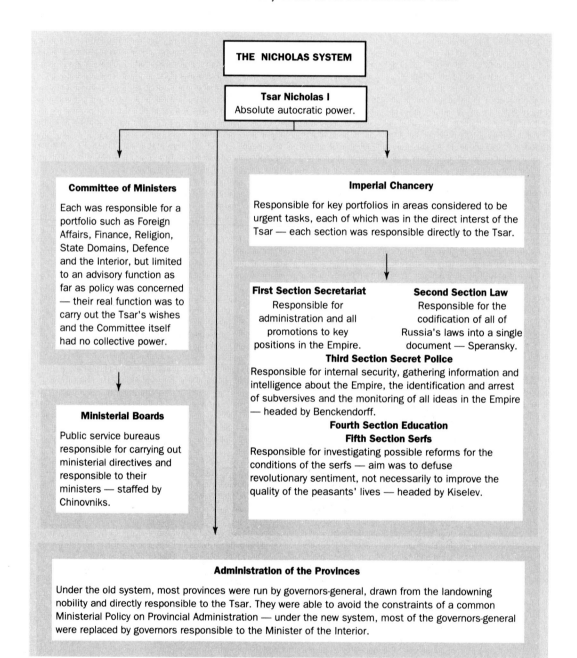

THE NICHOLAS SYSTEM

Tsar Nicholas I
Absolute autocratic power.

Committee of Ministers

Each was responsible for a portfolio such as Foreign Affairs, Finance, Religion, State Domains, Defence and the Interior, but limited to an advisory function as far as policy was concerned — their real function was to carry out the Tsar's wishes and the Committee itself had no collective power.

Ministerial Boards

Public service bureaus responsible for carrying out ministerial directives and responsible to their ministers — staffed by Chinovniks.

Imperial Chancery

Responsible for key portfolios in areas considered to be urgent tasks, each of which was in the direct interst of the Tsar — each section was responsible directly to the Tsar.

First Section Secretariat
Responsible for administration and all promotions to key positions in the Empire.

Second Section Law
Responsible for the codification of all of Russia's laws into a single document — Speransky.

Third Section Secret Police
Responsible for internal security, gathering information and intelligence about the Empire, the identification and arrest of subversives and the monitoring of all ideas in the Empire — headed by Benckendorff.

Fourth Section Education
Fifth Section Serfs
Responsible for investigating possible reforms for the conditions of the serfs — aim was to defuse revolutionary sentiment, not necessarily to improve the quality of the peasants' lives — headed by Kiselev.

Administration of the Provinces

Under the old system, most provinces were run by governors-general, drawn from the landowning nobility and directly responsible to the Tsar. They were able to avoid the constraints of a common Ministerial Policy on Provincial Administration — under the new system, most of the governors-general were replaced by governors responsible to the Minister of the Interior.

Fig. 2.18 Structure of power under Nicholas I—the Nicholas System.

Now, true power in Russia rested firmly in the hands of the Romanovs. Backed by the loyalty of the army and enforced by the **Chinovniks** (the name given to the emerging group of bureaucratic nobility dependent upon the Imperial purse for their income, not their own lands), the Tsar's word was truly law. Fig. 2.18 shows the structure of power under Nicholas I.

NATURE OF POWER

Over 150 000 of the critics of the Nicholas System were sent to Siberia and a secret police was established in the reorganisation of the administration to enforce these measures and policies. This secret police force was the Third Section of the Imperial Chancery, which shows how highly valued it was.

SECRET POLICE

Although an avowed opponent of any policy that even resembled liberalism, Nicholas I was not afraid to use prominent liberals to fulfil specific tasks—for example, Speransky was employed by Nicholas to write down all Russia's pre-existing laws and consolidate them into a single code. However, the intention was to strengthen the autocracy, rather than provide an avenue for liberals to gain substantial reform. The creed of the Nicholas System was 'Orthodoxy, Autocracy and Nationality'.

ORTHODOXY, AUTOCRACY, NATIONALITY

Limited Reform

Nicholas I was not completely blind to the need for reform. He restructured the currency, simplified Russian laws and passed a Factory Act specifying minimum employment conditions for urban workers. He was afraid to go

ECONOMIC REFORM

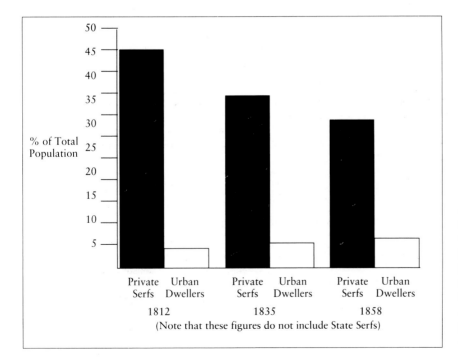

Fig. 2.19 Chart showing the comparison of percentages of private serfs and urban dwellers within the total Russian population 1812-1858.

further in case the political sentiment for change carried the reformist mood out of control.

Nonetheless, his desire for a centralised imperial system led to the reform of the administration and the establishment of the five Sections. This measure increased the bureaucracy in the Empire, with most positions filled by members of the lesser nobility, many of whom were prepared to enforce Nicholas I's conservative policies. Thus for Nicholas I reform was merely a way in which he could strengthen the position of his autocracy, rather than a change to the fundamental nature of the Tsarist regime.

Treatment of Serfs

To dilute the threat of peasant revolt, Nicholas I wanted to alleviate the condition of the serfs to a limited extent. He forbade the sale of serfs by their masters to settle private debts, or sales which broke up families. He allowed serfs whose masters went bankrupt to buy their freedom. The Minister of State Domains, Count PD Kiselev (1788–1872), introduced a limited state peasant welfare system of schools, medical and fire services and agricultural advisory centres. Kiselev improved the lot of state peasants and effected a more equitable distribution of land.

However, these reforms once again were designed to rectify what were perceived by the Tsar as weaknesses and potential sore spots in the institution of serfdom; they were in the style of benevolent paternalism, and certainly not

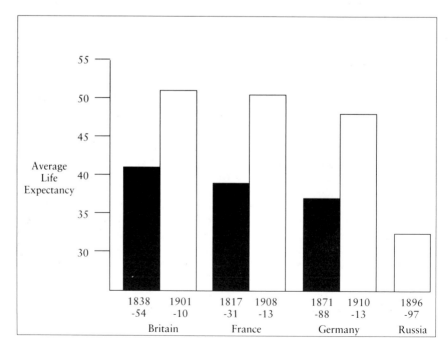

Fig. 2.20 Average life expectancy in Britain, France, Germany and Russia 1817-1913.

guided by liberal ethics. This can be seen further in Nicholas's way of dealing with over 400 peasant revolts that occurred during his reign. The result of serf frustration with oppressive treatment by their landlords and their poor living conditions, none of the revolts were really successful, due to their lack of organisation and poor cohesion between the different peasant groups. They were all stamped out quickly and ruthlessly, often by military intervention.

Primary Extracts and Questions – the Serfs before Emancipation

The appearance of several villages surprised me; they displayed signs of wealth, and even a sort of rustic elegance, which was very pleasing. The neat wooden houses form the line of a single street. They are painted, and their roofs are loaded with ornaments . . . [but] on examining them more closely, these habitations are discovered to be ill built . . . It was the first time I had seen the peasants in their own houses. [He enters an inn.] An immense wooden shed, plank walls on three sides, plank flooring and plank ceiling, formed the hall of entrance, and occupied a greater part of the rustic dwelling. Notwithstanding the free currents of air, I found it redolent of that odour of onions, cabbages, and old greasy leather, which Russian villages and Russian villagers invariably exhale . . . A low and confined room adjoined this immense shed; it reminded me of the cabin of some riverboat; walls, ceiling, floor, seats, and tables, were all of wood rudely hewn. The smell of cabbage and pitch was extremely powerful.

In this retreat, almost deprived of air and light for the doors were low, and the windows extremely small, I found an old woman busily serving tea to four or five bearded peasants, clothed in pelissers of sheepskin, the wool of which is turned inwards . . . There is ignorance and misery among the people . . .

All [the women] I have hitherto seen have appeared to me repulsive . . . Here as in Petersburg, they are broad and short in figure. . . which spreads freely under the petticoat. It is hideous! Add to this voluntary deformity, large men's boots and a species of riding coat . . . falling indeed literally in rags.

DE CUSTINE, FRENCH WRITER, COMMENTS ON THE CONDITION OF THE SERFS IN THE 1830s—1843

(a) What evidence of poor living conditions among villagers does De Custine reveal?
(b) Which sentence do you feel summarises the conditions?

The population varies probably as much as the appearance of the village. It consists usually of serfs (*panskiye liudi*) of free peasants (*kasakki*), of priests, and of nobles. The free peasants and the serfs always keep carefully aloof from each other, usually occupy the opposite portions of a village, rarely intermarry, and differ from each other both in manner and appearance. The panskiye liudi pride themselves on the power and wealth of their lords — the kasakki on their own independence. Among the latter will generally be found not only the wealthiest inhabitants of the village, but likewise all the beggars. This is natural enough. If a free peasant be a drunkard, as most of them are, he is likely to sink into abject poverty; and having no lord on whose bounty he can fall back, his only reliance must be on the alms of the benevolent; if, on the other hand, he be a careful, industrious man, he will be likely to accumulate property, without being liable to the extortions of a lord.

VILLAGES IN THE UKRAINE ACCORDING TO KOHL, ENGLISH WRITER—1842

(c) How does Kohl show the class divisions between the peasants?
(d) What does Kohl see as the main advantage of the free peasant?

SERFDOM IN THE EARLY NINETEENTH CENTURY ACCORDING TO HEBER, ENGLISH WRITER

The peasants belonging to the nobles have their *abrock* [*obrok*] regulated by their means of getting money; at an average throughout the empire of eight or ten roubles . . . Each male peasant is obliged by law, to labour three days in each week for his proprietor. The law takes effect on his arriving at the age of fifteen. If the proprietor chooses to employ him the other days, he may; as, for example, in a manufactory; but then finds him in food and clothing. Mutual advantage, however, generally relaxes this law; and, excepting such as are selected for domestick servants; or, as above, are employed in manufactures, the slave [*sic*] pays a certain *abrock*, or rent, to be allowed to work all week on his own account. The master is bound to furnish him with a house and a certain portion of land. The allotment of land is generally settled by the *starosta* (elder of the village) and a meeting of the peasants themselves. In the same manner, when a master wants an increase of rent, he sends to the starosta, who convenes the peasants; and by that assembly it is decided what proportion each must pay. If a slave exercises any trade which brings him in more money than agricultural labour, he pays a higher abrock.

(d) What obligations did the obrok peasant face?
(e) How does the use of the word 'slave' in the last sentence affect your reading of the extract?

HAXTHAUSEN ON THE RUSSIAN COMMUNE—1840

The Russian communes evince an organic coherence and compact social strength that can be found nowhere else and yield the incalculable advantage that no proletariat can be formed so long as they exist with their present structure. A man may lose or squander all he possesses, but his children do not inherit his poverty. They still retain their claim upon the land, by a right derived, not from him, but from their birth as members of the commune. On the other hand, it must be admitted that this fundamental basis of the communal system, the equal division of the land is not favorable to the progress of agriculture, which . . . under this system could for a long time remain at a low level.

(f) What does Haxthausen see as the major strength of the commune system?
(g) How do Haxthausen's opinions match Karl Marx's opinion that Russia was not suitable for an urban revolution led by a proletariat?
(h) How does the strength of the commune system tie in with Pan-Slavism?
(i) What reasons can you suggest for Haxthausen's opinion that the commune system prevented the growth of agriculture in Russia?

BENCKENDORFF, FIRST HEAD OF THE THIRD SECTION, ON THE PEASANTRY

The powder-magazine under the state.

(j) From the extracts you have read above, provide evidence in support of Benckendorff's statement.

Foreign policy

ACQUISITIONS

Nicholas I's foreign policy was guided by the two goals of expanding the territory of the Empire and crushing foreign liberalism. He added territory to the south in Kazakhstan and Turkistan through the defeat of Persia in 1826.

The Polish revolt of 1830-1 was crushed and further Russian control was established by denying the Poles the liberal reforms Alexander I had promised fifteen years earlier. In 1849 he supported Austria in suppressing

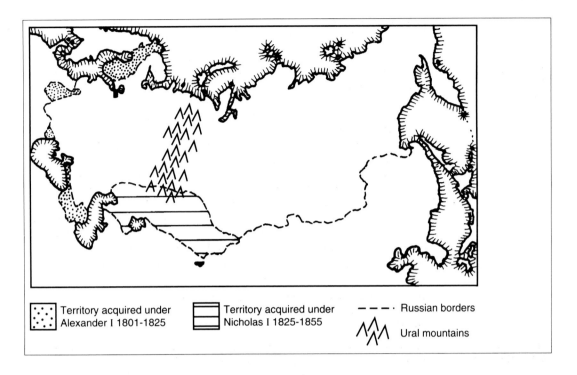

Territory acquired under Alexander I 1801-1825

Territory acquired under Nicholas I 1825-1855

— — — · Russian borders

Ural mountains

Fig. 2.21 Map showing imperial acquisitions under Alexander I and Nicholas I 1801–1855.

Fig. 2.22 The Nobel oil fields in the Azerbaijan in the late nineteenth century. By gaining these territories, Nicholas gained for the Empire the then unrealised potential of the Baku oil reserves.

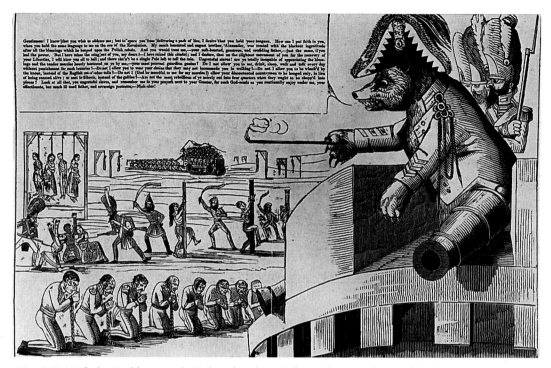

Fig. 2.23 Nicholas I addressing the Poles after the rebellion of 1831. This English cartoon (c1832) shows Nicholas as a bear, the symbol of Russian orthodox nationalism, and is called The Clemency of the Russian Monster.

revolts in Hungary. Note that in 1833, Nicholas re-affirmed the Holy Alliance with Prussia and Austria through the Muchengratz Convention, thereby confirming his support for the doctrines of the Metternich System. This commitment to European conservatism won him the nickname 'The Gendarme of Europe.'

THE GENDARME OF EUROPE

Intellectuals and the Superfluous Men

NATURE OF INTELLECTUAL MOVEMENTS

Some intellectuals were the sons of merchants from the small middle class, but most were younger nobles who had travelled abroad during the reign of Nicholas's brother, adopted liberal views, and returned to Russia either to teach or to study at the universities. The intellectuals attempted to discuss and spread some liberal ideas borrowed from Western European liberals. Most of the liberal ideas they adopted were aimed at redressing the poverty and misery among the workers, but, these early Russian liberals were largely ineffective due to the strict control of the Nicholas System, under which critics could be imprisoned, banned, exiled, declared insane or executed.

At this stage the basis of the desire for reform was the fear that the conditions of the serfs would deteriorate to the extent that the peasants would revolt and the system would collapse—thus the foundation of the belief in reform was still rooted in approval of the Tsarist regime. The liberal intellectuals of the 1830s and 1840s wanted to improve the system in a different way from the government's policies. A relatively sober group, their major weapon of dissent was the written word and their most dominant literary influence was VG Belinsky, possibly the most vocal, and influential critic of the Nicholas System.

VG Belinsky (1811–1848) was the son of a Finnish doctor and was rejected from university on the grounds that he was intellectually limited. He was one of the first of the middle class to make a living from writing, pioneering the style of critical realism, in which he advocated the social responsibility of the writer in portraying life as it actually occurred and the adoption of Western practices as the cure for the political, social and economic problems of Russia.

Increasingly, this land-owning intellectual elite, stripped of real power by the Chinovniks, came to be seen as the **Superfluous Men** of Russia. Bound to the St Petersburg court by the suspicious Tsar for most of the year so as not to build up personal followings on their estates, and not permitted to engage in trade or administration, they were left with the choice of either drunken socialising in the army or occasional travel within the Empire. They began to write of their experiences and the suffering of the peasants, but were not able to infiltrate the corridors of power. Among the most important of these literary figures were Pushkin, Gogol, Belinsky and Lermentov.

SUPERFLUOUS MEN AND LITERATURE

Thus this upper class intellectual elite, preferring words to actions, shunned by the autocracy and alienated from the middle class, failed to achieve any substantial reform during the reign of Nicholas I. By the time of his death, many of the younger nobles had gambled away their family fortunes; many others instead turned to the new ideas of socialism and began to formulate the revolutionary creeds of the 1860s and 1870s.

Intellectual Debate — Pan-Slavism and Westernisation

The major intellectual and philosophical debate in Russia in the middle of the nineteenth century concerned these two philosophies. Pan-Slavism was a popular movement which wished to create a separate 'Slav' culture under Russian leadership, which celebrated the Russian feudal system and which was free of any of the influences of Western culture. It was opposed to Westernisation and supported Russian expansion, especially into the Balkans. Its main proponents were writer and poet Khomyakov, Ivan Aksakov, and the Kireyevsky brothers, and as it was supported by Nicholas I and the bureaucracy, it became the philosophy that guided Russian foreign policy.

PAN-SLAVISM

Westernisation, the second major cultural movement of nineteenth century Russia, aimed to introduce Western culture, ideals and reform to

WESTERNISATION

Fig. 2.24 Intellectual suppression under Nicholas I. Gustave Doré comments on the secret police state set up by Nicholas and its preoccupation with arresting the most charismatic of the young radical thinkers.

Fig. 2.25 The Superfluous Men. From the left, Aleksandr Pushkin (1799–1837), Nicolai Gogol (1809–52) and Mikhail Lermentov (1814–41).

Russia and followed on from the program of Peter the Great in the eighteenth century. During the time of the Nicholas System, the main supporters of Westernisation were Chaadayev at first and later Petrashevsky. They believed that the technical and industrial strength of the West was too great to be ignored so limited concessions should be made by the Tsar to match these strengths. Their proposals included economic modernisation and industrialisation, freeing the serfs, and the granting of limited political reform towards a more liberal government. However, without the support of Nicholas I, this process did not begin until the 1860s, when Russia was well behind Europe economically and socially. Nicholas's treatment for these leading Westernisers and critics of his regime was harsh: Chaadayev was declared insane and put under house arrest; Petrashevsky and his circle of friends were arrested in 1849. Some of the Petrashevsky circle were sentenced to death, but their sentences were commuted to hard labour in Siberia, where they joined the rest of their colleagues.

MV Butashevich-Petrashevsky: A junior official in the Ministry of Foreign Affairs, Petrashevsky was deeply influenced by the pre-Marxian socialists. He believed strongly that peasant revolt was the only way for the people to overcome the military superiority of the Tsarist autocracy. From 1845 to 1849, he conducted discussion sessions for similar intellectuals, poets and writers (including Dostoievsky) in which they condemned the autocracy, serfdom and military discipline and supported the establishment of free speech, equality before the law and a democratic republic. This Petrashevsky circle never progressed beyond informal Friday evening soirées, but over 100 were arrested by the Third Section in 1849 and put on public trial. Some were sentenced to hard labour and 15 were sentenced to death although their sentences were commuted to exile to Siberia by Nicholas at the last moment an action which only served to bring greater public attention to their plight.

PA Chaadayev (1793–1856): Although from a military and aristocratic background, he favoured the liberal social circles in Moscow and St Petersburg. His *First Philosophical Letter*, written in 1829 and published in 1836, in which he condemned Russia as being sterile due to its dissociation with the West and with Catholicism, provoked the whole Westernisation debate. He believed in free thought, rationalism, science and personal liberty. The government's response to his letter was to declare him insane.

AS Khomyakov (1804–1860): A noble-born writer and poet who travelled widely outside Russia in his youth, Khomayakov was an ardent supporter of a society based on the traditional Russian values of the land, the village community and piety.

Primary Extracts and Questions — the Intelligentsia and the Superfluous Men before Emancipation

PUSHKIN, RUSSIAN NOVEL-IST, IN *A NOVEL IN LETTERS* ON THE PLIGHT OF THE SUPERFLUOUS MEN—1829

I shall, retire, marry and go off to my village in the Saratov district. The profession of a landowner is not unlike that of the Service. To be concerned with the management of three thousand souls, whose well-being depends entirely upon us, is more important than commanding a platoon or transcribing a diplomatic dispatch . . .

The state of neglect in which we leave our peasants is unforgivable. The more rights we have over them, the greater must be our responsibility towards them. We leave them to the mercy of a dishonest steward, who oppresses them and robs us. We mortgage our future incomes and ruin ourselves, and old age catches us worrying and in want.

This is the cause of the swift decline of our nobility: the grandfather was rich, the son is needy, the grandson will go begging. Ancient families fall into decay; new ones arise and in the third generation go again. Fortunes are merged, and not one family knows who its forebears were. To what will such political materialism lead? I do not know. But it is time to put a stop to it.

I was never able to see without regret the decline of our historic families; no one among us, beginning with those who belong to them, thinks much of them . . . But our Fatherland has forgotten even the real names of its saviours. The past does not exist for us. A miserable people . . .

A gentry stemming from meritorious bureaucracy cannot replace an hereditary aristocracy, whose family traditions ought to be part of our national heritage. But what sort of family traditions would one get from the children of a collegiate associate?

(a) What does Pushkin identify as the preferred life of the aristocrat? What does this say about his concerns for the peasantry?
(b) What reasons does Pushkin give for the decline of the aristocracy?
(c) What options does this extract suggest there were for a young male aristocrat to occupy his time? From your own knowledge, give more options.
(d) What does Pushkin see as replacing the land-owning aristocracy in terms of importance?
(e) From your own knowledge, explain why these events were occurring.

SOME EXTRACTS FROM MIKHAIL LERMENTOV'S *A HERO OF OUR TIMES*—1834

A conversation between the hero Pechorin and an old acquaintance, Maxim:

'Delighted to see you, dear Maxim Maximych,' said Pechorin. 'How are you?'
'And what about you?' the old man mumbled, with tears in his eyes, put out by Pechorin's formal tone. 'It's been a long time . . . Where are you heading now?'
'Persia. Then on from there.'
'But you're not going this minute, are you? My dear fellow, you must stay on for a bit. We can't part straight away after not seeing each other all this time.'
'I must be going, Maxim Maximych,' replied Pechorin.
'But merciful heavens, man, what's all the rush? I've got so many things to tell you. And a lot of things to ask as well. How is it then? Left the army have you? What have you been doing?'
Pechorin smiled. 'Being bored,' he said.

[Pechorin comments at the end of a failed romantic adventure:]
'And anyway, the joys and tribulations of mankind are of no concern to me, an itinerant officer with a travel warrant in my pocket.'

[Pechorin comments on a conversation with a friend:]
'Is it my sole function in life, I thought, to be the ruin of other people's hopes? Through all my active life fate always seems to to have brought me in for the denouement of other people's dramas. As if nobody could die or despair without my help. I've been the indispensable figure of the fifth act, thrust into the pitiful role of executioner or betrayer. What was fate's purpose? Perhaps I was meant to be a writer of domestic tragedies or novels of family life, or a purveyor of stories, perhaps for the Reader's Library? Many people start life expecting to end up as Alexander the Great or Lord Byron, then spend their whole lives as minor civil servants.'

(f) Lermentov stated that his hero, Pechorin, was based on the people of his class he saw around him. From the extracts given, choose three sentences and explain how they demonstrate the figure of the 'Superfluous Man'.

Confined in our schism, nothing of what was happening in Europe reached us. We stood apart from the world's great ventures . . . while the world was building anew, we created nothing: we remained crouched in our hovels of log and thatch. In a word, we had no part in the destinies of mankind. We were Christians but the fruits of Christianity were not for us.

CHAADAYEV, RUSSIAN WRITER IN FAVOUR OF WESTERNISATION, ON THE ISOLATION OF THE WESTERNISATION MOVEMENT—1836

(g) What impression does Chaadayev give of the traditional Russian way of life?
(h) From this extract, state reasons for the desire of some intellectuals to Westernise.

What a blessing it is for Russia that the rural commune has never been broken up, that private ownership has never replaced the property of the commune: how fortunate it is for the Russian people that they have remained outside all political movements, and, for that matter, outside European civilisation

HERZEN, RUSSIAN WRITER AND EX-WESTERNISER, ON THE BENEFITS OF THE RUSSIAN VILLAGE SYSTEM—1850s

(i) Herzen was at first a supporter of Westernisation, but on touring the West in 1847 and 1848, and seeing the chaos of the year of revolutions in Europe, he returned a supporter of Pan-Slavism. Based on the extract and your own knowledge, what reasons can you give for this conversion of belief?
(j) From your own knowledge, explain why Nicholas I championed the Pan-Slavists.

A life of wealth and bliss, to cover this beggar's earth with palaces and fruits and to adorn it with fruits—this is our aim. In our country we will begin this revolution, and the whole world will bring it to fulfilment. Soon the whole of mankind will be freed from unbearable suffering.

ONE OF THE PETRASHEVSKY CIRCLE COMMENTS ON ITS AIMS—1847

(k) What is the tone of this extract?
(l) What does this extract reveal about the aims of the Petrashevsky Circle?
(m) How realistic were these aims?
(n) From the extract and your own knowledge, explain the nature of the threat to Nicholas I posed by the Circle.

Economic Policy

Before the 1870s Russia was still predominantly a primitive agricultural society. Under Nicholas I, almost all the land was owned by the state or landlords, and worked communally by the peasants. Land was issued by local village authorities to male peasants to work to pay for the rent and taxes owed to the states and the landlords. Almost no attention was paid to industry and there was no public railway system at all before the 1850s, only a private rail link from St Petersburg to the Tsar's residence at Tsarkoye Selo, opened in 1837.

AGRICULTURE AND INDUSTRY

ECONOMIC POLICY

Nicholas I discouraged economic growth and development because he was afraid that rapid industrialisation would create instability and a desire for reform that would endanger his authority and position. There was common support among the wealthy for this view that an industrial society would lead to the questioning of the position of the Tsar and thus the aristocracy as well. The policies of Kankrin, Nicholas I's Finance Minister, were designed to foment economic stagnation. Any development of enterprise became part of the state's monopoly and was not to be shared with the traders.

Because Nicholas's economic policy provided no encouragement for the growth of a middle class, there was no large middle class to apply pressure to the regime for industrialisation. The government's reliance on pre-existing economic institutions, meant that the vodka tax farming system became even more consolidated, providing between 26 and 38% of total government revenues. Especially towards the end of Nicholas's reign, to meet the costs of fighting the Crimean War, liquor taxes became vital and the government increased the rate and frequency of taxation on the tavern-renting retailers. They in turn were becoming more adept at watering down their product and increasing their profit margins.

With these two sources for increased prices for the drinker, costs for this most Russian of products began to rise to the level where the lower classes could not afford to consume the quantities they desired. The mood in the countryside became virtually mutinous in the mid-1850s, with mass rioting and boycotting in response to the government's liquor policies in 1859.

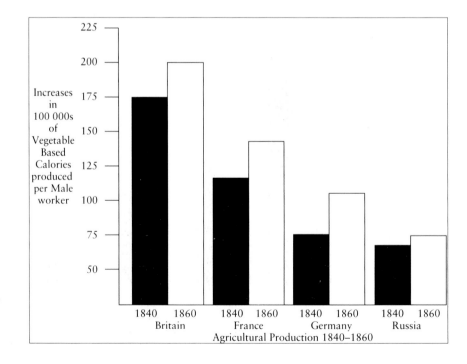

Fig. 2.26 Agricultural production in Britain, France, Germany and Russia 1840-1860.

Fig. 2.27 1838 engraving of the opening of Russia's first railtrack in 1837 from Tsarkoye Selo to St Petersburg.

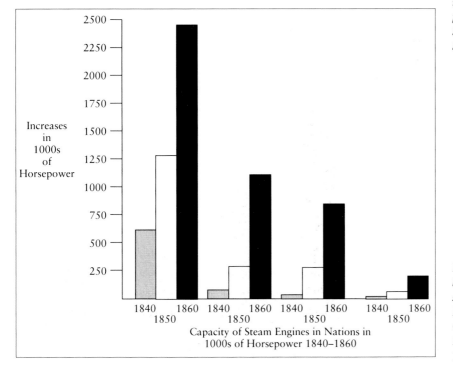

Capacity of Steam Engines in Nations in 1000s of Horsepower 1840–1860

Fig. 2.28 Total horsepower of steam engines in Britain, France, Germany and Russia 1840-1860.

Fig. 2.29 Russia's position in the Industrialisation in Major World Producers 1810-1860. (These figures are based on per capita consumption of raw cotton and coal, production of smelted iron, development of railways and industrial engine-driven machinery.)

	RUSSIA	FRANCE	GERMANY	BRITAIN
1810	10=	4=	7=	1
1840	10=	5	7=	1
1860	10=	5	6=	1=

Weak Middle Class

Without urbanisation and modernisation of industry, with monopolies held by the state, with manufacturing privileges granted to the aristocracy, with restrictions on education and reliance on state-sponsored feudalism, there could be no effective middle class. There were a few traders and professionals, but Kankrin's policies discouraged them from identifying themselves as a separate class. They felt that there was no prospect of change, so the liberal parliamentary ideas so popular in the rest of Europe in the 1840s had no appeal to the small middle class because they seemed unachieveable.

EF Kankrin (1774–1845): A German soldier who had acted capably as Quartermaster-General during the War of 1812, he was Minister of Finance for 21 years and served under both Alexander I and Nicholas I. He was an efficient administrator who was an extremely conservative and at times unimaginative director of state finance.

Orthodox Church

The Russian Orthodox Church was still the major pillar of the Tsarist system. Under the most unmystical Nicholas, most priests were from the upper classes, well educated, conservative and obedient to the Tsarist autocracy, which allocated to them the responsibility for upholding social as well as religious doctrine.

Crimean War

In 1853 Russia went to war against the Ottoman Empire led on by Nicholas I's policy of expansion in the Balkans. By 1856, Russia had lost, due to the intervention of Britain and France on the side of Turkey.

Despite its massive resources and manpower, Russia lacked the industrial capacity to supply a modern army, the communications to transport men and products to the front line and Russian generals were more concerned with the appearance of the soldiers on the parade ground than with their training for the battleground. Clearly, the lack of modernised industry was affecting the last defence of the autocracy — the army.

The Succession of Alexander II

Nicholas I died in 1854 and left his successor, Alexander II, with many problems. Many Russians, including members of the aristocracy, now realised that Russia's only hopes for military survival lay with modernisation. This in turn meant industrialisation for military purposes at least — improvements to communications and the need for a railway system. Also, there were increased demands from the peasants for improved conditions as a reward for their mil-

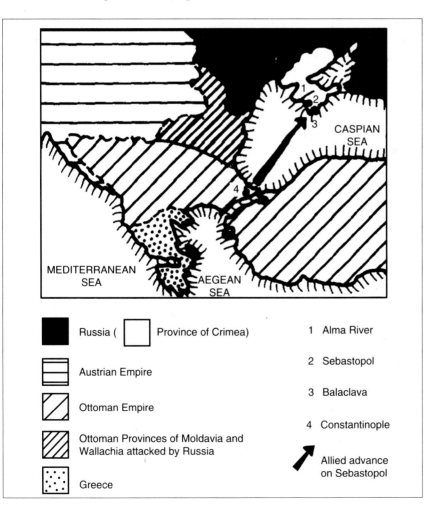

	Russia (		Province of Crimea)	1 Alma River
Austrian Empire				2 Sebastopol
Ottoman Empire				3 Balaclava
Ottoman Provinces of Moldavia and Wallachia attacked by Russia				4 Constantinople
Greece				Allied advance on Sebastopol

Fig. 2.30 Map showing Crimean War.

itary services and as recognition for their role in the survival of Russia. Many nobles and also the new Tsar, were in favour of these demands — though more because they feared revolt than wanted liberal reform.

Boycotts and riots in 1859 over the price of vodka meant that the tax-farm, the government's main source of income was no longer viable and serious consideration had to be given to reforming this economic anachronism. Above all, failure in the Crimean War was seen as symptomatic of a crisis in the Tsarist political, social and economic structure of Russia, making the need for some form of change vital, even if it only took the form of symbolic change.

Primary Extracts and Questions — the Nature of the Autocracy 1800–1861

KARAMZIN, RUSSIAN NOBLE, ON THE NEED FOR UNLIMITED AUTOCRACY IN RUSSIA — 1811

Autocracy has founded and resuscitated Russia. Any change in her political constitution has led in the past and must lead in the future to her perdition, for she consists of very many and different parts, each of which has its own special civic needs; what save unlimited monarchy can produce in such a machine the required unity of action? If Alexander, inspired by generous hatred for the abuses of autocracy, should lift a pen and proscribe himself laws other than those of God and his own conscience, then the true, virtuous citizen of Russia would presume to stop his hand, and to say: 'Sire! you exceed the limits of your authority. Russia, taught by long disasters, vested before the holy altar the power of autocracy in your ancestor, asking him that he rule her supremely and indivisibly.' . . . [Let us] affirm that there is only one true method for a sovereign to make certain that his subjects do not abuse their authority: let him rule virtuously, let him accustom his subjects to goodness. In this manner he will engender salutory customs, principles, and public opinions which will keep future sovereigns within the bounds of legitimate authority far more efficiently than all the ephemeral forms. How? By inspiring them with a fear of arousing universal hatred with a contrary system of government.

(a) What arguments does Karamzin put forward in favour of autocracy in Russia?
(b) What does Karamzin say that an autocrat should use to decide issues of state?
(c) What does Karamzin say ultimately will be the effect of autocracy on the ruler's subjects?
(d) What features of society does Karamzin fail to take into account in his defence of autocracy?

DE MAISTRE, FRENCH WRITER, ON THE ROLE OF SERFDOM — 1812

The Emperor cannot rule without slavery.

(e) List the reasons De Maistre might have said this.

COUNT UVAROV, RUSSIAN MINISTER, ON THE CONSERVATISM OF HIS POLICIES

If I can succeed in delaying for fifty years the kind of future that theories are brewing for Russia, I shall have performed my duty and shall die in peace.

(f) What does this extract say about Nicholas I's choice of ministers?

NICHOLAS I'S ANNOUNCEMENT TO THE EUROPEAN REVOLUTIONARIES OF 1848

Give heed, O ye peoples, and submit, for God is with us!

(g) What is the tone of this extract?
(h) How does this extract help you to understand the nature of Nicholas I's government?

DE CUSTINE, FRENCH WRITER, ON THE FUNDAMENTALS OF AUTOCRACY AND RUSSIA — 1843

The government of Russia is an absolute monarchy moderated by assassination . . .
The more I see of Russia, the more I approve of the conduct of the Emperor in forbidding his subjects to travel, and in rendering access to his own country difficult

to foreigners. The political system of Russia could not survive twenty years' free communication with the rest of Europe . . .

Military discipline, applied to the government of a state is a powerful means of oppression . . . But this formidable force will sometimes turn against those who employ it . . . The more ignorant the people are, and the longer they have been patient, the more likely is their vengeance to be dreadful. A government which wields power by maintaining ignorance is more terrible than stable . . . Tranquillity is maintained among the people by the length and difficulties of communication, by the secrecy of government . . . the blind obedience of troops, and above all, by the complete ignorance of the country people themselves . . . The reader can form no conception of the manner in which a lord, when taking possession of some newly acquired domain, is received by the peasants . . . Men, women and children all fall on their knees before the new master — all kiss the hands, and sometimes the feet of the landholder . . .

If ever your sons should be discontented with France . . . tell them to go to Russia. It is a useful journey for every foreigner; whoever has well examined that country will be content to live anywhere else. It is always well to know that a society exists where no happiness is possible, because, by the law of his nature, man cannot be happy unless he is free.

(i) What methods of the Russian autocracy does De Custine reveal in this extract?
(j) How does this extract help to show the nature of Russian society as compared to that of Western Europe in the early 1840s?
(k) What does De Custine foreshadow? What arguments does he use to support this prediction?
(l) How can this extract be used to demonstrate Nicholas I's attitudes towards censorship and the West?

Count SS Uvarov: Minister of Education from 1833-1849, he formulated the policy and oversaw the introduction of the regulations and Education Statute which restricted access to education and brought the academics and administrators within the education system directly under the control of the Ministry.

Historians' Opinions — Nicholas I

- Nicholas I resolved to preserve the status quo intact — he was brave, honourable, totally dedicated to his job, a monstrous anachronism and controlled his empire to the minutest level   **KOCHAN AND ABRAHAM**
- in a situation where free expression of public opinion was not allowed, Nicholas I lived in an autocratic vacuum, plagued by uncertainty and insecurity Nicholas I feared serfdom and wanted to abolish it — he feared that if emancipation favoured the peasants too much the nobility would assassinate him and that if the emancipation favoured the nobility too much the peasants would revolt — he decided that the nobility was a greater threat and therefore did not free the serfs
- Nicholas I was admired by the people until about 1840 at which time the intellectual mood of Russia swung away from him towards Westernisation
- the domestic policy of 'Orthodoxy, Autocracy, Nationality' clashed with

foreign policy of attracting the support of the Turkish rebels in the 1850s. Nicholas I's reign brought out all of the reactionary potential of the Holy Alliance of the Congress of Vienna

WESTWOOD

- Nicholas I was in a permanent state of struggle against his personal limitations, sincerely trying to do what he thought was right and failing not through a lack of will but through a lack of perception
- Nicholas I liked the organisation, chain of command, order, discipline, obedience and acceptance of authority in the army and he admired and imitated Prussia
- his two major influences were both Germans — Nesselrode, his foreign policy advisor who advocated caution in foreign policy and militarism, and Benckendorff, the founder and head of the Third Section
- Nicholas's position as the Christian autocrat meant that he was supposed to be the Christian conscience of his people and that he was supposed to use his absolute power to soften the effect of harsh law upon individuals, to reward the deserving and to punish the undeserving — he believed that God had given him the task of controlling the people because although they were great, they could be dangerous if out of control
- centralisation of administration meant increased control for the Tsar but extra paperwork for his administration
- the Western press referred to Nicholas I as the 'Royal Gendarme' due to his pursuit of police state methods, especially after 1848

THOMSON

- Nicholas I was haunted for the whole of his reign by the spectre of revolution.

CRAIG

- Nicholas I was the kind of soldier who put more value on discipline and drill than initiative — his ideal nation was a disciplined state where all subjects recognised that their first duty was to obey authority — this change was reprehensible in itself, even for institutions (such as serfdom) which he regarded as evil

COWIE AND WOLFSON

- Nicholas I prohibited the knout [a plaited steel whip used for flogging] for private offences, but its use by his law courts was so frequent that he became known as 'Nicholas Flogger'
- the slow development of industry brought an increase in the incidence of serfdom in factories and mines

KV Nesselrode (1780–1861): A Protestant German, as Foreign Minister from 1815 to 1856, Nesselrode was largely responsible for the way Russia joined in and supported the Holy Alliance and the Metternich System. He did not favour military intervention, seeing negotiations and diplomacy as more effective means of international politics. A strong supporter of monarchical autocracy and Russian expansion, he was dismissed by Alexander II after the disastrous Crimean War.

General AK Benckendorff (1783–1844): A Baltic German, he was responsible for the introduction and organisation of the Third Section and was its first head. The Third Section incorporated both civil and military police and its activities were primarily the shadowing and collection of information on suspected enemies of the state. At first, the Third Section was very effective in identifying both radical elements and corrupt officials, but after the death of Benckendorff in 1844, it tended more towards the persecution of opponents of the Tsar, basing its investigations largely upon false accusations and punishment without investigation.

Fig. 2.31
Problems and
Issues—Nicholas I.

Problems and Issues — Nicholas I

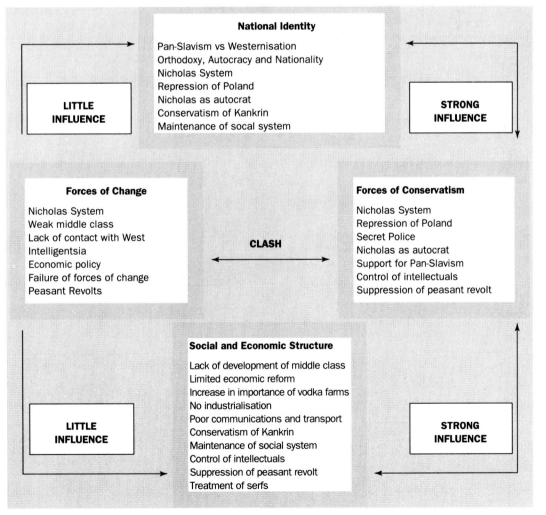

National Identity

Pan-Slavism vs Westernisation
Orthodoxy, Autocracy and Nationality
Nicholas System
Repression of Poland
Nicholas as autocrat
Conservatism of Kankrin
Maintenance of socal system

LITTLE INFLUENCE

STRONG INFLUENCE

Forces of Change

Nicholas System
Weak middle class
Lack of contact with West
Intelligentsia
Economic policy
Failure of forces of change
Peasant Revolts

CLASH

Forces of Conservatism

Nicholas System
Repression of Poland
Secret Police
Nicholas as autocrat
Support for Pan-Slavism
Control of intellectuals
Suppression of peasant revolt

Social and Economic Structure

Lack of development of middle class
Limited economic reform
Increase in importance of vodka farms
No industrialisation
Poor communications and transport
Conservatism of Kankrin
Maintenance of social system
Control of intellectuals
Suppression of peasant revolt
Treatment of serfs

LITTLE INFLUENCE

STRONG INFLUENCE

EXERCISES AND SKILLS REVISION

1. For each of the following questions, write a properly structured paragraph response:
   a. What was the significance of the Decembrist Conspiracy and why did it fail?
   b. How did the character of Nicholas I influence the way Russia was governed?
   c. What did the phrase 'Orthodoxy, Nationality and Autocracy' mean?
   d. What were the major instruments of government Nicholas I used to suppress opposition and the forces of change?
   e. What factors prevented significant social and economic change during the period 1825-1856?
   f. Why did Nicholas favour Pan-Slavism over Westernisation?
   g. What results did Nicholas I's war in the Crimea have upon the stability of Russia?
2. Construct a Mind Map to address the following issues:
   a. What was the Nicholas System?
   b. How did Nicholas I repress the forces of change in Russia in the period 1825 to 1854?
   c. What effects did the reign of Nicholas I have upon the political, social and economic institutions of Russia?

New Skills and Exercises

Writing Essays and Three Part Structured Responses

THE ESSAY IN HISTORY.

- An essay is an extended piece of formal writing in response to a particular question. It consists of a series of paragraphs of full sentences. In writing an essay for History you are presenting a logical argument in words to demonstrate:
  - knowledge and understanding of information and ideas
  - skills in the gathering, organising, analysis and written presentation of information and ideas

  Depending on the question, an essay may be *narrative* or *argumentative*. In other words, it can *re-tell facts*, or it can *re-tell and explain facts*.

In the Higher School Certificate examinations in New South Wales, you will not be required to write an essay on nineteenth century Russia — rather you will have to write a three part structured response.

THE STRUCTURE OF AN ESSAY

- Essays generally have three parts:
  - introduction
  - body
  - conclusion

- **The Introduction.** This is the first paragraph in which you provide your answer to the question and preview the issues you are going to discuss later in the essay. You may also wish to define any technical terms relevant to the whole essay here.
- **The Body.** This is a series of paragraphs to provide the evidence supporting your argument in answer to the question. In the body it is necessary to group information into paragraphs so as to avoid presenting random information and to knit your ideas into a fluid and logical sequence. You must have a clear idea of the logic behind the order of your paragraphs. Generally you should confine yourself to one major point per paragraph, but sometimes you may have to blend points together. If so, you will need to establish the link between these points within the paragraph. Some common ways of grouping information together include:
  - *Social, Economic and Political Factors S/E/P:* grouping events into social, economic and political factors. Although this is a simple breakdown and useful for broad-ranging questions where you have to compress a very large amount of information in a short period of time, it can become boring and unimaginative, and is inappropriate where you have to concentrate on one of these three areas by itself. It is also easy to fall into the trap of writing with insufficient detail with the S/E/P approach.
  - *Individual Factors:* allocating one significant factor (for example a reason why or a method how) to each paragraph and explaining it fully. This is very useful where you have between five and eight factors of equal importance and logical sequence to discuss but can become difficult where the factors concerned run over the chronology of a whole period or where there are too many factors to warrant individual treatment. You could order the paragraphs according to chronological order or the order of their importance.
  - *Highlighting One Factor:* taking one factor and explaining its significance to the question over several paragraphs. You then allocate the remaining paragraphs to discussing the other less important factors, usually by compressing them into two to three factors per paragraph. This approach is very useful if the question or the particular importance of one factor requires you to spend extra time explaining its contribution, but is less appropriate if a factor does not require special emphasis.
  - *Chronological Order:* allocating a specific time period of, say, 10 to 20 years of historical events per paragraph and discussing all the events of that period within the paragraph. The paragraphs should be in chronological order. This is especially appropriate where all the factors in a topic of history are separated into convenient and distinct changes over identifiable periods, and can lead to very sophisticated responses. However when using this approach, be careful to avoid simply saying 'and then this happened', without also carefully explaining the causes, course and effects of the event. This approach is

not really appropriate for emphasising a particular factor or where the chronology of a period does not break down evenly.

Be guided by the requirements of the question at all times and if given an unfamiliarly worded question, you may need a more flexible approach (especially where there are multi-part questions) or even a different one altogether.

- **The Conclusion.** This is the final paragraph in which you summarise and restate your answer to the question. Use it to expand and compare all the levels of the argument you developed in the body of your essay, tie up any loose ends, point out any difficulties or gaps in the evidence and perhaps give a brief prelude to the next phase of history to follow the topic of the question. Do not simply rewrite your introduction.

THE WRITING PROCESS

Successful, well drafted essay writing is the result of a series of steps:
- Identifying the nature of the question
- Brainstorming your ideas
- Planning and gathering evidence for the essay
- Writing the essay.

IDENTIFYING THE NATURE OF AN ESSAY TASK.

There are various types of essay question, requiring you to discuss information and ideas in a specific way. Each different type of essay question will set you a different task. Only rarely will you be asked to write down everything you know about a particular subject in the form of a narrative essay. Instead, most senior essays require different forms of interpretation of ideas and information. They require you to present an argument concerning methods, cause and effect, judgment and general discussion. It is important to be able to distinguish between the types of essay question, so that you are not confused about the exact nature of the task that an essay question sets.

TYPES OF ESSAY QUESTION

There are five types of essay questions:
- narrative questions
- method questions
- cause and effect questions
- judgment questions
- discussion questions

The following information will help you to identify the type of question and the approach to take in answering it.
- **Narrative questions:** Describe . . . State . . . What were?
  - State a full set of facts in chronological order, no detailed interpretation.
- **Method questions:** In what way . . . How did . . . What methods did . . . use?
  - Identify and explain the pattern of how something came about or the pattern of the action people took.
  - Identify and explain the way changes occurred by
    - deciding on the indicators/measuring factors

- assessing the indicators at the beginning of the subject
- assessing the indicators at the end of the subject stating the changes that occurred
- **Cause and effect questions:** Why was/were/did . . . What were the reasons for . . .? What were the causes of . . . For what reasons did?
  - Identify and explain the reasons that an event occurred. What effect/result . . . What were the effects/results of?
  - Identify and explain the effects of certain events. This may take the following forms:
    - full details of specific types of effects on events in general
    - full details of effects in general upon a specific event
    - full explanation of all the effects of a specific event
- **Judgment questions:** How far . . . How much . . . To what extent . . . How well? How important . . . How effectively . . . How significant?
  - Make a judgment about the contribution of one factor to a subject area. Look at
    - factors: identify the specific subjects and factors of the topic of the question
    - value words: your argument should correspond in size and extent of contribution relating to the idea of the Value Word in the question.
    - size of contribution: the degree of the contribution should be explained either in terms of full contribution, partial contribution or no contribution at all.
- **Discussion questions:** Do you agree with this statement? Discuss . . . What evidence is there to support this statement? . . . Discuss . . .
  Put forward all the issues associated with a statement or a happening, explain all the relevant points of view, make a judgement as the relative importance of the various pieces of evidence and give your opinions about the issues, with full reasons.

BRAINSTORMING

Once you have identified what the question requires, you will have to research the topic for the information and evidence for your answer. Then identify the main ideas and work out how they relate to the question. This is brainstorming. Write down the question on a spare sheet of paper, then let your mind go — write down every single idea that comes to you about the question. Use your notes and your research to help you if you like, but do not cross out yet.

When you have done this, check your research once again to see if you have missed anything. Then organise your list of ideas into a coherent set of notes:

- Look through your list of ideas.
- Combine ideas that are similar.
- Cross out those that do not relate to the question.
- Try to sort out the main ideas from the evidence needed to support them.

- Number the relevant ideas in order of importance.
- Rewrite the list, using the main ideas as headings, and the smaller ideas as notes under them. Write the ideas down in the order of importance, or chronological order if that is more appropriate.

PLANNING, GATHERING AND USING EVIDENCE TO WRITE AN ESSAY

You now have an outline plan for your essay. The next stage is to flesh out those ideas with full factual and source evidence and to form a detailed essay plan. One way of doing this is to use the outline scheme shown below:

QUESTION:

Topic:
Focus:
Task:

Key Issues	Evidence to support issue	Relevance?	Importance?

ANSWER:

There are five steps in the process:
- identify the question
- identify what the question requires
- assess the issues
- write the answer
- write the essay

- **Identify the question:** Write down the question in the space provided.
- **Identify what the question requires:** As usual, you must go through the process of working out what the question is asking. You must identify the topic of the question, the focus of the topic and then the nature of the task and write them in the space provided. Breaking down the question in this

fashion makes it easier to work out the most important issues in the question.
- **Assess the issues:** Write down the key issues (points central to the topic):
  - list the evidence in support of each issue
  - state how the evidence relates the issue to the topic
  - assess how important the evidence is and its overall weight in the topic in the spaces provided.

You will see that the first column on the chart contains a list of the most important issues which are part of the topic of the question. You should have arrived at these points through brainstorming. These points will later become the topics for the key sentences of the paragraphs in the body of the essay.

In the second column write a summary of each issue, which will provide the detail for the substance of the paragraphs in the body of the essay.

In the third column write a summary of how each issues relates to the topic as a whole and will provide the argument for the conclusions to the paragraphs in the body of the essay.

In the fourth column write an evaluation of each issue. This means valuing its importance to the topic and determining the specific areas in which it can be used.

Write a paragraph summary of your argument as briefly as possible in the space beneath the columns.

You can now write the essay based on this method. Notice that **WRITING THE ESSAY** although the essay is based on the notes made in the scheme, it does not follow quite the same format. This scheme is designed for developing ideas. The essay structure of introduction, body and conclusion is a more thorough way of presenting these ideas to a reader in the form of an logical argument.

Structure the essay as follows:

- **Introduction** (one paragraph)
  - Answer the question.
  - Outline the key points to the essay — these will become topics for the paragraphs in the body of the essay.
  - Define any terms crucial to the whole of the essay.
- **Body** Use properly written paragraphs, each with its own key sentence introducing the topic of the paragraph, a body giving all the relevant detail and opinions in a logical order and a conclusion summarising the evidence and referring the point back to the question.
  - The order of paragraphs should follow the outline presented in the introduction.
  - Try to keep to one important point per paragraph.
  - Try to use at least one relevant source per paragraph.

- **Conclusion** (one paragraph)
  - Summarise and develop your argument from the body.
  - Re-answer the question.

WRITING A THREE PART STRUCTURED RESPONSE

The three questions are narrative, method and interpretation. Each requires a separate answer, so information can be repeated. However, if you need to make a point you have already made in an earlier part, you must do so again. Structure your answer as follows:

- Part A: **Narrative.** One paragraph of straight narrative description, answering the question, mentioning the five most important points with no attempt to argue or summarise, no sources, worth 6/30 marks.
- Part B: **Method.** Three to four structured paragraphs usually in response to a Method question, one sentence introduction, evidence used in the Narrative part may be repeated, sources should be used, worth 12/30 marks.
- Part C: **Interpretation.** Three to four structured paragraphs in response to an interpretative question, one sentence introduction, evidence used in the Narrative and Method parts may be repeated, sources should be used, worth 12/30 marks.

THE DRAFTING PROCESS:

When writing an essay or three part structured response at home, write at least two drafts, allowing for some time to pass between the writing of the two drafts. This time will allow you to adopt a more critical approach to your first draft. This means that you will have to plan to write the essay more than one night before it is due!

EXERCISES

1. Write an essay of no less than 1000 words in response to the following:
Why was there no significant change in the nature of politics, the economy and the society of Russia in the period 1800 to 1861? By 1861, what needs for change had become apparent?

The following material will assist you in preparing for your essay:

FROM THE WRITINGS OF SHEVYREV, A PAN-SLAVIST AND CONSERVATIVE POET IN 1848

In Europe for a long time already there have existed just two real forces, revolution and Russia. These two forces are now opposed to each other and tomorrow they may enter into combat. No negotiations or treaties between them are now possible: the existence of one means the death of the other! . . . Russia, country of faith, will not lose her faith at the decisive hour. She will not shrink from the greatness of her calling, she will not shirk her mission.

Consider also each of the following key areas:

- Russian Geography and Social System
- The Nature of Russian Government
- Alexander I's Flirtation with Reform

- The Nicholas System
- Pan-Slavism vs Westernisation
- Intellectuals and the Education System
- The Orthodox Church
- The Nature of the Middle Class
- Russian Economic Policy
- The Crimean War

2. Write a three part structured response in answer to the following:

a. What were some of the major reasons for the lack of social and economic change in Russia between 1800 and 1825?

(100 words — 6 marks)

b. How did Nicholas I attempt to stop political change from 1825 to 1854?

(450 words — 12 marks)

c. How successful were the Tsars in repressing the forces of change between 1800 and 1854?

(450 words — 12 marks)

Glossary

Arakcheyev General Count AA: see page 31

Barschina: form of rent whereby peasants were required to provide free labour for the landlord in return for the privilege of farming a section of the landlord's estate.

Belinsky VG: see page 53

Benckendorff General AK: see page 65

Butashevich-Petrashevsky MV: see page 55

Chaadayev PA: see page 55

Chinovniks: a special caste of the nobility who acted primarily as the administrators of the empire, rather than as landowners.

Divine Right of Kings: a political theory which stated that a monarch gained the right to rule from God. Because the monarch's right to rule was divine and therefore enforced by the church as well as the state, to contradict it was an act of blasphemy as well as an act of political rebellion.

Duma: a Russian term for a parliament.

Golitsyn AN: see page 33

Kankrin EF: see page 60

Khomayakov AS: see page 55

Kiselev Count PD: an efficient Minister of State Domains, who relieved pressure on the peasantry by introducing a limited social welfare, improving the lot of state peasants and effecting a more equitable distribution of land.

Metternich System: see page 31

Military Colonies: a system of self-sustaining villages whose produce was used to support the small military garrisons stationed in them.

Nesselrode KV: see page 64

Obrok: a form of taxation whereby peasants paid rent for the privilege of farming the landlord's land by paying a sum of money based on the composition and number in the peasant's family — in short, Obrok was a form of poll tax paid to the landlord and should not be confused with the separate poll tax which peasants also had to pay to the Tsarist government.

Pan-Slavism: the social and political philosophy and popular movement which wished to create a separate 'Slav' culture under Russian leadership, which celebrated the Russian feudal system and which was free of any of the influences of Western culture. It was opposed to Westernisation and supported Russian expansion especially into the Balkans and received the support of the Nicholas System.

Pestel Colonel PI: see page 41

Society for Public Good: the military-based revolutionary group which unsuccessfully attempted the overthrow of the Tsarist regime in 1825.

Speransky Count MM: one of Alexander I's major liberal advisors and Ministers of State, Speransky was responsible for proposing many and instituting a few liberal constitutional reforms before he lost his influence due to the intrigues of his conservative enemies. Later, during the reign of Nicholas I, he was responsible for many of the proceedings against the Decembrist conspirators and for codifying Russian law.

Uvarov Count SS: see page 63

Westernisation: the second major cultural movement of 19th century Russia which aimed to introduce Western culture, ideals and reform to Russia and followed on from the program of Peter the Great in 18th century. It was not supported by Nicholas I.

Reform and Repression

Introduction

B Y 1861, Russia was in dire need of reform, a problem that had been recognised by the Tsar, Alexander II. During the first few years of the 1860s, he seemed to be the broad-thinking visionary that his country needed. He introduced a wide range of political, social and economic changes, the most important of which was the emancipation of the serfs. However, attempts on his life caused him to turn away from the cause of progress; he spent the rest of his days in fear for his life, still considering, but never implementing, constitutional change.

Eventually in 1881, one of the radical groups that had sprung up in the 1870s as a by-product of both the social frustration at the incomplete nature of the reforms and also the brief period of more liberal education policies, caught up with him and he was disintegrated by an assassin's bomb. His son, Alexander III, reacted with extreme conservatism and was determined to return Russia to the days of complete autocracy, especially through the policy of Russification.

Nonetheless, the reforms changed the nature of Russia, even though they were not enough to rectify the massive problems within society and the economy. In particular, they paved the way for the introduction of more modern industry and the growth of the urban population as discontented peasants, unable to meet redemption payments and no longer tied to the land, sought new lives in the cities.

The most important concepts for you to address concern the nature of these changes and the Tsar's roles in encouraging and suppressing them.

FOCAL ISSUES

- What changes to the nature of politics, the economy and the society of Russia came about as a result of the reforms of the early 1860s?
- How did the Tsars attempt to deal with these changes?
- By 1894, why was the response of the Tsarist autocracy to the forces of change inadequate to relieve social and economic pressure in Russia?

Alexander II
- What were some of the social, economic and political problems in Russia at the start of the reign of Alexander II?
- How did Alexander attempt to deal with these problems in the early years of his reign?
- Why was there a growth in radical and revolutionary movements during the 1870s?

Alexander III
- What were the major changes to the society and economy of Russia during the period 1881 to 1894?
- How did Alexander III repress the forces of change in Russia in the period 1881 to 1894?
- By 1894, to what extent had Alexander achieved his conservative aims?

Fig. 3.1 Mind Map Russia from 1855 to 1894.

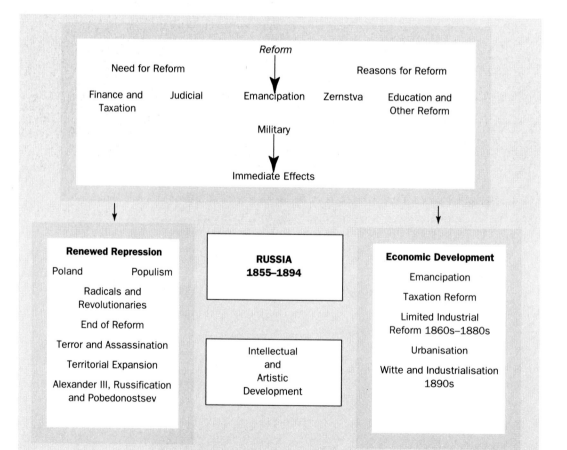

Reading list

The books listed below will provide a useful supplement to your reading on this area:

*Fig. 3.2
Alexander II and
Alexander III.*

D Christian, *Power and Privilege: Russia and the Soviet Union in the Nineteenth and Twentieth Centuries*, Pitman, 1987
L Cowie & R Wolfson, *Years of Nationalism — European History 1815-1890*, Edward Arnold, 1987
L Kochan & R Abraham, *The Making of Modern Russia*, Pelican, 1983
M McAndrew & D Thomas, *Century of Change*, Nelson, 1990
D Thomson, *Europe since Napoleon*, Pelican, 1987
J Westwood, *Endurance and Endeavour: Russian History, 1812-1992*, OUP, 1994

Guide To Note Making

For your notes on Russia between 1854 and 1894, you will need to consider:
- a chronological coverage of the area of concern
- an assessment of the problems and issues

Use the following key points as a source for your headings:
- Causes of 1860s reforms
- Nature of 1860s reforms
- Immediate effects of reform
- Radicals and revolutionaries
- Intellectual development
- Political repression
- Territorial expansion
- Russification
- Industrial and financial reform
- Urbanisation

Include sources in all of these notes and do not forget the focus questions for this section of the course:

What changes to the nature of politics, the economy and the society of Russia came about as a result of the reforms of the early 1860s?

How did the Tsars attempt to deal with these changes?

By 1894, why was the response of the Tsarist autocracy to the forces of change inadequate to relieve social and economic pressure in Russia?

The Reigns of Alexander II and Alexander III

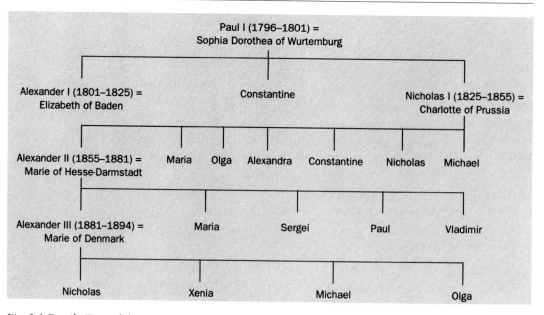

Fig. 3.3 Family Tree of the Romanovs 1796–1894.

TIME LINE

1855	Death of Nicholas I
	Accession of Alexander II
1856	Crimean War ends in Russian defeat
1858	Conquest of Amur River and Island of Sakhalin begins
1859	Vodka riots
1861	Emancipation Edict begins the process of emancipation
1862	Public budgeting of Department of Finance introduced by new Minister of Finance, MK Reutern
	Publication of Turgenev's *Fathers and Sons*
1863	Village officials previously elected now made state appointed bureaucrats
	Polish revolt defeated
	Judicial reform
	Abolition of the vodka tax farm
	University Statute
1864	Zemstva reform
1865	Censorship laws relaxed
1866	Unsuccessful assassination attempt on Alexander II
1868	Tightening of censorship and education laws
1870	Introduction of elective municipal government in towns
1872	First Russian translation of *Das Kapital*
1873	'Going to the people' begins
1874	Military reforms
	Failure of 'Going to the people'
1876	Formation of Land and Liberty
1877	Allocation of 80% of land under the mir system complete
	Russian victory in Russo-Turkish War
1878	Congress of Berlin
	Vera Zasulich trial
1880	Konstantin Pobedonostsev appointed Chief Procurator of the Holy Synod
1881	Assassination of Alexander II
	Accession of Alexander III
	Beginning of pogroms
	Appointment of NK Bunge as Minister of Finance
1882	Appointment of Dimitri Tolstoy as Minister of Interior
	Establishment of Peasants' State Bank
1885	Establishment of Nobles' State Bank
1887	Appointment of IA Vyshnegradski as Minister of Finance
1889	Establishment of Department of Railways within Ministry of Finance by Sergei Witte
	Establishment of 'land captains'
1890	Termination of Russo-German Alliance
1891	Franco-Russian Alliance
	Witte authorises the beginning of the construction of the Trans-Siberian Railway
1892	Sergei Witte appointed Minister of Finance
1894	Death of Alexander III
	Accession of Nicholas II

[Note: Because the topic of the reforms is mainly concerned with causes and effects, which are largely matters of analysis and interpretation, much of the following section is presented as a collation of the opinions of some of the leading historians in the field. They are shown as discrete areas, but you will notice that many of them are closely related to each other.]

Historical Developments — Reasons for Reform

CHARACTER OF ALEXANDER II

Craig argues that Tsar Alexander II was not a liberal or reformer seeking change for the sake of change. Rather, he wanted to regain imperial prestige and forestall the possibility of peasant revolt. This is supported by Alexander's statement to a committee of nobles in 1856: 'It is better to abolish bondage from above than to wait for the time when it will begin to abolish itself from below'. Kochan and Abraham believe that further to this, the Tsar wanted to restore Russia's shattered military pride after the disaster of the Crimean War.

CRIMEAN WAR

Fig. 3.4 Map showing imperial acquisitions under Alexander II and Alexander III 1855-1894.

Thomson believes that under some incompetent leadership during the Crimean War, Russia suffered the humiliation of defeat and its economy strained under the pressures of war, to the brink of bankrupting the country. The only thing that saved Russia in the war was the courage and determination of the peasant soldiers, who started to realise that their contribution warranted better treatment than serfdom. Westwood shows that after Crimea, many nobles realised that Russia's social structure was inefficient and archaic.

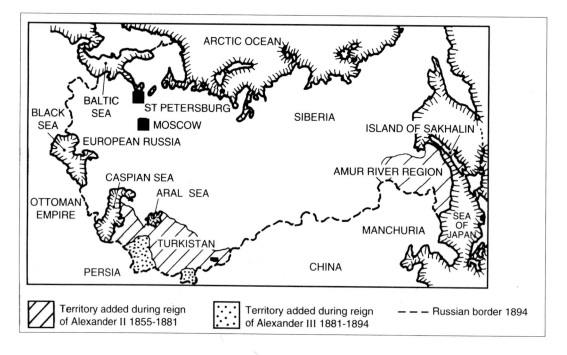

| Territory added during reign of Alexander II 1855-1881 | Territory added during reign of Alexander III 1881-1894 | – – – Russian border 1894 |

Thomson also states that serfdom, which relied on the personal and collective suppression of over 40 million people by privileged landowners and the state, could not be justified, even by the sporadic humane and paternalistic treatment of some of the serfs by some of the landlords. From an administrative point of view, Westwood says that the government of Russia was separated from the peasants by a huge cultural and geographical gap which meant that the Tsar's administration only really came into contact with the serfs when putting down peasant revolts and that for the vast majority of serfs, the only law they saw was that of their local nobility.

As well as this threat of revolt, there was a common fear that it would be possible for a revolt on the scale of Purgachev's Revolt (1773-5) to recur if the condition of the serfs became too dire. In addition, Craig shows that the increased use of peasant soldiers to suppress the 228 minor peasant revolts between 1835-54 was not necessarily a sound policy for the Tsarist government, especially after the increasing realisation by the soldiers in the late 1850s that they and their families deserved something better than serfdom. Where it was necessary to rely on peasants to suppress other peasants, such feelings loomed dangerously. Cowie and Wolfson conclude that social reform was needed to prevent peasant revolution and that political reform was necessary to modernise the administration and to make Russia once again a great power in Europe.

INHERENT WEAKNESSES OF THE RUSSIAN SOCIAL SYSTEM

LATEST INTELLIGENCE.

THE SIEGE OF SEBASTOPOL.

(BY SUBMARINE AND BRITISH TELEGRAPH.)

VIENNA, MONDAY MORNING.

The *Morgen Post*, which is a paper of no great authority, has the following :—

"CZERNOWITZ, Nov. 11.

"On the 6th the whole garrison of Sebastopol, amounting to 65,000 men, made a sortie.

"A furious battle ensued, which was not ended when the messenger left ; but the allies had the advantsge."

We have received, at half-past 4 o'clock this morning, the following despatch, dated yesterday afternoon, from our correspondent at Vienna :—

"The news forwarded this morning relative to the sortie was but too true.

"Reliable information has been given me that the English suffered a very heavy loss, and had three Generals wounded.

"It is said that later intelligence has been received, according to which the Russians had at last been repelled with a loss of 3,000 men."

Fig. 3.5 The Times *reports the Siege of Sebastopol during the Crimean War.*

*Fig. 3.6
Photographs
showing peasant
housing:
(a) the wattle and
daub izba of the
Ukraine
(b) log-built
khata of the
northern and
central regions
where more
timber was
available for
peasant use.*

ECONOMIC FACTORS

Christian identifies five major economic reasons for reform. The first related to natural disasters. The famines in 1820, 33, 39, 45, 48, 55 and 59 were due largely to the fact that peasants had to give away too much produce in the form of taxes and therefore not enough food was left for the families to survive. In addition, serfdom did not provide enough revenue for either the government (1855: 54 million rouble debt) or the landlords (1859: 60 per cent of private serfs had been mortgaged by their owners). Thus the serf system was not

Soon, appreciating the correctness of the motto of Robert the Devil, the Russian lords change their stakes, betting first their landed property and then their human property.

Fig. 3.7 Debt and the Peasantry. Gustave Doré comments on the level of debt among the Russian nobility during the mid-nineteenth century and the way serfs were viewed as valuable property, capable of being mortgaged.

producing enough to sustain both ends of the social structure.

Thirdly, serfdom required an immobile population. The need for improved communications and a railway system revealed by the inadequate conduct of the Crimean War was incompatible with this immobility of the working class. Economically, many nobles began to accept the liberal economic ideas that freed, hired labour was more productive and would produce more profit.

Finally, Alexander realised that the tax-farming of vodka had become an institutionalised system of corruption for both government officials and tavern-keepers. It was depleting government revenue and, in combination with higher tax rates to compensate for the cost of the War, was forcing vodka prices up. Large-scale liquor riots and boycotts in 1858-59 were a measure of peasant dissatisfaction with this state of affairs, and also with the condition of the serfs as a whole.

ARMY

The peasant army was a very brave and disciplined force which looked good on parade. But Christian demonstrates that because they were poorly equipped, poorly supplied and poorly led, they fought largely unsuccessfully. It was very expensive to maintain a standing army, requiring between 40 and 50 per cent of the peacetime budget, and even more during times of conflict. Clearly, there was a need for a smaller standing army, with a shorter period of service, and a large reserve force in case of war. Finally, the existence of a large, trained, armed group of peasants who traditionally were freed on completing their military service was incompatible with the general mood of unhappiness among the serf population.

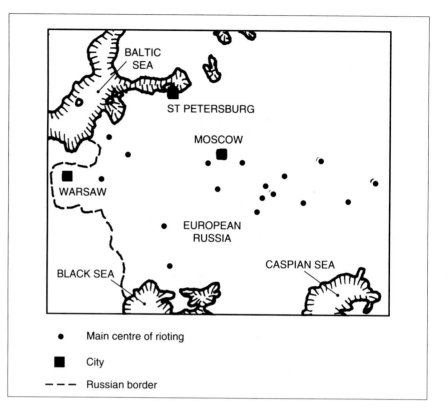

Fig. 3.8 Map showing the location of Vodka Riots 1859.

- ●   Main centre of rioting
- ■   City
- – – –   Russian border

Primary Extracts and Questions — the Need for Reform 1855–1863

ALEXANDER II ADDRESSING A GROUP OF MOSCOW NOBLES ON THE NEED FOR EMANCIPATION — 1856

But you yourselves are certainly aware that the existing order of serfdom cannot remain unchanged. It is better to abolish serfdom from above than to wait for a time when it will begin to abolish itself from below. I request you, gentlemen, to reflect on how this may be achieved.

(a) From the extract, identify Alexander II's main reason for emancipating the serfs.
(b) Who did Alexander intend to benefit by emancipation?

THE NEED FOR REFORM ACCORDING TO A PAMPHLETEER OF THE 1850s QUOTED BY MACKENZIE WALLACE, SCOTTISH WRITER—1877

And what did we Russians do all this time? We Russians slept! With groans the peasant paid his yearly dues; with groans the proprietor mortgaged the second half of his estate; groaning we all paid heavy tribute to the officials. Occasionally, with a grave shaking of the head, we remarked in a whisper that it was a shame and a disgrace — that there was no justice in the courts — that millions were squandered on Imperial tours, kiosks, and pavilions — that everything was wrong; and then with an easy conscience we returned to our apathy . . .
[But] we had at least one consolation, one thing to be proud of — the might of Russia in the assembly of kings. 'What need we care' we said, 'for the reproaches of foreign nations?' . . .

And lo! After all our boasting we were taken by surprise, and caught un-
awares . . . Where were our millions of soldiers? . . . The army wandered about
without real aim or purpose . . .

(c) What does the pamphleteer identify as the major problems in Russian society
before the Crimean War?
(d) From your own knowledge, state more problems in Russian society at that
time.
(e) According to the extract, how important was the Crimean War to the mood for
reform?

The cornerstone of all abuses has been removed: serfdom has been abolished. But
there is still much to do in order to rebuild the shaken edifice of the state on firm
foundations . . .

1. The greatest possible expansion of the elective principle in state service, and greater
scope for local self-government. In addition: strict observance of the laws, not only
by subordinates but also by superior authorities; and strict personal accountability
and responsibility before the law for each and every official in state service.
2. Security of personal and property rights for all citizens of the state through the
introduction of verbal and public court procedure and a jury court.
3. Elimination of hostile relations between the nobility and their peasants by means
of obligatory, immediate separation of resources, simultaneous with grant of
land charters, securement of obrok and redemption payments by the government (with a guarantee for the entire amount, not of 80 percent).
4. Publication of state debts and the budget for state revenues and expenditures in
order to allay fears of financial crisis.
5. Public discussion in the press of questions in all spheres where the government
contemplates change . . .

ADDRESS OF THE MOSCOW
NOBLE ASSEMBLY—1862

(f) What does the extract identify as the most important problem facing Russia before
1862?
(g) Rewrite each of the five demands in your own words.
(h) Read more of this chapter and identify how adequately Alexander II met these
demands.

Somehow, our officers have little interest in studying their military profession, but
instead seek to acquire an encyclopaedic knowledge. They want, in a stroke,
without effort and toil, to be initiated into all the secrets of contemporary
learning. Such an aspiration is of course laudable. But, since the positive,
general educational background of most officers is too weak, they grab at
everything and grasp onto nothing—not only at an advanced level, but even at a
middling one. Meanwhile they completely neglect what they should know
above all else . . . But at the same time, are many of our officers familiar with military literature, not to mention foreign, but even our own Russian military literature, which is by no means rich? It is after all embarrassing to say that there are
even officers in the guards who do not know, for instance, what journals are published in Petersburg for soldiers . . .
It is vital that our officers have greater love and desire to make a serious
study of the cause they serve, that our military family develop and strengthen a
spirit of collegiality, and finally, that we establish true discipline, based on
mutual respect and trust of all military service people among themselves and
toward their military work . . .

AN OFFICER COMMENTS ON
HIS FELLOW OFFICERS—
1862

(i) What problems among Russian officers does the extract identify?

1. The parish in the village of Skhomorokhovo has one free school, established by the local priest, with the permission of diocesan authorities, on 1 February 1860. It is housed, without compensation, in the priest's own home; the school has no fixed income; the priest himself provides heating.

2. The priest himself supervises the school and gives instruction to the children. There are constantly ten to twelve pupils . . .

3. The primary shortcoming of our school is the lack of means for a firm existence. All the efforts on behalf of the school rest solely with the priest; there is neither assistance from superior nor support from the parishioners.

(j) What solutions could you propose to the problems identified in the extract?

Historical Developments — Preparation for Reform

ALEXANDER II'S OBJECTIVES IN 1858

In 1858, Alexander II stated his aims for reform:
- *Stage 1*: The peasant must immediately feel that his life has improved.
- *Stage 2*: The estate owner must immediately be reassured that his interests are protected.
- *Stage 3*: The government must never waiver for a moment at any point in ensuring against any disturbance of law and order.

PREPARATION OF LEGISLATION

In 1858, provincial assemblies of nobles were called together to advise the Tsar on reform. There was some considerable conflict between liberal and conservative nobles but Christian states that the Tsar eventually leaned towards the liberal nobles and pro-peasant reform. He used his own bureaucracy of liberal intelligentsia to formulate legislation from 1859-61. Westwood believes that when this legislation was eventually presented to the nation, it was in the nature of a *fait accompli*, giving the conservatives no chance to object.

Fig. 3.9 The reading of the Emancipation Edict to Georgian peasants.

Historical Developments — Details of Reform

[*Note: emancipation took the form of 22 separate pieces of legislation working as a scheme.*]

EMANCIPATION ACT 1861

- **Stage 1:** between 1861 and 1863, 23 million private serfs were freed. There was no change in economic status as the landlords still owned all of the land except the peasants' houses and **usad'ba** (garden vegetable patches). All feudal dues remained.
- **Stage 2:** from 1863 ex-serfs became 'temporarily obligated'. This meant that feudal punishment and the justice system were handed over to communal courts. Feudal dues still had to be paid to the government, but the peasants were no longer obliged to pay those owed to the landlords once they had assumed control of their land in Stage 3. Negotiations occurred as to the details of the hand over of land (around 50 per cent of all the nobility's lands). The government set the price ranges and quantities of land to be bought, with the landlords compelled to sell and peasants compelled to buy from the nobles. The financial arrangements for this were usually that the peasants bought the right to farm land with a 49-year mortgage, the government used these payments to pay redemption levies as compensation to the nobles. The land was actually owned by the village **mir** (village community) and individuals only had the right to farm land. Household and domestic serfs were freed with no rights to land.

Fig. 3.10 Private serfs being freed. Notice how this contemporary engraving shows the reverence of the freed peasants towards their former master.

- *Stage 3*: this stage marked the completion of negotiations, assumption of new land rights and the cessation of local feudal dues. Ex-serfs now had roughly the same legal status as state peasants, in that legal ties were with the state and the village commune.

JUDICIAL REFORM 1863

The judicial reforms created the notion of nominal equality of all before the law. They included open courts, the admission of oral evidence as well as documentary evidence, jury trials, an independent judiciary, and the introduction of justices of the peace and a Bar of lawyers, giving the peasants at least two sources of legal support. Government officials retained wide administrative powers, and officials could only be tried under special circumstances and with the government's permission. In addition, military courts retained their own jurisdiction, ex-serfs were restricted to special courts and the government kept informal pressure on the judges to comply with official policies and attitudes.

POLAND

The failed attempt for liberty by the Polish nobles in 1863 prompted Alexander II to introduce very liberal reforms, giving the Polish peasants more land than the Russian peasants received. This was aimed at reducing the nobility's power (Alexander also increased his Russification program to crush Polish nationalism, to be discussed later). However, these measures failed to appease any of the Poles.

ZEMSTVO REFORM 1864

Zemstva (Zemstvo in the singular) were district and provincial elected local government assemblies and represented the first form of popular involvement in the government of Russia. All classes of men could vote but the assemblies were dominated by upper class members (74 per cent in

Fig. 3.11 Mir leaders.
These men were the starotsy or leaders of their mir. The bronze medals around their necks are their badges of office.

1866). The zemstva had very limited powers over public health, public education and prisons and they had small budgets funded by local rates. Their decisions were subject to veto by the provincial governor if the legislation was 'contrary to the laws and to the general welfare of the state'.

Other reforms introduced included: OTHER REFORMS
- the introduction of a public budget of government finances (1862)
- a university statute giving universities greater autonomy over their curricula and opening up admission to lower classes (1863)
- the abolition of vodka tax farms, the introduction of a revenue collection system based on excises on the production of vodka and allowing retailers to open up their own distilleries, thus removing the upper class privilege on the production of spirits (1863)
- legislation limiting censorship (1865)
- elective municipal government in the towns (1870) and
- military reforms making service compulsory for all classes and reducing the term of service in the standing army from 25 years to 6 years (1874).

Note however, that the change in the status of village officials in 1863 from being elected officials to state-appointed bureaucrats meant that the state exerted a greater centralised control over the administration of the nation.

Historical Developments — Immediate Effects of Reform

Christian says that, as a result of the reforms, the nobility lost their traditional   NOBILITY
advantages of a free labour force, feudal dues, their traditional justice and police powers and some social status. They also lost some input into local government to the zemstva. These losses reflected the fact that landed nobility were becoming less important to the autocracy than the official bureaucracy which the Tsar now required to administer the new socio-economic system in order to provide a more centralised form of government. Poorer nobles could not afford to pay for labour and thus had to accept an even lower standard of living.

There were some short term economic advantages with the redemption payments creating ready cash to pay back the nobility's debts (by 1871, 248 out of 543 million roubles had been used to pay off bad debts). However, the long term economic effects were not so good since most nobles failed to modernise their estates and many were forced to sell their land (between 1867 and 1911, as a class, the gentry lost 49 per cent of their land). Kochan and Abraham believe that the economic effects of the reforms were so drastic that it was only because the Tsar employed large numbers of the nobility within the bureaucracy that they were able to retain their status up to the revolution in 1917.

PEASANTS

According to Christian, the peasants were not immediately pleased with the reforms. There were many riots from 1861 to 1863 until the ex-serfs were able to secure their land rights. There was considerable resentment that they had to pay for land which they considered theirs by right. The system of land distribution was not really fair — on average, most received 4 per cent less land than they had rented before. However, this overall statistic includes Poland, where the peasants received more land as a means of punishing the rebellious gentry. Note that in the fertile south and central plains, peasants lost up to 25 per cent, yet they paid on average 134 per cent of the free market value of land.

Cowie and Wolfson point out that emancipation brought no economic freedom for the serfs and that mir ownership of land meant that there was no incentive to improve the land, resulting in a decline in productivity. Kochan and Abraham believe that the collapse in landlord authority meant poorer women married earlier and the birthrate increased, resulting in a peasant population increase of 72 per cent between 1861 and 1901. At the same time, land ownings declined, so there was a serious land hunger by 1900. From 1870 onwards, there was a population shift towards towns when many peasant families found that they could not

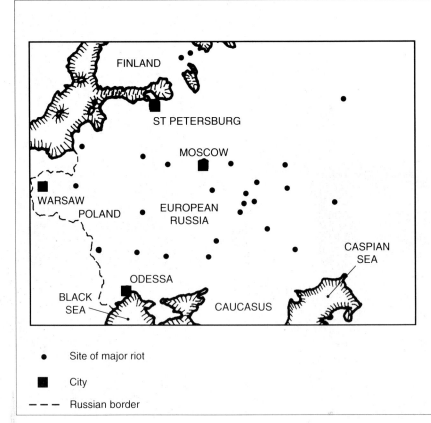

Fig. 3.12 Map showing locations of peasant riots after emancipation in the 1860s.

succeed at running their own land, due to primitive techniques. This drift helped to provide an urban working population for later industrialisation.

In the rural areas, the increasing and prolonged debt to pay off the redemption of land created by low productivity meant the peasants had to export grain to cover this debt, depleting their reserve grain stores. With no emergency supplies, frequent crop failures resulted in the mortality rate increasing from 24-27 in 1000 in 1800 to 35 in 1000 in 1880.

Fig. 3.13 Economic backwardness in 1868. This photograph shows a stall in the St Petersburg market, which was the largest and most important commercial centre in the whole empire.

Fig. 3.14 During times of famine, thatched roofs were often used to sustain livestock.

Primary Extracts and Questions — the Peasants after Emancipation

MACKENZIE WALLACE, SCOTTISH WRITER, ON THE CONDITIONS OF THE PEASANTRY — 1878

The present money dues and taxes are often more burdensome than the labor dues in the old times. If the serfs had a great many ill-defined obligations to fulfil . . . they had on the other hand a good many ill-defined privileges . . . All this has now come to an end. Their burdens and their privileges have been swept away together, and have been replaced by clearly defined, unbending, unrealistic legal relations. They now have to pay the market price for every stick of firewood they burn, for every log they require for repairing their houses, and for every rood of land on which they graze their cattle. Nothing now is to be had gratis . . .

The spinning, weaving, and other home industries have been killed by the big factories, and the flax and wool have to be sold to raise a little ready money for the numerous new items of expenditure. Everything has to be bought — clothes, firewood, petroleum, improved agricultural implements, and many other articles which are now regarded as necessities of life.

(a) What does this extract reveal of the financial burden faced by the peasants after their emancipation?
(b) From your own knowledge, what reasons can you suggest for the government's failure to anticipate this problem?

KRAVCHINSKY, RUSSIAN WRITER, ON THE FAILURE OF EMANCIPATION — 1894

Emancipation has utterly failed to realize the ardent expectations of its advocates and promoters. The great benefit of the measure was purely moral. It has failed to improve the material conditions of the former serfs, who are on the whole worse off than they were before emancipation. The bulk of the peasantry is in a condition not far removed from starvation . . . The frightful and continually increasing misery of the toiling millions of our country is the most terrible indictment against the Russian Government, and is the paramount cause and justification for the rebellion against it . . .

The universal expectation, as proved by the universal disappointment, was that freed peasants would have all the land that they had previously tilled . . . The freed peasants were endowed with small parcels of land, carved out of the estates of their masters, who retained, however, the greater part of their properties . . . The land was so parsimoniously apportioned that the enfranchised peasants were utterly unable to provide themselves with the first necessities of life. With few exceptions, the bulk of the peasantry are compelled to look to wage labour, mainly agricultural, on their former masters' estates, as an essential, and often the chief source, of their livelihood.

(c) What does this extract identify as the main problems with Emancipation?

(d) How does this extract help you to understand the rising dissent against the government among the peasants?

The mir means a commonality of interest among the inhabitants. The Russian peasant family has a head; the heads of the families form the mir . . .

The arable land, part of which [the peasant] must work, is not his actually; it belongs to the mir. The arable land is divided into three parts to suit the triennial rotation of crops, so that that which is used for winter grain this year is used for summer grain the next, and the third year lies fallow. Each family possesses in each of the two fields under cultivation so many strips, according to the richness of the soil and the working capacity of the family. Thus the fields are divided up into innumerable long narrow strips parallel with one another, and these difficult proportional distributions are done by the peasants themselves with measuring-sticks.

Each family must work according to the rules of the mir. Ploughing, reaping, sowing, harrowing — work of any sort — must be done at the time ordained by the mir, neither before nor after. Every family is responsible for every member of that family. If there is a drunkard and ne'er-do-well in the family, the onus of the non-fulfilment of his duties falls on the family. Similarly, if a family is lazily inclined, that family has a very bad time of it, for if it does not do its share of the mir work, till its share of the mir land, and pay its share of the mir taxes, which the mir must pay to the government, then the mir, ie the village as a whole, is held responsible by the government.

A peasant may not leave his village for other regions without having obtained leave from the mir, and, having gone, he is required to pay his taxes when away, and may be recalled at the will of the mir.

KENNARD, BRITISH WRITER, COMMENTS ON THE ROLE OF THE MIR AT THE END OF THE NINETEENTH CENTURY — 1907

(e) It has been said that Emancipation replaced one form of slavery with another. Does this extract support this statement? Give reasons for your answer.

(f) What evidence can you find from this extract and the previous extracts to support the opinion that 'the mir-system was in fact harder on the peasants than the serf system'?

From reports reaching the ministry of the interior it is seen that in certain provinces, predominantly southern and south-eastern, there has recently emerged a series of peasant disorders in the form of systematic damage to the landowners' fields

A MINISTRY OF THE INTERIOR CIRCULAR ON PEASANT UNREST — 1898 and meadows, together with the driving away of cattle under the protection of men armed with sticks, staves and pitchforks, and attacks on the landowners' watchmen and guards or considerable illegal timber-cutting in the landowners' woods, and brawls with foresters. When the guards seize the peasants' cattle, the peasants, hoping to free it, often by moving whole villages, carry out armed attacks on the buildings and farmhouses of the landowners and divide up the working and even the living quarters, attacking and wounding servants and guards.

(g) What does this extract reveal of the mood of the peasantry at the end of the nineteenth century?

(h) What indirect evidence does the extract provide of the causes of peasant unrest at the end of the nineteenth century?

(i) What are the likely reasons that no comment is made in the extract on the causes of peasant unrest?

The Effects of Emancipation

GOVERNMENT AND
ADMINISTRATION

According to Kochan and Abraham, the introduction of the zemstva meant that liberal professionals employed as experts had more contact with peasants and saw their miserable conditions, especially after 1878 as the zemstva spread to more provinces. Westwood believes that zemstva showed that peasants could manage their own local affairs with great success, but the failure of the government to extend this responsibility on a broader scale created resentment. This provides support for Thomson's generalisation that the reforms of Alexander II were not motivated by sentiment or nationalism, but were designed to strengthen the autocracy and were implemented from above in an authoritarian manner.

Therefore it should come as no surprise when Christian says that the two sectors of society who retained the greatest power after the reforms and who gained the most from them overall, were the monarchy and the rapidly expanding bureaucracy. This adjustment to the balance of power occurred at the expense of the nobility. However, these reforms were not completely successful in securing the position of the Tsar and his administration; although the government's power increased, its control decreased and it became ineffective at winning popular acceptance for its authority. The growth of the liberal nobility and revolutionary tendencies among the peasants provide further evidence of the alienation of the government from the people.

PROMOTION OF LIBERAL
THOUGHT

The reform and liberalisation of education in the 1860s encouraged freer thinking and a desire for an even more radical level of reform. As in other European countries, this trend increased demands for a liberal constitution and national legislative parliament. However, unlike many other European monarchs, the Tsar refused to accede to these more fundamental proposals, which only spurred on the growth of liberalism, revolutionary movements and secret societies. Kochan and Abraham believe that the reforms failed to integrate society as the bureaucracy had hoped, making the tension between the forces of autocracy and Western liberal democratic institutions, which the reforms had attempted to resolve, even more apparent.

Fig. 3.15 Three great Russian writers (a) Fyodor Dostoievsky (b) Ivan Turgenev and (c) Leo Tolstoy

Leo Tolstoy (1828–1910): Widely regarded as the greatest of all the Russian writers, Tolstoy was a noble Russian whose influence on the course of Russian intellectual debate has extended right into this century. At first a law and languages student and later a soldier and administrator, he retired to his estates in 1862, where he put into practice ideas on peasant education and welfare that he had seen whilst travelling overseas. At this time he began his most famous series of novels, including *War and Peace* (1865-68) and *Anna Karenina* (1874), which demonstrate the nature of the effect of historical events and social patterns on the individual, as well as the internal conflict between a love of life and a sense of duty. In the 1870s he turned to a simple form of Christianity and disavowed violence in his quest to lobby the Tsarist governments for social and economic reform. His views on non-violence and social justice led him to even wider recognition as a philosopher and thinker. Later still in life, he turned his back on his noble background and tried to renounce all his property, much to the chagrin of his family. Fleeing them with his daughter, Tolstoy died on the platform of Astapovo railway station in 1910.

Ivan Turgenev (1818–1883): Born into the nobility, Turgenev was university educated and worked for a while as a civil servant. He turned to writing, including *A Sportsman's Sketches* (1852), in which he showed upper and middle class Russia that the Russian peasant was after all a human being. After a fruitless but lengthy passion for a Parisian singer, which even involved co-editing works with her husband, he settled in Paris and died there in 1883. Among the most important of his novels were *Fathers and Sons* (1862), in which he first described the Russian nihilist and *Virgin Soil* (1877), which shows the naive and doomed attempt of the young narodni who attempted to bring populism to the people in 1873-74. His novels are characterised by their sympathetic, yet bleak view of radical life in Russia.

Fyodor Dostoievsky (1821–1881): Born into a middle class family, Dostoievsky trained as an engineer, but as one of the Petrashevsky Conspiracy, he was sentenced to death for his radical beliefs, later to have his sentence commuted to exile by Nicholas I. On his return to society in 1859, he had read the New Testament and now supported a more harmonious and ordered view of society. This was reflected by his attempt to publish a newspaper which united Slavophil and Western intellectual thought. Although reasonably successful between 1860 and 1863, it was banned in 1863 for unpatriotic sentiment. It is for his novels that he is best remembered, including *The Possessed* (1872) and *The Brothers Karamazov* (1880). In these novels, he shows an extraordinary ability to portray the psychological make-up of what many consider to be the archetypical Russian identity, as well as more generally commenting on the value of Christian humility.

Wide currents of popular feeling emerged in the 1870s with the capitalists and rich peasants opposing revolution but also denying support to the autocracy. The poorer peasants loved the Tsar but hated his government, and the intelligensia and newly emerging press also remained hostile to the autocracy. Westwood notes that the decade of the 1870s was the 'golden age' of Russian literature, especially with the writers Tolstoy, Turgenev and Dostoievsky who wrote with a realism that was more often than not critical of the injustices and contradictions within Russian society.

Unlike other reforms, those relating to the army had a great deal of **ARMY** success. Cowie and Wolfson state that the introduction of a literacy campaign in the army led to a rate of education five times greater than that of the general population. The reduction in the compulsory term of military service and further reductions for educational qualifications added to the incentive for city students to become more educated. Westwood describes a system of admission to the officer corps which was increasingly based on ability not privilege — by 1871, 12 per cent of officer cadets were drawn from classes outside the nobility, which in turn assisted in breaking down archaic class privileges within the army. These reforms also contributed to the demise of the prestige and position of the nobility.

Craig believes that within the judiciary the spirit of reform was hampered by **JUDICIARY** three factors. Firstly, the system was complicated by the existence of separate military, ecclesiastical and municipal courts. Secondly, the crown retained the prerogative to amend courts' decisions, which deprived them of the absoluteness of their decisions. Lastly, the Ministers of Justice were opposed to the spirit of reform and the independence of the judges. However, Westwood points out that the more open system resulted in courts where the judges and defendants could criticise the government actions and policies in cases where there were important issues at stake and which received wide coverage. Lawyers were free to speak and to be reported.

The ultimate result of judicial reform could be seen in the Vera Zasulich trial of 1878 where a judge who could not be sacked at the whim of local officials, eloquent lawyer and jury combined to find Zasulich (1851–1919) not guilty even though she had shot the governor of St Petersburg, General Trepov. This had such a profound effect that the Tsarist administration never again tried a major political case in the courts. Many emigrés in 1917 claimed that without this result there would have been no revolution.

Repression under Alexander II—the Growth of the Radical and Revolutionary Movements

In 1866, following his attempted assassination by Polish rebels, Alexander II **POLAND, IMPERIALISM AND** turned away from reform and towards reaction to the demands for **RUSSIFICATION** change. He reversed some of the liberal reforms both in Russia and

Poland by reintroducing some censorship and education restrictions as well as limiting further constitutional reform.

In addition, it was Alexander II who began the policy of Russification, with the conquest and cultural persecution of the Amur River region and the Island of Sakhalin in 1858-1860. The aim of this policy was to impose a universal Russian culture as a means of control over outlying provinces. Russian language, religion and culture were forced upon non-Russian provincials at the expense of their own heritage. In Poland after the attempted revolution, Alexander II introduced a policy of limited Russification — a policy that was intensified during the reign of his son, Alexander III.

UNDERLYING REVOLUTIONARY SENTIMENT AND POLITICAL DISSENT

Despite his reputation as the 'Tsar Liberator', Alexander II confirmed his belief in autocracy with his attitude towards dissent — over a quarter of a million prisoners were exiled to Siberia between 1855 and 1875.

The revolutions which shook Russia in 1905 and 1917 were the results of nearly 100 years of changing attitudes. The advent of industrialisation, the freeing of the serfs and the effects of reforms and education on the common people all played their parts in this. The distant origins of Revolution can be found in the failure of reform to go far enough to alleviate the conditions of the people, and also in the intellectual movements which developed from those of the early decades of the nineteenth century.

The dissent articulated by these movements helped to feed and sustain Russian revolutionary ideas. The increasingly intense debate between the Westernisers and Slavophils questioned whether Russia should follow the path of Western industrialisation or build a uniquely Russian society based

Fig. 3.16 Map showing areas of Russification and places of exile in Siberia 1855-1894.

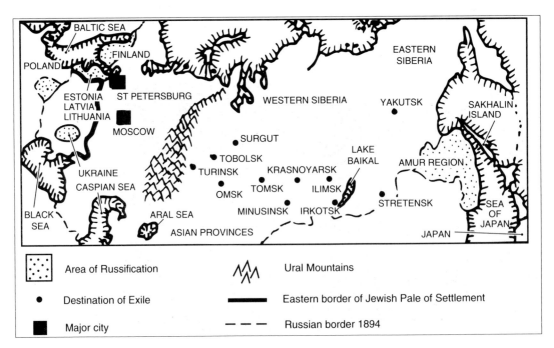

upon its own model of development. Many groups formed around each argument and they exercised considerable influence upon the growth of future revolutionary movements in Tsarist Russia. The philosophies which dominated the political opposition of the monarchy from the 1860s onwards were as follows:

- Narodnism (Populism)
- Nihilism, Hell and Anarchism
- Marxism

POPULISM

During the 1870s, revolutionaries called **Populists (narodniks)** actively began to work for socialism among the peasantry. Their philosophy was derived from Western European socialism and the debates of the Westerners and Slavophils of the 1840s. Count Uvarov (1786–1855), Minister of Education under Nicholas I, is credited as the author of the theory of official narodnost. Narodniks were anxious to take advantage of peasant discontent over restrictive conditions attached to emancipation. Populism, the forerunner of later revolutionary movements, argued that the state should be composed of a free federation of peasant communities and that the village commune or mir would provide the basis for economic progress.

Much of the populist economic analysis of Russian society was sound. It recognised the uniqueness of Russian conditions — in particular the strong commune, with its collective life, which would enable the country to evolve its own form of socialism without undergoing the capitalist phase of exploitation required before a Marxist revolution. This analysis was largely a local response to generalisations advanced by Marx, who had already begun to realise that Volume I of *Das Kapital* could not be applied indiscriminately to every society and that local conditions must be taken into account.

Fig. 3.17 Lavrov and colleagues working on a populist newspaper.

Fig. 3.18 A freed peasant in Simbirsk 1865. The populist theories revolved around peasants such as this.

Fig. 3.19 Alexander Herzen.

Fig. 3.20 Peter Lavrov.

Alexander Herzen (1812–1870) was the most significant early influence for the populists. He idealised the agricultural commune, seeing it as means of preparing people for social revolution. In 1847 he was exiled and spent the rest of his life in Geneva and London, where his home became a centre for revolutionary exile. In 1857, Herzen founded a newspaper, *Kolokol (The Bell)*, which was smuggled into Russia. His ideas had a strong impact upon liberal opinion throughout Russia during the first years of Alexander II's reign.

Peter Lavrov (1823-1900) was a professor of mathematics who believed that ordinary people, not professional revolutionaries, could bring about their own liberation. He opposed violence and encouraged educated people to move among the masses to awaken them to their plight.

From about 1870, the populist movement split into two factions — **FACTIONALISATION** some embraced the peaceful ideas of Lavrov, which was reflected in the movement of 'Going to the People', while others formed more radical groups, heavily influenced by Bakunin's anarchism.

• **'Going to the people'** was a spontaneous mass movement of populists organised during the 'mad summers' of 1873 and 1874. Over 2000 upper and middle class young men and women dressed as peasants, moved to the country and settled in villages and industrial areas. They urged peasants to become politically active, but the movement proved to be futile, failing to convince peasants either to rise in revolt or become populists. The peasants saw the bright young idealists as insincere and did not trust their motivation, nor were the peasants yet ready to accept such open criticism of a Tsarist regime, which they had become conditioned to accept and support. However this time was not far away.

The secret police saw populism as a conspiracy and arrested students who encouraged and promoted its beliefs. Such arrests resulted in two mass trials in 1877, where many populist missionaries were convicted and exiled to Siberia. The trials made a great impression on the educated public who remarked on the courage, honesty and idealism of these young people. In January 1878, the day after the second trial ended, Vera Zasulich shot General Trepov, the St Petersburg Chief of Police. Trepov recovered from his wounds and Zasulich was acquitted, due to sufficient popular support to protect the liberal views of the judge hearing the case. The police tried to re-arrest her but a sympathetic crowd arranged her escape and helped her to flee abroad.

• **Land and Liberty** was a secret group of radical populists which became prominent in the early 1860s. It was deeply influenced by the socialist Chernyshevsky but following the failed Polish Revolt of 1863, Land and Liberty was crushed by the establishment. In 1876, the organisation was resurrected to become the first proper revolutionary party. The failure of 'Going to the People' convinced the members of Land and Liberty that the

Fig. 3.21
Peasants from the
Upper Volga.
Despite their
good intentions,
populists never
fully won the
trust of the
peasantry. The
social conditions
of the poor
provided an
impenetrable gap
for the well-
meaning wealthy
radicals.

state must be destroyed and that the land must be handed back to the peasants. They staged mass demonstrations including a meeting outside Kazan Cathedral in St Petersburg, where the revolutionary symbol of the red flag was unfurled for the first time by Georgy Plekhanov (1857-1918). He later established the first Russian Marxist party but was opposed to indiscriminate violence. In 1879, after a series of gun attacks, Land and Liberty split into:

– **The People's Will** (Narodnaya volya): this group was composed mainly of young middle class men and women. Their aims were the murder of the Tsar, the violent destruction of the state and the redistribution of economic power on socialist lines. The People's Will later became the basis for the powerful Socialist Revolutionary Party.

– **Black Repartition:** this smaller group associated with Plekhanov aimed to redistribute land but later turned to Marxism and became assimilated with the socialist groups.

THE DEMISE OF POPULISM

Populism continued to influence political debate in Russia after the 1870s. It experienced a modest revival at the turn of the century and the influence of Russian populism on twentieth century revolutionary ideology was profound. With respect to the trend towards terrorism, the government made a public appeal for support among liberals. Initially most populists detested violence, but arrests, imprisonment and hanging of activists led many of them to accept it as a necessary measure — nonviolence had achieved nothing. However, terrorism alienated the populists from sympathetic liberals in government positions and from public support.

NG Chernyshevsky (1828–1889): The son of a priest, Chernyshevsky was educated at St Petersburg University and became one of the editors of the radical newspaper, *The Contemporary*. He believed that the sources of misery in the world were economic and that socialism provided the cure for them. Arrested following some student demonstrations in 1862, he remained imprisoned until 1882. In 1862, whilst in gaol, he wrote the novel *What is to be Done?*, which through its strikingly portrayed heroes and the story of the emancipation of women through socialist principles, became an inspiration to many future revolutionaries, including Lenin, who gave his 1902 treatise on Bolshevik revolution the same name.

Georgy Plekhanov (1857–1918): Born into the gentry, he dropped out of a career as an officer to support peasant revolutionary causes in the 1870s. He was a founder of Liberation of Labour and the despite overseas exile until 1917, he assisted with the formation of the RSDWP in 1898, he sided with the Mensheviks in 1903, and gradually became an irrelevant figure, as men such as Lenin and Trotsky stole the intellectual initiative from him.

Fig. 3.22 Georgy Plekhanov.

Fig. 3.23 Members of The People's Will party.

Primary Extracts and Questions — Populist Revolutionary Thought in the 1860s and 1870s

THE OFFICIAL GOVERNMENT AIMS FOR THE REFORMS — 1861

The peasant should immediately feel that his life has been improved; the landowner should at once be satisfied that his interests are protected; and stable political order should not be disturbed for one moment in any locality.

(a) What does this extract reveal of the primary aims behind the Emancipation reforms?

(b) Is this extract naive? Give reasons for your answer.

DOSTOIEVSKY, RUSSIAN NOVELIST, ON POPULISM IN THE 1860s

They talked of the abolition of the censorship, and of phonetic spelling, of the substitution of the Latin characters for the Russian alphabet . . . of splitting Russia into nationalities, united in a free federation: of the abolition of the Army and Navy, of the restoration of Poland as far as the Dnieper, of the peasant reforms and of the Manifestoes, of the abolition of the hereditary principle and of the family, of children, of priests, of women's rights.

(c) What does this extract reveal of the aims of the populists in the 1860s?

AN ANONYMOUS REVOLUTIONARY MANIFESTO — 1861

Are the economic conditions and the land situation in Europe the same as they are here? Does the agricultural commune exist there...? Can every peasant and every citizen there own landed property? No, but here he can. We have enough land to last us tens of thousands of years.

We are a backward people and in this lies our salvation. We should thank our good fortune that we have not lived the life of Europe. Her misfortunes and desperate straits are a lesson to us. We do not want her proletariat, her aristocracy, her state principle, or her imperial power . . .

We want all citizens of Russia to enjoy equal rights; we do not want privileged classes to exist; we want ability and education, rather than birth, to confer the right to high position; we want appointments to public office to follow the elective principle. We do not want a nobility and titles. We want everyone to be equal in the eyes of the law and equal in [the assessment of] exactions, taxes, and obligations by the state . . . We want the land to belong to the nation and not to individuals; we want each commune to have its allotment, without the existence of private landowners; we do not want land to be sold like potatoes and cabbage . . .

(d) What does this extract reveal of attitudes towards shortcomings in the reforms?

(c) What does this extract reveal of the nature of Populism and its pro-Russian stance?

Gradually they came to the idea that the only way was to settle among the people and to live the people's life. Young men went into the villages as doctors, doctors' assistants, teachers, village scribes, even as agricultural labourers, blacksmiths, woodcutters, and so on, and tried to live there in close contact with the peasants. Girls passed teachers' examinations, learned mid-wifery or nursing, and went by the hundred into the villages, devoting themselves entirely to the poorest part of the population.

PRINCE KROPOTKIN, RUSSIAN ANARCHIST, ON POPULISM IN THE EARLY 1870s

(f) What does this extract reveal of the Populist idea of 'Going to the People'?

(g) What does this extract reveal of the weaknesses of Populism?

Nihilism, Hell and Anarchism — The Radical Groups

Nihilism was a particularly radical line of thought, named after an expression used by Ivan Turgenev in *Fathers and Sons* (1862). It rejected authority, social and moral restraints and relied on the notion of reason and the principles of natural science as the sole guides to conduct. The practical expression of the philosophy was a crude utilitarianism: nature was only there to be dominated, art was worthless in itself, and the practical should triumph over the philosophical.

BASIC PHILOSOPHY

Fig. 3.24 Mikhail Bakunin, was the most prominent of the Russian anarchists in the 1860s and 1870s, emphasizing the notion of individual revolution. However in the 1880s he became convinced that the organised class revolution proposed by the Marxists was more likely to succeed. He remained a prominent figure in Russian socialism for the rest of the century.

DIMITRI PISAREV

Dimitri Pisarev (1841-86) exercised an early influence upon the development of nihilism. He realised that a successful revolution would require careful planning to win over the conservative and backward peasantry. His radical political philosophy soon became popular with many young people who, before long, were deemed by the government to be godless, immoral, and dissolute. Although there was a fashionable and appealing element to nihilism, the movement was committed and serious. Few of its critics noticed that through nihilism, young people were searching for an acceptable alternative to the old order in Russia.

MIKHAIL BAKUNIN AND ANARCHISM

Mikhail Bakunin (1814-76) was the most significant influence upon nihilism and anarchism. The archetype of Russian revolutionaries in the pre-Bolshevik era, he participated in the European revolutions of 1848 and 1849, after which he was extradited to Russia and exiled to Siberia. In 1861 he escaped and fled abroad where he became a convinced anarchist. Anarchism took nihilism one step further and advocated the destruction of centralised government, preferring instead that nations be organised purely at a local level. Bakunin received generous financial support from his friend Herzen. From 1869 to 1872 Bakunin clashed with Marx and Engels at the First International, the first organised conference of world socialist groups. Between 1870 and 1873, he participated in unsuccessful anarchist revolts in Lyons and Spain. He was successful in obtaining government attention — both Prussia and Austria sentenced him to death for revolutionary activities within their borders. Through anarchist journals, his ideas continued to influence contemporary Russian writers and thinkers, but he was limited in his ability to organise an effective political movement.

HELL

Hell was an extremist group, closely allied to the nihilist movement and Bakunin's ideas, as well as borrowing heavily from the ideas of Chernyshevsky. It attracted student Romantics who justified assassination as a political weapon. In April 1866, Karakazov, a mentally unbalanced former student, attempted to shoot Alexander II. Karakazov's arrest and interrogation led to members of Hell being named as conspirators against the Tsar and to renewed supervision of universities and press censorship.

PN TKACHEV

PN Tkachev (1844-85) was a former student and journalist, who was among the first Russians to take an interest in Marx and extremist groups such as Hell encouraged him to agitate for political change and reform. Tkachev was also a follower of the French revolutionary, Louis Blanqui. Tkachev saw violent revolution as the only solution to Russia's problems — due to his subversive activities among students, he was imprisoned in 1869 and soon after escaped to Germany.

SG NECHAYEV

SG Nechayev (1847-82) was another radical supporter of violence and an admirer of Tkachev. He master-minded cell organisation of two or three revolutionaries as a means of spreading revolutionary sentiment. He collaborated with Bakunin on *Catechism of the Revolutionary* (1860s), which demanded that revolutionaries totally subject themselves to the authority of the group and claimed that social happiness could only be achieved in the long term by increasing the misery and suffering of peasants in the short term. Corrupt and oppressive officials were to be spared assassination in the hope that they would contribute to the onset of revolution. Nechayev's solution demanded the murder of liberals who obstructed revolution and of those others who doubted his views. After the murder of a bureaucrat in 1869, Nechayev fled to Switzerland but in 1872 he was extradited to stand trial. When the *Catechism* was read aloud in court, it shocked the public and seriously discredited the entire reform movement, even though Nechayev represented only the anarchistic fringe.

Marxism in Russia

By the 1880s, with the apparent failure of the other movements for change, more intellectuals in Russia began turning to the Marxist view of society and its code of political conduct. It came to dominate political debate among revolutionary groups. The nature of Marxism attracted a wide variety of people including former populists, Social Democrats and liberals. The consequent history of social democracy in Russia was one of intense doctrinal disputes, splits and party disagreements. At first, the Tsarist regime failed to understand the potential threat posed by Marxist doctrine and even allowed a Russian translation of the first volume of *Das Kapital* in 1872.

EARLY HISTORY

An early convert to Marxism was Georgy Plekhanov, a leading figure in the populist movement and the Black Repartition. In 1883, he abandoned populism and the following year in Switzerland with assistance of exiles Vera Zasulich and Peter Akselrod he established the group known as Liberation of Labour which believed that:

LIBERATION OF LABOUR

- capitalism would collapse of its own accord
- a bourgeois revolution would lead the masses in revolution
- Marxists must organise and spread propaganda among the working class to prepare for revolution
- Russia suffered from both the development of capitalism and the scarcity of that development
- Russian capitalism required the overthrow of Tsarism — revolution in Russia would only succeed when Russia was fully industrialised from which would flow the development of consciousness among industrial proletariat and eventually the establishment of socialism.

These beliefs differed fundamentally from those of the successful Bolshevik revolutionaries of 1917, especially in the area of the role of the party and its elite in organising the revolution.

The Assassination of Alexander II

Despite opposition from non-violent populists, the People's Will maintained terrorist activity. After several attempts on Alexander II's life, the movement finally succeeded. On 1 March 1881, the Tsar was bombed in his carriage while returning from a military parade. It was characteristic of Alexander the autocrat that despite severe wounds — one of his legs had been blown off and he was bleeding from the legs, stomach and head — his main concern was to be taken back to the palace so that he would not be seen to be dying in the street among his peasants.

Fig. 3.25 Death of Alexander II.

According to Treadgold, Alexander II did more to improve the lives and conditions of the Russian people than any other single person in their history. Despite his return to more conservative measures, on the morning of his death Alexander had approved the first tentative steps towards a Russian constitution, which had resulted from the 1880 appointment of a commission under General MT Loris-Melikov (1825–1888) to investigate the causes of unrest and find ways to alleviate them.

Far from encouraging revolt, the assassination shocked and appalled the nation. Alexander III hunted down the conspirators with a fanatical vengeance and reversed many reforms inspired by his father Alexander II. The assassination also had a significant psychological impact on the nine year old future Tsar Nicholas II, who witnessed the bloody scene of Alexander's eventual gory death from the corner of the royal bedroom.

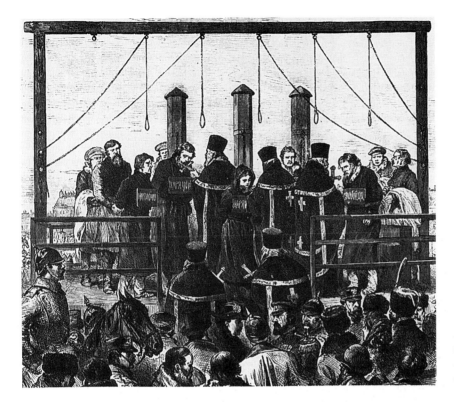

Fig. 3.26 The execution of Alexander II's assassins.

Fig. 3.27 Michael Loris-Melnikov. Melnikov was an aristocrat who was largely responsible for domestic policy in the last years of Alexander's life. He pursued a twofold policy of suppressing political radicals but broadening reform where it had already been granted in order to preserve popular support for the Tsar.

Fig. 3.28
Alexander III
with his family.

The Reign of Alexander III

Alexander III's Beliefs and Values

PERSONALITY

Alexander III was determined to wage war against all political opponents. Physically he was immensely strong, a quality he wanted to reflect in his style of government. He relished power as an autocratic ruler, believing in the old Nicholas System creed of orthodoxy, autocracy and nationality. Increasingly he failed to recognise the unstable nature of Russian society.

POBEDONOSTSEV

Most of Alexander III's ideas were borrowed from his close adviser, Konstantin Pobedonostsev (1827-1907), the Chief Procurator of the Holy Synod. Appointed Professor of Constitutional Law at Moscow University 1860-1865, Pobedonostsev tutored the two sons of Alexander II. Pobedonostsev was conservative, theocratic, deeply suspicious of the West and resistant to change. He was an ardent champion of the reactionary Russian Orthodox Church and referred to the notion of parliamentary democracy and a constitution as the 'greatest lie of our time'. He believed that autocracy was the only possible basis of government for Russia and that Alexander II's reforms were 'criminal acts'.

Domestic Policy — Education, Rural Controls and Local Government

Under the influence of Pobedonostsev, Alexander III introduced a number of reactionary measures. Pobedonostsev wanted to make secondary and higher education the preserve of the elite, so qualifications for education were subjected to even more strict conditions and consequently the number of high school enrolments fell. By 1904, only 27 per cent of school-age children were being educated. Universities were deprived of their independence and student organisations were suppressed. Dimitri Tolstoy (1823–1889) was Alexander's Minister of the Interior, and was enthusiastic to support the policies of Alexander and Pobedonostsev. In 1889, 'land captains' were appointed to oversee peasants, with powers to whip and prosecute farmers for minor misdemeanours. This measure earned Alexander III the bitter resentment of peasants who saw it as a return to serf law. In 1890, Pobedonostsev reduced the powers of the zemstva in favour of increased noble control of local affairs.

Primary Extracts and Questions — Political Repression under Alexander II and Alexander III

First of all, I was taken into a room where was stored everything necessary to the equipment of a convict under sentence. On the floor lay piles of chains; and clothes, boots, etc, were heaped on shelves. From among them some were selected that were supposed to fit me; and I was then conducted to a second room. Here the right side of my head was shaved, and the hair on the left side cut short . . . I experienced a sensation of personal degradation of something less than human. I thought of the days — in Russia not so long ago — when criminals were branded with hot irons. A convict was waiting ready to fasten on my fetters. I was placed on a stool, and had to put my foot on an anvil. The blacksmith fitted an iron ring around each ankle, and welded it together . . .

The fetters at first caused me intolerable pain in walking, and even disturbed my sleep. It requires considerable practice before one can easily manage to dress and undress. The heavy chains, about thirteen pounds in weight, are not only an encumbrance, but are very painful, as they chafe the skin round the ankles . . .

I asked my companions the reason of their banishment, and learned from them that . . . they had simply been accused by the police of being 'untrustworthy'. This word has become classical in Russian police affairs, and has a conveniently vague signification. Literally it means 'of whom nothing good can be expected'. A young man or girl associates with so-and-so, reads such and such books; this is enough to awaken suspicions that the said young man or girl is 'untrustworthy'. The police or the gendarmerie pay a domiciliary visit, find a suspicious letter or a prohibited book, and then the course of events is certain — arrest, imprisonment and Siberia. It may be scarcely credible that people languish for years in prison, without any pretense of legal procedure against them, simply by decree of an officer of the gendarmerie; and that at the good pleasure of these officers — most of them fabulously ignorant men — people are banished to the wilds of Siberia.

LEO DEUTSCH, RUSSIAN WRITER, COMMENTS IN 1903 ON HIS BANISHMENT TO SIBERIA IN 1874

(a) What does this extract reveal of the justice system with respect to political prisoners?
(b) What does this extract reveal of the treatment of political prisoners?
(c) From your own knowledge, what would have been the likely effects of this sort of treatment upon surviving ex-prisoners?

There had recently been much insubordination amongst the students of the different colleges in the capital, which had given serious agitation to the Government, and it appeared . . . that in the middle of the previous night, General Trepoff, the head of the metropolitan police, had sent his agents to make a descent on one of the colleges, a number a students in which, taken indiscriminately, were hurried into car-

POLITICAL REPRESSION OF STUDENTS IN 1878 ACCORDING TO COLONEL WELLESLEY, BRITISH MILITARY ATTACHÉ TO THE BRITISH EMBASSY IN ST PETERSBURG — 1905

riages and taken to General Trepoff's offices. There the General, after having upbraided them in no measured terms, informed them that he was about to hand them over to the tender mercies of the secret police.

It so happened that my informant's nephew, a boy of eighteen, was among those who had thus been arrested. The lad . . . had neither the wish nor the time to join in any of the boyish disloyalty of his comrades . . . When the turn of my friend's nephew came, he found on entering the next room Count Schouvaloff, who . . . was then chief of the secret police, sitting at a table close to which was [a] chair, on which the Count invited him to sit. No sooner had he done so than a trapdoor, on which the boy's chair was placed, was gradually lowered until only the upper half of his body remained above the floor, and in this position he received a severe flogging, after which he was sent about his business, being told by Count Schouvaloff that he had received a lesson which would teach him not to meddle in politics again.

(d) What does this extract reveal of secret police methods?
(e) From your own knowledge, what would have been the likely effects on those who had been subjected to these methods?
(f) From your own knowledge, how effective were these methods in suppressing opposition to the regime?

CENSORSHIP IN THE 1880S ACCORDING TO KENNAN, BRITISH WRITER — 1891

[It is] the censorship of the Press in Russia . . . precisely this forcible repression of thought, speech and discussion in Russia that drives so many men — and especially young men — into political crime. The whole Russian revolutionary movement is nothing but a violent protest against cruel injustice and gag-law. Below will be found a list of cases in which Russian periodicals have been punished, or wholly suppressed, for giving voice to ideas and sentiments regarded as objectionable by the ruling class . . .

1882 June 17: The *Riga Visnik* publishes the following in lieu of a leading edito-

Fig. 3.29 Political Prisoners on the Island of Sakhalin 1890. These men are being chained up by their guards — notice the man on the left who has been chained to his wheelbarrow.

Fig. 3.30 Volga porters on a lunch break of bread and tea.

Fig. 3.31 Contemporary engraving of political prisoners working in the mines of Siberia.

rial' 'In today's issue it was our intention to have had a leading editorial, urging the Estonians to unite more closely among themselves, and with the Russians, and to work with energy for the Fatherland; but we have not been allowed to print it.'

1882 July 1: The humorous illustrated newspaper *Gusla* is seized by order of the censor, and its 24th number is suppressed, for making fun of an irrigation scheme in which the censor is interested . . .

1886 May 6: The editor of the *St Petersburg Police Gazette*, a purely official Government organ, is arrested and imprisoned because, in an article in his paper referring to 'a requiem for Alexander II', there was a typographical error which made it read 'a requiem for Alexander III'.

(g) To what does this extract attribute the majority of revolutionary activity in Russia at the time?
(h) How realistic is this assessment?
(i) What do the examples of censorship reveal of government attitudes to criticism of the Tsarist government?

Ethnic Minorities

RUSSIFICATION

Alexander III's repressive domestic policies were matched by his persecution of religious and ethnic minorities. Pobedonostsev pursued a policy of Russification in which he aimed to make the Russian people and language pre-eminent in the empire, forcing peoples from all the other varied ethnic groups within the empire to relinquish their own cultural identities. The minorities endured many restrictions:

- Russian was imposed as the main language in Ukraine, Russia, Lithuania and Poland — local languages were banned
- similar restrictions were applied to German inhabitants in the Baltic provinces of Livonia, Estonia and Courland — forced conversions from the Lutheran faith to Russian Orthodoxy were common despite the fact that before this they had served the Russian Empire with unquestioning loyalty
- obscure and nonconformist Russian sects such as the Molokany, the Doukhobors and the Stundists were deported or imprisoned
- after the Polish Revolt in 1863, the Russification of Poland had intensified with closure of Warsaw University in 1869 — under Alexander III, Russian replaced Polish as the language of instruction, except in scripture and the teaching of native Polish. The onset of the economic revolution in Poland became yet another opportunity for Russia to exercise its dominance. The bulk of civil servants' positions were open only to Russians — overall, the officialdom did its utmost to prevent the local people from running their own affairs
- inhabitants of Muslim Tartar areas were forcibly converted to Russian Orthodox religion and the regime encouraged separatism especially among Crimean Tartars — Muslims in other areas were treated just as poorly
- the industrialising nation of Finland, annexed by Russia during time of Alexander I, was subjected to new and harsher restrictions — Russian tariffs discriminated against Finnish products — the Finnish post office and railway system were absorbed into the Russian administration —

finally, in 1899 the imperial government abrogated Finland's constitutional rights, a move which united the Finnish nation in a campaign of passive resistance under a liberal leadership.

The Jews

Under the policy of Russification, the harshest treatment was reserved for Jews, of whom there were five million in the Russian Empire at the time of Alexander III's accession. Theoretically, from 1815 onwards they had been limited to living in the Pale of Settlement in the Western European provinces, although wealthier Jewish families by and large ignored this proscription. Pobedonostsev encouraged anti-semitism among the ignorant, frustrated mass of peasants, actively seeking to divert their anger away from the government. Jews living in the Pale of Settlement were tormented by the surrounding population, whose suffering and misery were blamed on Jewish customs and their activities as moneylenders (one of the few occupations that Jews were permitted to practise in Russia). Ridiculous charges were trumped up — Jews were even accused of murdering children to obtain blood for secret rituals.

ANTI-SEMITIC POLICIES

This suspicion and superstition united the peasants in a xenophobic hatred and succeeded in directing their hostility towards the Jews and away from the state during this time of crisis. Periodically this hatred erupted in outbreaks of extreme violence organised by Alexander III's officials against defenceless Jews. These outbreaks, known as pogroms were appalling in their savagery, shameful in their intent and resulted in the death of many thousands of innocent Jewish people. Frequently pogroms were planned in advance with the active support of Pobedonostsev. At the insti-

POGROMS

Fig. 3.32
Contemporary engraving of the Kiev Pogrom following Alexander II's death.

gation of the government, newspapers often carried obscene anti-semitic stories before these campaigns. Overall there were 215 pogroms in the reign of Alexander III, starting in July 1881. Numerous foreign governments protested to the Russian government, but to no avail.

Results of Russification

The policy lacked any semblance of common sense. Loyal minorities like the Baltic Germans and Finns were treated with the same disregard as the potentially disloyal Ukrainians and Tartars, or those in open revolt such as Poles. Thus by the outbreak of World War I, the Finns, Armenians, Georgians, and some Baltic Germans were in active opposition to the Tsarist regime. With the Jews, the systematic program of repression and violence resulted in mass emigration to Eastern Europe, the United States and Palestine.

Economic Development 1855–1894

Causes

The Crimean War revealed the extent of Russian backwardness and that it was primarily responsible for the change in government attitude towards industrialisation. Thus the leading role played by the state was a response to the conditions of economic backwardness. In addition, Christian shows that the vodka riots of 1858-1859 proved to be a salient message to the state that, unless it changed the nature of its revenue-collecting activities and its overall financial policy, peasants were capable of mass action in protest, which could lead to violence and even political upheaval.

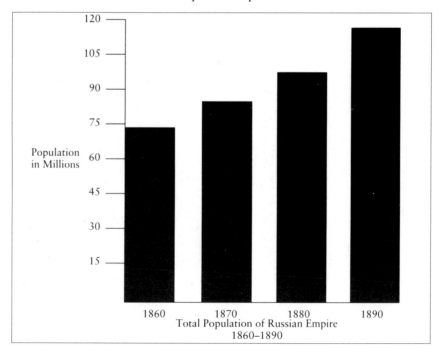

Fig. 3.33 Population statistics in Russia 1860-1890.

Financial Reform

The needs of the state, rather than private capital, were the determining factor in guiding industrial development. In 1860 Alexander II established the State Bank with a primary role to provide credit for industrial enterprises. MK Reutern, Minister of Finance from 1862 to 1876, was eager to restrict government spending and encouraged the extension of a network of private banks. Between 1799 and 1853 only 72.1 million roubles had been invested in joint stock banks, but from 1855 to 1860 investments reached more than 317 million roubles. Reutern also encouraged railway construction, using private companies funded through foreign loans. National accounts were published and serious effort made to prevent wasteful expenditure.

EARLY REFORM

The replacement of the vodka farms from 1863 onwards with a system of direct excises on production improved the revenue-raising capacity of liquor for the government to the extent that during the remaining years of the century, liquor often provided over twice the revenue of the obrok and poll tax combined, as well as separating systematic private profit from public accounts. It eliminated much of the bureaucratic corruption from the vodka industry and freed up large amounts of capital, which the former vodka tax farmers began to divert into industrialisation projects.

VODKA

NK Bunge, Minister of Finance from 1881 to 1887, also realised the importance of fiscal reform and introduced measures to reform the antiquated taxation system. The Peasants' State Bank was set up to help relieve the redemption payment crisis among the rural peasants and to help them buy more land from the nobility and the Nobles' State Bank was established to assist nobles whose estates were in danger of being dismantled. As Chairman of the Committee of Ministers from 1887 to

FINANCE

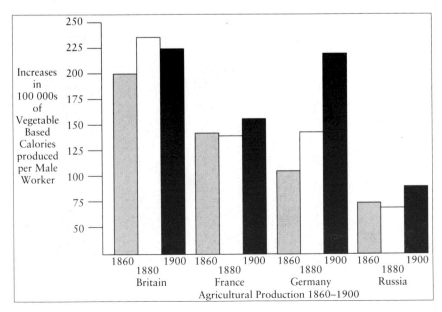

Fig. 3.34 Agricultural production in Britain, France, Germany and Russia 1860-1900.

1895, Bunge was responsible for these and other progressive and expansionist policies, such as the abolition of the poll tax, protectionism of industry through the establishment of tariffs and the formation of the Factory Inspectorate. He even planned to introduce an income tax, but never quite succeeded in doing so.

FISCAL REFORM

IA Vyshnegradski (1831–1895), Minister of Finance from 1887 to 1892, was an experienced financier who introduced the highest tariffs Russia's commercial history had seen. During his term as minister, the state came to play a more active role in the economy and encouraged foreign investment, imposed tariff protection to protect domestic producers and promoted heavy industry in the Ukraine and the oil industry centred upon Baku on the Caspian Sea.

Industry

From 1856 onwards, there was a surge in enterprise (notably in foreign trade), mechanisation in the textile industry and an increase in railway building. Between 1860 and 1870, industrial output increased by 60 per cent and the value of exports rose from 181 million to 359 million roubles. Yet, by 1880 the industrial labour force still numbered less than 500,000, most of whom were unskilled.

Fig. 3.35 A blast furnace in Central Russia around 1890.

Although Witte had begun the process of modernising and expanding industry by 1894, most industry was still performed in the homes of the

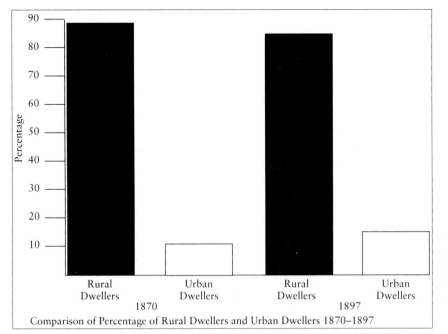

Comparison of Percentage of Rural Dwellers and Urban Dwellers 1870–1897

Fig. 3.36 Rural and urban populations as percentages of total population statistics in Russia 1870-1897.

peasants. Some peasants, driven off the land by crippling mortgage repayments, wandered to the cities to find work in the factories where they suffered greatly from the appalling conditions.

Fig. 3.37 A woman working at the loom. During the reigns of Alexander II and Alexander III, despite the pressure to modernise, most industry was still cottage-based.

Fig. 3.38
Peasants at the
Kamenka Fair in
1862.

Trade Fairs

Trade fairs were an effective means of circulating consumer goods and encouraging light industry and in circumstances where there was no developed retail network, the fairs were useful for the collection of agricultural raw materials and the distribution of finished manufactured goods. During the 1860s, over 6500 trade fairs were held in the empire.

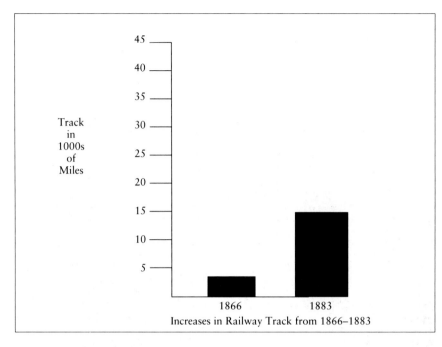

Fig. 3.39
Increases in
Russian rail track
1866-1883.

Railway Construction

More than any other industry railway construction stimulated Russia's economic growth. In 1838, the first railway was built, running 25 km from St. Petersburg to Tsarskoye Selo, funded by private entrepreneurs. Later, railway lines from Warsaw to the Austrian frontier (1843), and

PRE-1885

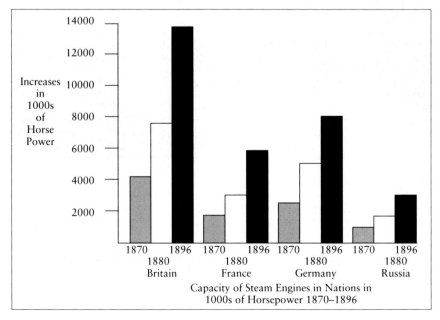

Fig. 3.40 Total
steam engine
horsepower in
Britain, France,
Germany and
Russia 1870-
1896.

Fig. 3.41
Lubayanska
Square in
Moscow in the
1880s. The
archway in the
rear of the
photograph is the
entrance to the
Kitai-Gorod,
which had been
the main
commercial
centre of Moscow
since the 16th
century.

Fig. 3.42 A child
dying of typhus,
made more
deadly by
starvation, in the
plague of 1891-2.

from St. Petersburg to Moscow (1847-51) were undertaken by the state. The high cost of this last rail line was the major reason for the government seeking venture capital from French companies for future projects.

Between 1855 and 1860 almost half of the 317 million roubles invested in joint stock companies went into railways. Rail track increased from 1448 km in 1860 to 10,731 km in 1870 and to 20,800 km by 1880. A network of rail lines linked the chief grain-growing areas with Moscow and St Petersburg and the Baltic and Black Sea ports. In 1891, Witte authorised the beginning of the construction of the Trans-Siberian Railway, in order to spread the rate of development to the eastern provinces as well as to develop communications within Russia. The impact of the spread of urbanisation and the resulting creation of pockets of proletariat workers in industrial towns along the network was significant. Yet, considering Russia's vast size and the progress made in other European countries in rail track, Russia was still far behind in improving her communications network.

GROWTH 1855–1894

	Russia	France	Germany	Britain
1860	10=	5	6=	1=
1880	11	6	5	1
1900	10=	6	5	1=

Fig. 3.43 Rank Order of Industrialisation in major world producers 1860-1900. These figures are based on per capita consumption of raw cotton and coal, production of smelted iron, development of railways and fixed motive power.

Results

Although finance had been reformed and the industrialisation process had started, by 1894 Russia was still largely the same agricultural nation it had been for centuries. Little had been done to change the real social and economic distress of the peasantry. Despite their new legal status following Emancipation, the conditions of the rural poor were still very difficult, especially since they now faced the added burden of redemption payments as well as poor land. Many could not afford their land payments and scratched out a meagre living from wage-labour in the countryside or drifted to the city in the vain hope of a better life there.

There was still no evidence of a real desire to improve the lives of the workers, either in the villages or in the towns, Factory hours and conditions were still unregulated. There were few health services — the typhus plague of 1891-1892 carried off thousands of undernourished children. Wages remained low and dissatisfaction high, yet the autocracy retained tight control. It seemed that Alexander III had succeeded in following Nicholas I's prescription of little social and economic change and harsh political repression in order to preserve the system. However the events of the twenty five years following Alexander's death would show how this traditional policy was at best only a temporary remedy for containing the long-term suffering of the poor.

Historians' Views

CHRISTIAN

- the government's attitude to industrial development after 1861 was still hostile — railway-building was the only real concession to this policy, but this laid the path for the industrial policy of the 1890s — it also encouraged the development of iron industry and coal mining
- peasants had three options to cope with the economic changes: finding work in domestic industry; rural wage-labour; and urban wage-labour — the latter was the most drastic as it meant a complete upheaval and change in living and was usually taken up by only the poorest of the peasants — even when they did, they still clung to many of their rural peasant habits and customs, especially holidays
- by the end of Alexander III's reign it seemed that the government had temporarily won the battle with the revolutionaries

WESTWOOD

- the loosening of entry regulations into universities and censorship in the 1860s allowed poorer students and Western texts into universities — it promoted the radicalism of 1870s
- many of the readers of the radical writers did not realise that as well as criticising the old regime they also proposed a new and better form of society
- the 1870s was the great decade for revolutionaries seeking socialism based among the peasantry — the failure of 'Going to the People' and the arrests prominent in the latter years of Alexander II and also Alexander III encouraged more extreme solutions to Russia's problems
- the policy of Russification was supported by the bureaucracy, the army and the Church and corrupted zealous Slavophilism — the intensification of repression among the national minorities only furthered dissent in the Empire
- Alexander III's reign was notable for the persecution of minorities and the partial reversal of some of Alexander II's reforms — he kept Russia out of war (although he laid the foundation for the Russo-Japanese War) — the promotion of industrial development was mainly due to the work of Bunge

COWIE & WOLFSON

- the encouragement offered by the initial reforms of the early 1860s and the frustrations created by Alexander II's return to more reactionary policies led to intellectuals turning away from liberalism to more radical theories — in addition the abstract Slavophile vs Westernisation debate encouraged by Alexander II only made them seek more practical and revolutionary policies
- the most serious economic problem facing Russia during the 1870s was rural over-population and agricultural stagnancy
- Alexander III was a powerful personality, conscientious in devotion to duty but narrow-minded and opposed to all forms of liberalism
- the government's method of financing foreign debt (taxation of the peasants) led only to more dissent

KOCHAN & ABRAHAM

- a measure of Alexander II's priorities can be seen in the fact that he sacked his liberal bureaucrats as soon as the emancipation legislation was drafted and implemented, but he did retain the services of the liberal War Minister Dmitry Miliutin
- although they gained some greater personal freedom, Russian peasants did not gain the rise in standards of living occurring elsewhere in Europe — in fact living standards declined, and land hunger and rural over-population increased — this had the effect of hampering industrial development
- railway-building was one of the most impressive aspects of post-reform decades — although funded largely by overseas capital, it was a major encouragement for Russian heavy industry and it improved communications enormously

- industrial development was determined by the needs of the state and not those of private capital
- the cultural development of the period from writers such as Turgenev, Dostoievsky and Tolstoy provided a broad intellectual vote of approval for the ideas of Populism
- Alexander III wanted to return to Nicholas I's slogan of 'Orthodoxy, Autocracy and Nationality' — to do this he had to be far more more repressive than Nicholas I due to the maturing and radicalisation of Russian thought since the 1830s and 1840s

Problems and Issues

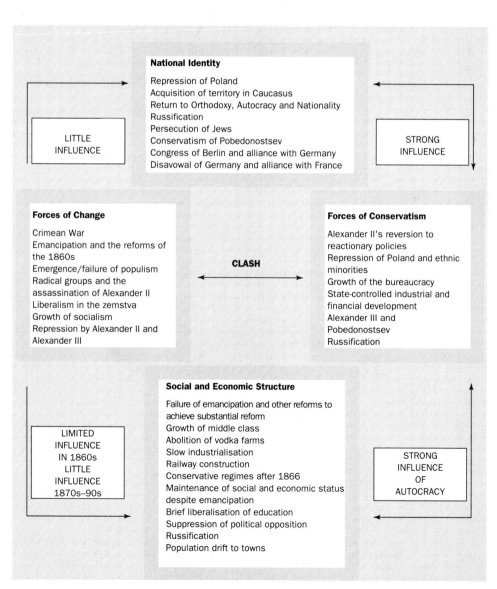

Fig. 3.44 Problems and Issues — Alexander II and Alexander III.

EXERCISE AND SKILLS REVISION

1. Paragraphs

Write properly structured paragraph responses for each of the following questions:

a. Why was it necessary for Alexander II to institute reform in Russia?
b. How were the serfs emancipated?
c. How did Alexander II reform other areas of his empire?
d. What were the major radical and revolutionary movements in the 1870s?
e. What financial reform did the administration of Alexander III introduce into the empire?
f. How did Alexander treat the ethnic and religious minorities in his empire?
g. Why had the conditions of the peasants not improved in Russia by 1894?
h. What improvements in Russian industry and communications were apparent in the period 1854 to 1894?

2. Mind maps

a. Construct a mind map explaining the origins, policies and activities of the radical and revolutionary movements of the 1870s.
b. Construct a mind map demonstrating the development of Russian literature from 1854 to 1894.

3. Three part structured responses

• Alexander II

a. What were some of the social, economic and political problems in Russia at the start of the reign of Alexander II? *(6 marks)*

b. How did Alexander attempt to deal with these problems in the early years of his reign? *(12 marks)*

c. Despite the reforms of Alexander II, why was there a growth in radical and revolutionary movements during the 1870s? *(12 marks)*

• Alexander III

a. What were the major changes to the society and economy of Russia from 1881 to 1894? *(6 marks)*

b. How did Alexander III repress the forces of change in Russia from 1881 to 1894? *(12 marks)*

c. By 1894, to what extent had Alexander achieved his conservative aims? *(12 marks)*

4. Essay topics

a. Write an essay of no less than 1000 words in response to the question: What changes to the nature of politics, the economy and the society of Russia came about as a result of the reforms of the early 1860s? How did Alexander II and Alexander III attempt to deal with these changes?
b. Write an essay of no less than 1000 words in response to the question: By 1894, why was the response of the Tsarist autocracy to the forces of change inadequate to relieve social and economic pressure in Russia?

The following will assist you in preparing material for your essays.

Consider carefully each of the following key areas:

Causes of 1860s Reform
Nature of 1860s Reforms
Immediate Effects of Reform
Radicals and Revolutionaries
Political Repression

Territorial Expansion
Russification
Industrial and Financial Reform
Urbanisation

Consider this quotation from the *Revolutionary Manifesto*, written by radical students in September 1861:

> The sovereign has betrayed the hopes of the people; the freedom he has given to them is not real and is not what the people dreamed of and need.

Consider this quotation from one of the characters of Tolstoy's *War and Peace*:

> Thoughts that have important consequences are always simple. All my thinking could be summed up with these words: 'Since corrupt people unite amongst themselves to constitute a force, then honest people must do the same'. It's as simple as that.

Consider this quotation from Turgenev's *Fathers and Sons*:

> A Nihilist is a man who does not bow before any authorities, who does not accept any single principle on trust, no matter how respected this principle.

Consider this extract from the poem 'Revenge', written by Alexandr Blok about the reign of Alexander III:

> In those mute and distant years
> A dull gloom filled all hearts.
> Pobodonostsev had unfurled
> His owlish wings over Russia.
> There was neither day nor night,
> Only the shadow of his giant wings.

New Skills and Exercises

Reading Texts

When you study a textbook, approach the job of reading in a clear and pur-   **APPROACHING TEXTS**
poseful manner. You must know:
- Why you are reading
- What information are you looking for?
- Where are you going to find it?
- How does it relates to the task at hand?
- How it relates to what you have done in class.
   Once you have established these firmly in your mind, you have a focus for your reading. Write down your focus questions; you are now ready to

read the text book. There are some steps to follow to increase the effectiveness of the way you study a text book:

- Surveying
- Detailed reading
- Restating
- Reviewing

Studying this way means actively asking yourself questions all the way through.

SURVEYING

Surveying is the preliminary reading process, which focuses your mind specifically on the text. Quickly read through the text, using your skimming and scanning skills, in order to answer these questions:

- Which sections will help me?
- Which sections are relevant to me?
- What is the general outline of the information in the text?
- Where is the important information?
- *The process.* Look for titles, sub-headings and section headings. Read the introductory paragraphs carefully — they will usually contain an outline of the information in the material. Take note of all illustrations, maps and diagrams — don't forget to look at their captions. Read any summary paragraphs and review questions — these will usually be at the end of sections, and they may be specially marked.

DETAILED READING

Read through the text thoroughly and patiently. This is where you are going to obtain the information to answer the questions. Therefore ask yourself:

- What is the task that I have to do?
- What information do I need to do this task?
- Does the text provide this information to me?
- *The process.* Read in small chunks of a few paragraphs at a time. Pause where you feel there is a natural break and go through the questioning and thinking process shown here to confirm this information in your mind.
  –Search for answers to the specific questions of the task.
  –Question what you are reading: Is it relevant? Will it help me? Does it answer the question? How much of it do I need?

READ ACTIVELY

Think about what you are reading, don't just let the words flow over your head. Link the information to what you already know — how does it fit in? What does it help to explain? How useful is it to your understanding? If you are reading *your own book*, underline the important points as you go.

BE SELECTIVE

Look at the information carefully and decide what you need, what is important and what is essential. Don't get lost in long slabs of less important supporting detail. Ask yourself how the information relates to the general outline of the text — use the key terms and concepts to group information into categories, and don't be afraid to say the important terms and sentences out loud to yourself. This will help you to remember them.

Try to visualise the information. Try to picture the events in your mind, rather than just looking at letters and numbers on a page.

If the text is getting too much for you, give yourself a short break and when you return to it, read the text in smaller chunks.

- **Restating** means taking the time during your detailed reading to stop, think and make brief notes on what you have just read.   **RESTATING**
- *The process*. When you reach a natural break in your reading, STOP. Ask yourself what you have just read. How is it important to the question? How can you use this to answer the question?

In your notepad, *briefly and in your own words*, summarise or outline the information. Leave room for a heading at the start of each section of your notes. Continue this process all the way through your reading. When you have finished reading, you will have made a series of notes, which follow the outline of the text, but are expressed in your own words.

When you have finished the text, read through your notes again. As you read each section, stop and ask yourself what that section was about. Formulate a key term or phrase and write that above the section as its heading.

Reviewing is the final process where you concentrate on placing the information into your memory.   **REVIEWING**
- *The process*. As soon as you have finished 'Restating', go back through your notes. Start with the first key term open to your view and ask yourself what this key term means. If incorrect, go over the section of notes again until you know the answer.

Work through each key term this way. When you have finished, go back and write down all the key terms on a separate piece of paper. Again, go through them all in turn, and see whether you can remember them. Re-study your notes if need be. Next, try to write down all the key terms from memory.

By the end of your reading session, you can write down the list of key terms by heart, and you also know by heart what they mean. Every now and then go back to these notes and revise them. See whether you can remember them after a day, a week, a month.

Be aware: this process will take some time for you to use easily. It may be slow at first, but using it frequently and consistently, you will find the steps will become automatic. You will be able to read and take notes more quickly and more efficiently, obtain far more meaning and store far more information in your memory.

EXERCISE

Research Task: Russian Foreign Policy 1855-1894

There has been no assessment of the foreign policy of either Alexander II or Alexander III in this text. Research and write an account of no less than 750 words to outline and explain the major events of Russian foreign policy between the years 1855 and 1894. Use the following focus questions as a guide to the analysis of your account:

- What were the major events of foreign policy in the years 1855-1894?
- Where did the Tsars wish to acquire extra territory for their empire?
- Why did the Tsars wish to acquire extra territory for their empire?
- How and why did the Tsars react to the foreign policies of the other major European powers?

  Be sure to include both primary and secondary sources in your account.

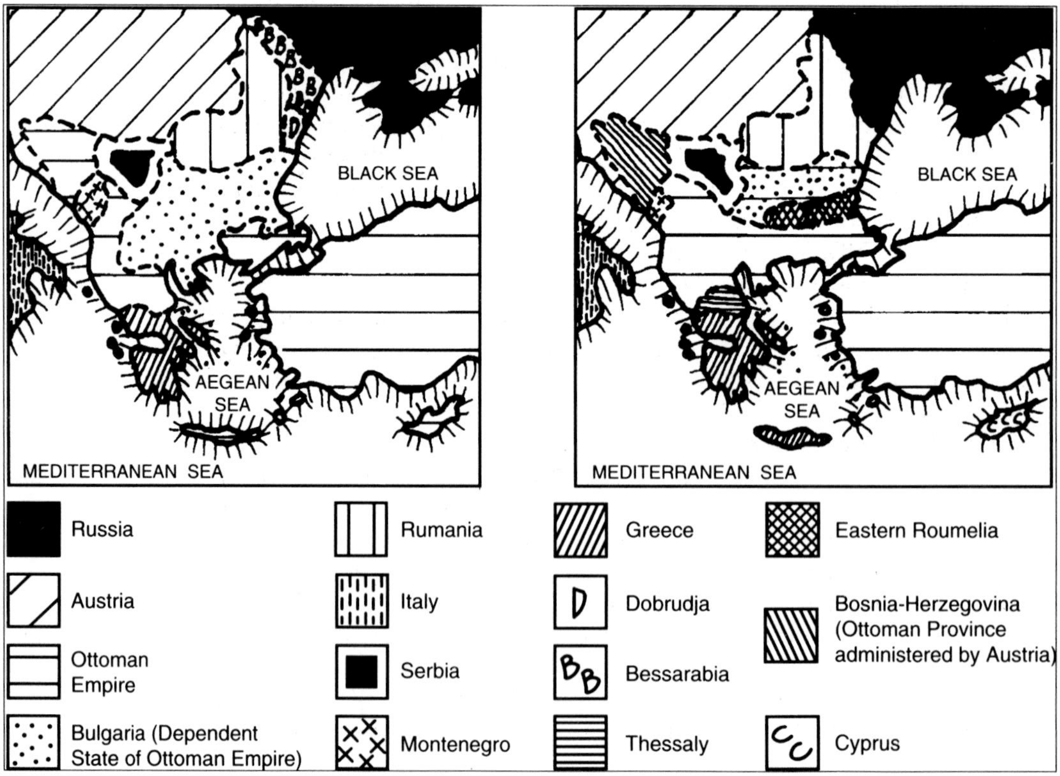

BLACK SEA
AEGEAN SEA
MEDITERRANEAN SEA
BLACK SEA
AEGEAN SEA
MEDITERRANEAN SEA
Russia
Austria
Ottoman Empire
Bulgaria (Dependent State of Ottoman Empire)
Rumania
Italy
Serbia
Montenegro
Greece
Dobrudja
Bessarabia
Thessaly
Eastern Roumelia
Bosnia-Herzegovina (Ottoman Province administered by Austria)
Cyprus

Fig. 3.45 Maps showing the territorial settlements after the Treaty of San Stefano and the Treaty of Berlin 1878.

Glossary

Bakunin Mikhail: the most significant influence upon nihilism and anarchism. The archetype of Russian revolutionaries in the pre Bolshevik era, he participated in the European revolutions of 1848 and 1849, after which he was extradited to Russia and exiled to Siberia. In 1861 he escaped and fled abroad where he became a convinced anarchist. Anarchism took nihilism one step further and advocated the destruction of centralised government, preferring instead that nations be organised purely at a local level. Bakunin received generous financial support from his friend Alexander Herzen, a nobleman and an active propagandist. From 1869 to 1872 Bakunin clashed with Marx and Engels at the First International. Between 1870 and 1873, he participated in unsuccessful anarchist revolts in France and Spain. Through anarchist journals, his ideas continued to influence contemporary Russian writers and thinkers, but his ability to organise an effective political movement was limited.

Black Repartition: this small group associated with Plekhanov broke away from Land and Liberty and aimed to redistribute land. It later turned to Marxism and became assimilated into the socialist groups.

Bunge NK: Minister of Finance from 1881 to 1887, Bunge realised the importance of fiscal reform and introduced measures to reform the antiquated taxation system. He was also responsible for introducing the Peasants' and the Nobles' State Banks, in an effort to reduce the financial crises that both these sections of the population were experiencing. As Chairman of the Committee of Ministers from 1887 to 1895, he was responsible for these and other progressive and expansionist policies, such as the abolition of the poll tax, protectionism of industry through the establishment of tariffs and the formation of the Factory Inspectorate.

Chernyshevsky NG: See page 103.

Dostoievsky Fyodor: See page 96.

Hell: an extremist group, closely allied to the nihilist movement and ideas of Bakunin. The group also borrowed heavily from the ideas of Chernyshevsky. It attracted student Romantics who justified assassination as a political weapon.

Herzen Alexander: Herzen was the most significant early influence for the populists. He idealised the agricultural commune. He saw it as means of preparing people for social revolution. In 1847 he was exiled and spent the rest of his life in Geneva and London. His London home became a centre for revolutionary exile. In 1857, Herzen founded a newspaper, *Kolokol* (*The Bell*), which was smuggled into Russia. His ideas had a strong impact upon liberal opinion throughout Russia during first years of Alexander II's reign.

Land and Liberty: a secret group of radical populists which became prominent in the early 1860s. It was deeply influenced by the socialist

Chernyshevsky but, following the failed Polish Revolt of 1863, Land and Liberty was crushed by the establishment. In 1876, the organisation was resurrected, becoming the first proper revolutionary party. The failure of 'Going to the People' convinced the members of Land and Liberty that the state must be destroyed and that the land must be handed back to the peasants.

Lavrov Peter: a professor of mathematics who believed that ordinary people, not professional revolutionaries, could bring about their own liberation. He opposed violence and encouraged educated people to move among the masses to awaken them to their plight.

Liberation of Labour: an early Marxist group formed by Plekhanov which believed that capitalism would collapse of its own accord and that a bourgeois revolution would lead the masses in revolution. They thought that Marxists must organise and spread propaganda among the working class to prepare for revolution — Russia suffered from both the development of capitalism and the scarcity of that development. This meant that Russian capitalism required the overthrow of Tsarism — revolution in Russia would only succeed when Russia was fully industrialised from which would flow the development of consciousness among industrial proletariat and eventually the establishment of socialism.

Nechayev SG: another radical supporter of violence and admirer of Tkachev. He master-minded cell organisation of two or three revolutionaries as a means for spreading revolutionary sentiment. He collaborated with Bakunin on *Catechism of the Revolutionary* (1860s), which demanded that revolutionaries totally subject themselves to the authority of the group and believed that social happiness could only be achieved in the long term by increasing the misery and suffering of peasants in the short term. Corrupt and oppressive officials were to be spared assassination in the hope that they would contribute to the onset of revolution. Nechayev's solution demanded the murder of liberals who obstructed revolution and of others who doubted his views. After the murder of a bureaucrat in 1869, Nechayev fled to Switzerland from where he was extradited to stand trial. When the Catechism was read aloud in court, it shocked the public and seriously discredited the entire reform movement, even though Nechayev represented only the anarchistic fringe.

Nihilism: a particularly radical line of thought named after a term used by Ivan Turgenev in *Fathers and Sons* (1862). It rejected authority, social and moral restraints and relied on the notion of reason and the principles of natural science as the sole guide to conduct. The practical expression of the philosophy was a crude utilitarianism: nature was only there to be dominated; art was worthless in itself, and the practical should triumph over the philosophical.

The People's Will: this group was composed mainly of young middle class men and women. Their aims were the murder of the Tsar, the violent destruction of the state and the redistribution of economic power on socialist lines. The People's Will later became the basis for the powerful Socialist Revolutionary Party.

Pisarev Dimitri: Pisarev exercised an early influence upon the development of nihilism. He realised that a successful revolution would require careful planning to persuade the conservative and backward peasantry. His radical political philosophy became popular with many young people who were soon deemed by the government to be godless, immoral, and dissolute. Despite its fashionable and appealing element, nihilism was committed and serious. Few of its critics noticed that through it, young people were searching for an acceptable alternative to the old order in Russia.

Plekhanov Georgy: see page 103.

Pobedonostsev Konstantin: Appointed Professor of Constitutional Law at Moscow University 1860-1865, Pobedonostsev tutored the two sons of Alexander II, including Alexander III, for whom he became a mentor and later, his chief advisor. Pobedonostsev was conservative, theocratic, deeply suspicious of the West and resistant to change. Appointed Chief Procurator of the Holy Synod in 1880, he was an ardent champion of the reactionary Russian Orthodox Church and referred to the notion of parliamentary democracy and a constitution as the 'greatest lie of our time'. He believed that autocracy was the only possible basis of government for Russia and that Alexander II's reforms were criminal acts.

Pogrom: the systematic, officially approved and planned destruction of a community through violent attack

Purgachev's Revolt (1773-5): a peasant revolt of the eighteenth century. Led by the Cossack Purgachev, it nearly resulted in the overthrow of Catherine the Great's rule, and was only suppressed by the army after much bloodshed and destruction. The causes of the revolt were linked to the conditions of the serfs, conditions which had not really changed up to the time of Alexander II.

Russification: the policy of Russian social and cultural imperialism introduced by Alexander III to cement his control over his empire.

Tkachev PN: a former student and journalist, he was among the first Russians to take an interest in Marx and extremist groups such as Hell encouraged him to agitate for political change and reform. Tkachev was also a follower of the French revolutionary, Louis Blanqui. Tkachev saw violent revolution as the only solution to Russia's problems, but despite his subversive activities among students, he was imprisoned in 1869 and soon after escaped to Germany.

Tolstoy Dimitri: as Alexander II's last Minister of Education and Procurator of the Holy Synod, Tolstoy supported the reactionary backlash of Alexander's growing fear of revolution. Later, as Alexander III's Minister of the Interior, he was enthusiastic to support the conservative policies of his master, and his master's mentor, Pobedonostsev.

Tolstoy Leo: see page 96.

Turgenev Ivan: see page 96.

Vyshnegradski IA: Minister of Finance from 1887 to 1892, he was an experienced financier who introduced the highest tariffs yet in Russia's commercial history. During his term as minister, the state came to play a more active role in the economy and encouraged foreign investment, imposed tariff protection to protect domestic producers and encouraged heavy industry in the Ukraine and the oil industry centred upon Baku on the Caspian Sea.

Zasulich Vera: the cause of the famous show trial of 1878 where an irremovable judge, eloquent lawyer and jury combined to find her not guilty even though she had shot the governor of St Petersburg, General Tropov. This had such a profound effect that the Tsarist administration never again tried a major political case in the courts and many emigrés in 1917 claimed that without this result there would have been no revolution. She later helped Plekhanov form Liberation of Labour.

Zemstvo: a local parliamentary body.

Nicholas II—The Last of the Tsars

Introduction

O N NICHOLAS II'S accession to the throne, the inadequacy of earlier reforms was apparent to many — but not to the Tsar. His reign can be seen as the attempts of a remote and conservative man, more interested in his family than his nation, to preserve the autocracy handed on to him by his father. Reluctantly, he allowed Witte to expand Russia's industry in the 1890s, but he did little to relieve social and economic distress in the countryside and the new cities. A disastrous attempt to promote Russia's image in the East saw a humiliating defeat at the hands of the Japanese in 1905.

Finally the social protest of Father Gapon turned into a bloody slaughter. Revolution, though disorganised, erupted all over Russia, and it was only through the loyalty of the army and the lure of economic and constitutional reform that order was eventually restored. Nonetheless, despite the introduction of quasi-parliamentary government and the efforts of Stolypin to eradicate opposition and reform the agrarian economy, the Tsar's commitment to autocratic power meant that he was reluctant to allow the drastic changes needed to save his reign and his dynasty from collapse.

Despite huge industrial growth, Russian industry was plagued with increasing levels of debt. Nicholas then allowed his nation to be lured into the morass of the First World War, an occurrence which applied so much strain to the political, economic, social and military structures of the country that the Romanovs were unable to hold back the tide of revolution any longer. Yet, in 1914 this disaster was predicted by few.

FOCAL ISSUES

- Why was there an attempted revolution in Russia in 1905? How did Nicholas II deal with the threat to his autocracy?
- To what extent had Russia industrialised successfully by 1914?
- By 1914, how successful had Tsar Nicholas II been in solving the problems faced by his country?

The autocracy of Nicholas
- What were some of the reasons for the 1905 Revolution?
- How did the Tsarist autocracy survive this threat to its position?
- To what extent was Nicholas II in control of his country in 1914?

Social and economic development
- What were the major problems facing Russia's agricultural economy from 1890-1905?
- How did Russia attempt to industrialise between 1890 and 1914?
- Why was Russia's economy weak, despite apparent growth, by 1914?

Fig. 4.3 on page 138 shows the areas to concentrate on when you address the issues.

Reading List

Books to supplement your reading on this area include:

D Christian, *Power and Privilege: Russia and the Soviet Union in the Nineteenth and Twentieth Centuries*, Pitman, 1987
R Cowie, Years of Change — *European History 1815-1890*, Edward Arnold, 1987
L Kochan & R Abraham, *The Making of Modern Russia*, Pelican, 1983
M McAndrew & D Thomas, *Century of Change*, Nelson, 1990
M. McAndrew & D. Thomas, *Russia/Soviet Union 1917–45*, Hodder, 1995
D Thomson, *Europe since Napoleon*, Pelican, 1987
J Westwood, *Endurance and Endeavour: Russian History, 1812-1992*, OUP, 1994

Fig. 4.1 Family Tree of the Romanovs 1796–1917.

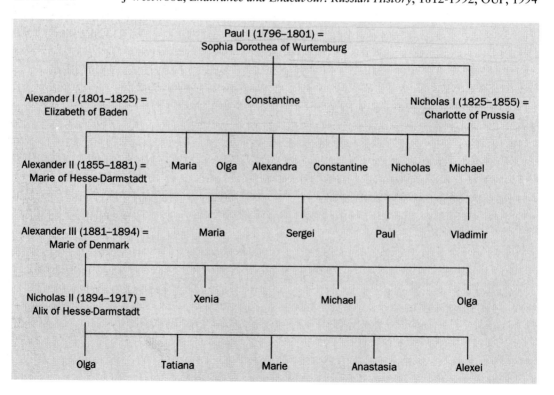

Guide To Note Making

For your notes on Russia between 1894 and 1914, you will need to consider
a chronological coverage and an assessment of issues of concern.
Use the following key points as a source for your headings:

- Causes, Course and Results of 1905 Revolution
- Radicals and Revolutionaries 1894-1905
- Radicals and Revolutionaries 1905-1914
- Constitutional Reform and The Dumas
- Foreign Policy
- Nationalism and Minorities
- Industrial and Financial Reform
- Agrarian Reform
- Russia on the eve of World War I

Do not confine yourself to linear notes — mind maps may prove more
useful for some areas in assessing of the problems and issues.

*Fig. 4.2 Tsar
Nicholas II
outside one of his
hunting lodges.*

Do not forget to include sources in these notes and do not forget the focus questions for this section of the course:

- **Why was there an attempted revolution in Russia in 1905? How did Nicholas II deal with the threat to his autocracy?**
- **To what extent had Russia industrialised successfully by 1914?**
- **By 1914, how successful had Tsar Nicholas II been in solving the problems faced by his country?**

4.3 Mind Map of Russia from 1894 to 1914.

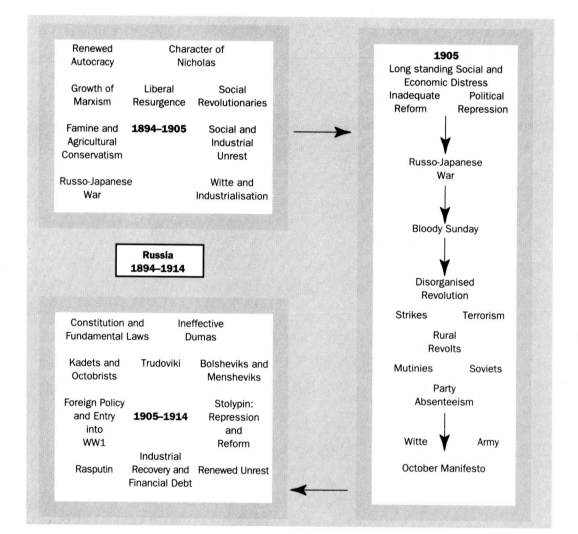

TIME LINE

1894	Death of Alexander III
	Accession of Nicholas II
1896	Industrial Strikes
1897	Witte introduces Factory Act
	Famine
1898	Formation of RSDWP
	Famine
1900	Russia acquires Liaotung Peninsula
1901	Formation of SRs
	Famine
	Formation of police-sponsored unions
1902	Industrial Strikes
1903	Formation of Liberation League
	Industrial Strikes
1904	Outbreak of Russo-Japanese War
1905	Bloody Sunday
	Revolution
	Potemkin Mutiny
	End of Russo Japanese War
	Witte appointed Prime Minister
	October Manifesto
	St Petersburg Soviet
	Main urban resistance crushed
	Agrarian reform
1906	Goremykin then Stolypin appointed Prime Minister
	Agrarian reform
	First Duma
1907	End of rural revolts
	Second and Third Dumas
	Agrarian reform
	Electoral changes
	End of Redemption Payments
	Triple Entente signed
1908	Education reforms
	Austria annexes Bosnia-Herzegovina
1910	Education Reforms
1911	Stolypin Assassinated
1912	Formation of Bolshevik Party
	Health and Insurance Law gives insurance to all workers
	Lena Goldfield Strike
	Kerensky becomes leader of Trudoviki
	Fourth Duma
1913	Russian agricultural and industrial capacity increasing
1914	Industrial Strikes
	Entry into World War I
	Goremykin appointed Prime Minister

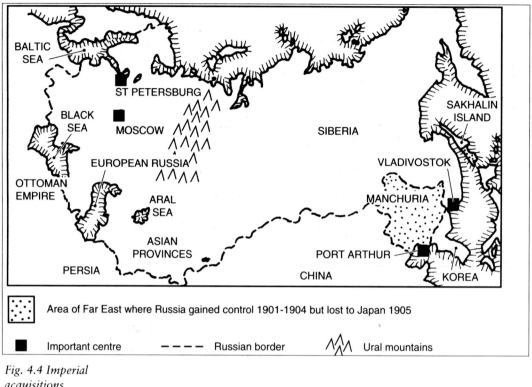

Area of Far East where Russia gained control 1901-1904 but lost to Japan 1905

■ Important centre   – – – – Russian border   ⋀⋀⋀ Ural mountains

Fig. 4.4 Imperial acquisitions under Nicholas II 1894-1914.

Political Repression to 1905

Beliefs and Character of Nicholas II

In October 1894 Nicholas II succeeded to the throne following the natural death of Alexander III. His coronation in 1896 was marred by the death of over 1000 people during celebrations at Khodynka Meadow near Moscow. The reaction the army officers to the over-excited and drunk celebrators was to open fire on them to restore order. Nicholas II continued to rule with the support of an alliance of bureaucracy, autocracy and religious orthodoxy. Like Alexander III, Nicholas II was a pupil of Pobedonostsev, but unlike his father, he was weak in character and intellect, and politically naive. He was ill-suited to the role of Tsar. He did not trust his ministers and preferred to rely on advisers of dubious ability and reputation. His dislike of government business prevented him from understanding the Russian Empire with its complexity of problems and his poor knowledge and understanding of affairs of state encouraged intrigue within the bureaucracy. The power struggles that ensued often paralysed effective decision making.

Fig. 4.5 Nicholas II leaving the Church of the Dormition after his coronation, 14 May 1894.

Influence of the Royal Family

FAMILY LIFE

Nicholas preferred the life of a squire on one of his country estates to the role of Tsar. He was very much a family man and a loving father to his children — his interest in photography has left the world with a fascinating glimpse of a happy, imperial, family life. But this all meant that he was far removed from his subjects, with little understanding of the outside world; he was ignorant to the point of arrogance and he helped to isolate the monarchy from the whole of Russian society.

TSARINA ALEXANDRA

In 1894, Nicholas married Princess Alix of Hesse-Darmstadt (granddaughter of Queen Victoria of Britain) who became Alexandra Feodorovna (1872-1918), Empress of Russia (1894-1917). Nicholas II was devoted to but dominated by his manipulative wife, a highly emotional and bigoted woman, whose increasing interference in government affairs was ultimately a disaster for Russia. In addition, the royal family's concern over Prince Alexei's condition of haemophilia meant that the royal attention was often diverted completely from matters of state.

Treatment of the Jews

PLEHVE AND POGROMS

The systematic use of pogroms begun by Alexander III continued unabated and indeed intensified after the 1905 Revolution. The earlier anti-semitism of Pobodenostsev was now matched by that of the Minister of the Interior, Vyacheslav Plehve (1846-1904). His officials produced a forged document, *The Protocols of the Elders of Zion*, which purported to be the plans for Jewish domination of the world alleged to have been drawn up by the Zionist Congress of 1897. In April 1903, Plehve's vicious methods incited a particularly brutal pogrom at Kishinev, Bessarabia (now known as Romania). It is also certain that Nicholas II joined the Black Hundreds, a society established in 1905 to unite the causes of Russian nationalists and anti-semites.

Fig. 4.6 The Royal Family. The royal princesses (a) Olga, Tatiana, Marie and Anastasia; (b) Nicholas and Alexandra, and (c) Alexei, with his sailor-protector Derevenko, is riding a cycle specially designed to lessen the risk of a fall.

*Fig. 4.7
Vyacheslav
Plehve.*

JEWISH REACTION

Thus both public policy and the private views of the government had a distinctly anti-semitic tone. Largely as a reaction to this official censure, during this period many Jewish intellectuals became attracted to socialist and revolutionary parties, while the Zionist movement, a political movement formed internationally in the 1890s with the express purpose of returning the Jewish people to a Jewish homeland in Palestine, was strengthened considerably. Many Jews chose what they saw as their only safe alternative and emigrated in their thousands to the United States and South America.

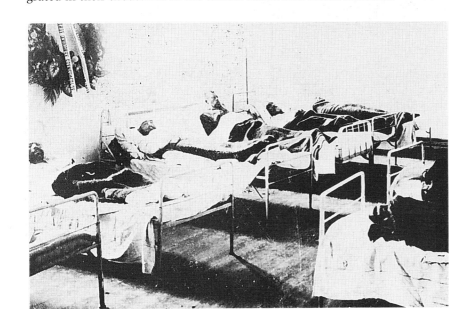

*Fig. 4.8
Pogrom
victims in
hospital.*

Vyacheslav Plehve: Nicholas's unpopular Minister of the Interior, Plehve used violence freely in his attempts to control the Russian peoples, especially with his program of pogroms, with which he sought to 'drown the revolutionaries with Jewish blood'. He was largely responsible for encouraging Nicholas to pursue an aggressive policy with Japan, and thought that this 'little war' would result in a patriotic swelling of support for the regime. How wrong he was can be measured by the reaction to his assassination by the SRs in 1904: very few mourned his violent demise.

Liberalism

HOPES FOR REFORMS

Since the 1870s, the zemstva, under guidance of the gentry, had been active in implementing piecemeal local reforms. The zemstvo remained one of the few institutions through which liberals could work together for wider change. Between 1895 and 1905 Russian liberalism broadened its base to include members of the new industrial professional classes (doctors, lawyers, journalists, students). Many had already been involved with the zemstva before 1894, but their hopes for a new style of government were dashed soon after the accession of Nicholas II. In a speech to an assembly of zemstva delegates in January 1895, Nicholas II described hopes of liberals for constitutional government as 'senseless dreams'. This speech provoked the opposition of many zemstva executives who met under the leadership of the conservative nobleman, D.N. Shipov. A 'bureau' was established to coordinate their activities and formulate suggestions for reform.

LIBERATION LEAGUE

A succession of Ministers of the Interior tried to obstruct these developments — finally under Plehve the last remnants of local self-government were eliminated. This did not deter a group of radical intellectuals, led by Peter Struve (1870-1944). In June 1902, they began to publish an illegal newspaper, *Liberation*, which played a vital part in shaping moderate opinion and in establishing a coherent political party, the Liberation League, in 1903. This party, which attracted the support of members of the gentry, senior ranking military and bourgeoisie, promoted policies of constituional monarchy and civil liberties. For those liberals for whom this organisation proved to be too radical, a delegation of zemstva members formed a less radical forum for liberal thought, and were even allowed by Plehve to meet, although only in private.

Marxism

By the early 1890s, the Marxist emphasis had shifted from the peasantry to industrial workers as the main revolutionary force. Julius Ossipovich Zederbaum aka Martov (1873-1923), advocated the tactic of working and living among industrial workers, with the aim of winning their trust and assisting in the struggle for higher wages and better conditions. This worked and from 1895-1897 widespread strike action gained many concessions from employers. However, many activists suffered arrest and exile to Siberia.

In 1898 at a secret congress in Minsk, the Russian Social Democratic Workers' Party (RSDWP) was founded to unite Marxists. However, a dangerous rift soon developed in the party with emergence of 'economism', a policy which urged the party to support the Liberals' campaign for a constitution through which socialism could be introduced and at the same time, work towards obtaining better conditions for the workers. In 1899, the party was infiltrated by the police and disbanded.

RUSSIAN SOCIAL DEMOCRATIC WORKERS' PARTY

The failure provoked a bitter dispute among Russian Marxists. Some believed that workers, organised in a mass movement, should conduct the political struggle. Others, such as Lenin and Martov, were opposed to democratic mass movement — they believed that an elitist vanguard of professional revolutionary intellectuals was needed to plan the struggle. They believed that party organisation and policy, rather than size, were the two crucial issues. Within five years, disagreements over the nature of the party led to the division of Marxists into two factions, the Bolsheviks and the Mensheviks.

Lenin (1870-1924) became a revolutionary in 1887 after the execution of his elder brother for his participation in revolutionary activities. He was expelled from the Kazan University for revolutionary activities in December 1887 but passed his law exams by studying at home and practised as a lawyer in St Petersburg. In 1895 he was gaoled for 15 months and then exiled for three years in Siberia.

VLADIMIR ILYICH ULYANOV (LENIN)

Fig. 4.9 Martov, an early leader of the Marxist movement.

Released in 1900, Lenin went to London, Munich and Geneva where he tried to rebuild the RSDWP. He helped to publish a newspaper called *Iskra (The Spark)* which was smuggled into Russia, and in 1902 he wrote an article 'What is to be Done?' which became the blueprint for the future Bolshevik party and Leninism from 1917 to 1924. In this article he stated that intellectuals were to play an important role in the leadership of the working class and that they would form an elite of dedicated professionals. He stressed that the party must understand completely the works of Marx and that the peasant masses would play a significant role in the coming revolution.

BOLSHEVIKS AND MENSHEVIKS

In 1903 at the second congress of the RSDWP held in London, the party broke apart in disagreement. The Jewish socialist union (**Bund**) walked out after they were denied the right to represent Jewish workers. Lenin's proposal to reduce the board of Iskra from six to three members created controversy. The vote split the party into the supporters of Martov (Mensheviks, or minority) and supporters of Lenin (Bolsheviks, or majority). The vote itself was controversial, with the Mensheviks claiming Lenin had rigged the numbers and did not have sufficient support to claim the title of Majority. Lenin characteristically rejected this with nonchalance. Nevertheless, the split brought into the open long-standing disputes about doctrine:

- **Mensheviks:** Led by Martov and Plekhanov, they wanted a less radical socialist party. They were regarded as 'legal Marxists' and wanted to await the evolution of capitalism and a proletariat prior to the incitement to revolution.

Fig. 4.10 A group of prominent young Marxists in St Petersburg in 1897. Lenin is in the front row, second from the right. Martov is next to him on his right. This photo was taken after the two returned from exile together in Siberia. They were to be the major figures in the RDSWP and the leaders of the subsequent Bolshevik and Menshevik factions.

Bund: The anti-Semitic policies of the Tsarist government encouraged Jewish revolutionary sentiment and the socialist movements by and large welcomed the participation of Jewish intellectuals such as Trotsky. So prominent were they that by 1898, they had formed their own Bund or League. However, more due to factional infighting rather than anti-semitic feeling, they were denied an effective group voice in socialist affairs.

- **Bolsheviks:** Under Lenin's leadership, the Bolsheviks called for a 'dictatorship of the proletariat', a state structure, controlled by the party, designed to be implemented through a proletariat revolution whereby Russian agriculture would support the industrial workers who supported the Bolshevik revolution. This would be brought about by an elitist party of professional revolutionaries.

Lenin's arguments prevailed, but his victory was short-lived. Despite attempts at reconciliation, the RSDWP had split irrevocably by 1905, although notionally, it remained intact until 1912, when Lenin formed his own party based on the Bolshevik ideology. Leib Bronstein, aka Lev or Leon Trotsky was one of the few activists to see the consequences of Lenin's theory of organisation and pointed out that under this system 'the Party is replaced by the organisation of the party, the organisation by the central committee and finally the central committee by the dictator'. The accuracy of this vision was borne out by future events.

SPLIT OF RSDWP

Fig. 4.11 Lenin. These photos were from Okhrana (secret police) files.

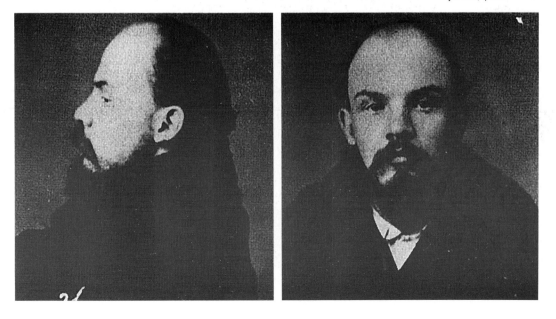

Fig. 4.12 Convict barracks at the Alexandrovsky Central Prison near Irkutsk in Siberia.

Leon Trotsky: Trotsky came to prominence as a leading Jewish Social-Democrat used by Lenin to help deny the Bund a voice at the RSDWP Congress of 1903. He was also an admirer of Martov, but, disgusted by the Machiavellian infighting of the Congress, managed to avoid committing himself to either faction of the RSDWP, until 1917 when Lenin recruited him to the cause of Bolshevism. Trotsky was admired widely within the socialist movement as a formidable intellectual and writer, and spent many years in Siberia after his trial for his part in the 1905 Revolution, returning only for the events of 1917.

Renewed Repression and Government Trade Unions

These internal divisions within the socialist left provided Plehve with a perfect chance to exploit the situation — government–sponsored legal trade unions were established in Moscow by the local secret police chief, Colonel Zubatov (1864-1917) with the aim of removing the popular support base from the apparently fractious socialists and attracting it towards 'police socialism'. These unions, as well as non-government unions like that of Father Gapon in St Petersburg, attracted thousands of recruits, most of whom remained unaware of the true identities of their leaders.

Some concessions were made by employers who favoured this type of moderate trade union. These attempts to control tensions among the working classes backfired when, to maintain credibility, limited strike action was endorsed and in July 1903 a similar fiasco accidentally sparked a general strike in the Ukraine.

Socialist Revolutionary Party

A number of former Populists, opposed to Lenin's narrow views, formed the Socialist Revolutionary Party in 1901. Led by Victor Chernov (1876-1952) and BV Savinkov (1879-1925), the Socialist Revolutionaries (SRs) soon became the largest party of the left. They attracted those who believed that peasants, not industrial workers, held the key to precipitating a successful revolution. The SRs had their disagreements about political strategies and lacked the tight discipline of the Social Democrats but were particularly feared by authorities for their terrorist activities.

POLICIES

The SRs remained remained a threat to the government until the Bolshevik revolution in 1917. Their victims included two Ministers of the Interior — on 28 July 1904 the assassination of Plehve brought popular support and

ASSASSINATION

Fig. 4.13 Russian cartoon of 1900 issued by the Union of Russian Socialists showing a view of the hierarchical nature of Russian society.

acclaim and in 1905 the hated Grand Duke Sergei (1864-1905), the Tsar's uncle and governor of Moscow, was struck down. It was eventually revealed that the leader of the terrorist section in the SRs was a police agent — a scandal which had damning consequences for both the authorities and the SRs.

Primary Extracts and Questions—Socialist and Reactionary Thought

FROM *THE COMMUNIST MANIFESTO* BY KARL MARX AND FREDERICK ENGELS — 1849

The modern bourgeois society that has sprouted from the ruins of feudal society, has not done away with class antagonisms. It has but established new classes, new conditions of oppression, new forms of struggle in place of the old ones . . .

Our epoch, the epoch of the bourgeoisie, possesses, however, this distinctive feature: it has simplified the class antagonisms. Society as a whole is more and more splitting up into two great hostile camps, into two great classes directly facing each other . . .

Modern industry has converted the little workshop of the patriarchal master into the great factory of the industrial capitalist. Masses of labourers crowded into the factory, are organised like soldiers. As privates of the industrial army, they are placed under the command of a positive hierarchy of officers and sergeants.

Fig. 4.14 Peter Stolypin's house after being damaged by a Socialist Revolutionary bomb in 1906. Stolypin, as Prime Minister from 1906-1911, was a key target for the SR death squads. An almost fanatical opponent of terrorism, he was eventually assassinated by a confused police agent in 1911.

Not only are they slaves of the bourgeois class, and of the bourgeois state; they are daily and hourly enslaved by the machine, by the overseer, and, above all, by the individual bourgeois manufacturer himself. The more openly this despotism proclaims gain to be its end and aim, the more petty, the more hateful and the more embittering it is . . .

The immediate aim of the Communists is the same as that of all the other proletarian parties: formation of the proletariat into a class, overthrow of the bourgeois supremacy, conquest of political power by the proletariat . . .

These measures [will be introduced]:

1. Abolition of property in land and application of all rents of land to public purposes.
2. A heavy progressive or graduated income tax.
3. Abolition of all rights of inheritance.
4. Confiscation of the property of all emigrants and rebels.
5. Centralisation of all credit in the hands of the State by means of a national bank with State capital and an exclusive monopoly.
6. Centralisation of the means of communication and transport in the hands of the State.
7. Extension of factories and means of production owned by the State . . .
8. Free education for all children in public schools. Abolition of children's factory labour in its present form . . .

When in the course of development, class distinctions have disappeared, and all pro-

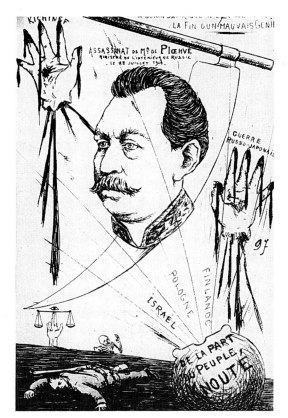

Fig. 4.15 French cartoon celebrating the assassination of Plehve.

duction has been concentrated in the whole nation, the public power will lose its political character. Political power is merely the organised power of one class for oppressing another.

(a) What do these extracts reveal of Marxist theories of the evolution of history?
(b) Where did Marxism claim that the revolution would come from?
(c) What did Marxism see as the aims and role of Communism in this process?
(d) What did Marxism see as the immediate solutions to social and economic justioce following the revolution?
(e) In what way did the fundamental nature of Russian society conflict with the Marxist view of the pre-conditions for revolution?

POBODONOSTSEV ON DEMOCRACY — 1898

We may well ask in what consists the superiority of Democracy. Everywhere the strongest man becomes master of the State; sometimes a fortunate and resolute general, sometimes a monarch or administrator with knowledge, dexterity, a clear plan of action, and a determined will. In a Democracy, the real rulers are the dexterous manipulators of votes, with their place-men, the mechanics who so skillfully operate the hidden springs which move the puppets in the arena of democratic elections. Men of this kind are ever ready with loud speeches lauding equality; in reality, they rule the people as any despot or military dictator might rule it. The extension of the right to participate in elections is regarded as progress and as the conquest of freedom by democratic theorists, who hold that the more numerous the participants in political rights, the greater is the probability that all will employ this right in the interests of the public welfare, and for the increase of the freedom of the people. Experience proves a very different thing. The history of mankind bears witness that the most necessary and fruitful reforms — the most durable measures — emanated from the supreme will of statesmen, or from a minority enlightened by lofty ideas and deed knowledge, and that, on the contrary, the extension of the representative principle is accompanied by an abasement of political ideas and the vulgarisation of opinions in the mass of the electors.

(f) What does the extract identify as the fundamental weaknesses of democracy?
(g) What does the extract identify as the strengths of autocracy?
(h) How does this extract support the notion that the government was unable to distinguish clearly between the different forms of opposition to the regime?

LENIN IN *ISKRA* — 1900

Not a single class in history has reached power without thrusting forward its political leaders, without advancing leading representatives capable of directing and organizing the movement. We must train people who will dedicate to the revolution, not a spare evening but the whole of their lives. . .

(i) What does Lenin say about the role of the party before and during the revolution in this extract?

FROM LENIN'S *WHAT IS TO BE DONE?* — 1902

Class political consciousness can be brought to the workers only from without, that is, only from outside the economic struggle, from outside the sphere of relations between workers and employers. The sphere from which alone it is possible to obtain this knowledge is the sphere of relationships of all classes and strata to the state and the government, the sphere of the interrelations between all classes . . . We must 'go among all classes of the population' as theoreticians, as propagandists, as agitators, and as organisers . . . The work of the West-European Social-Democrat is in this respect facilitated by the public meetings and rallies which all are free to attend, and by the fact that in parliament he addresses the representatives of all classes. We have neither a parliament nor freedom of assembly; nevertheless, we are able to arrange meetings of workers who desire to listen to a Social-Democrat. We must also find ways and means of calling meetings of representatives of all social classes that desire to listen to a democrat; for he is no Social-Democrat who forgets in practice that the Communists support every revolutionary movement, that we are obliged for that reason to expound and emphasise general democratic tasks before the whole people, without for a moment concealing our socialist convictions . . .

(j) What does this extract add to your knowledge of Lenin's beliefs in the role of the party before the revolution?
(k) What reasons does this extract give for support of all revolutionary causes?
(l) From your own knowledge, how consistent were Lenin's actions with this statement?

The 1905 Revolution

The Russo-Japanese War, 1904 and 1905

This war began on Plehve's misguided advice — Nicholas II agreed to fight a 'small, victorious war that would stop the revolutionary tide'. This was contrary to the warnings of Witte, who pressed for imperialistic expansion through economic measures and warned General Kuropatkin (1848-1925), Minister of War (1898-1904) against political adventures involving Japan. Long-standing tensions between Japan and Russia over claims to Manchuria and Korea were the pretext for war and on 8 February 1904 the Japanese attacked Port Arthur. After an eleven-month siege, Port Arthur fell in January 1905. Then in May 1905, with the sinking of the Baltic squadron in the Straits of Tsushima by Admiral Tojo (1847-1934) in less than six hours, the Russian military and naval powers were comprehensively beaten.

CAUSES AND COURSE

The effects of this loss were dramatic — it had been inconceivable that with the size of their forces the Russians could lose. Similarly, the racially charged views of the regime found it unthinkable that an Asian power could defeat the Imperial Russian Army and Navy. Realistically, size counted for little in the face of superior Japanese technology, tactics, supply and logistics. This was a huge blow to the image of the impregnability of the Russian Government in the eyes of its own people and the world at large, and resentment at privations forced on the people in the name of the war effort grew rapidly. The humiliating defeats unleashed the revolution of 1905 — unrest among every social class had reached the limit of endurance. Typically though, few of the wealthy citizens realised the imminence of revolution.

RESULTS

Causes of Revolution

The most important causes of the 1905 Revolution included:
- the military and naval defeats suffered at the hands of the Japanese
- agrarian discontent due to famines in 1897, 1898 & 1901

- problems with land distribution under the emancipation reforms of the 1860s and the resulting mortgage debt level for rural peasants
- unrest among the new industrial working class as a result of poor living and working conditions in the cities
- dissatisfaction among many of the landed gentry due to their loss of land to the peasants and their own rising debt levels
- agitation of radical political parties and frustrated attempts to introduce trade unions
- the growth of an ambitious but politically impotent middle class
- the development of a national consciousness among the Russian Empire's ethnic minorities.

Above all, the inflexible Tsarist government, out of touch with its people, had lost support throughout Russia. Half-hearted reforms during the century before the Revolution had had few significant or long term benefits, since they were designed in all cases more to preserve the autocracy than to introduce a more equitable political, social and economic system. The reforms of Alexander I in the 1810s, Nicholas I and Alexander II were really no more than stop-gap solutions. Although they received some support initially, eventually they were either reversed or revealed to be inadequate at relieving distress, generally creating more distress, often in new ways (especially the effects of industrialisation), rather than genuinely helping the people to improve their lives.

Fig. 4.16 Russia's reversal of fortune in the Russo-Japanese War 1904-5. Initial Russian confidence (as shown by a contemporary Russian cartoon) and an engraving showing the Japanese victory at Tsushima Strait.

The ultimate example of these failed reforms can be seen in the Emancipation Edict and its aftermath. Aimed at reducing peasant misery and land hunger, it actually had the reverse effect: the average size of landholding decreased from 21 acres in 1860 to 10 acres in 1905, while the average tax debt of peasants increased by 250 per cent between the 1870s and the 1900s. By failing to institute a workable economic solution, the Edict by and large made matters worse in the countryside, despite the legal freedom of the peasants. This latter notion was largely anathema to the Tsars and their advisors, who through a combination of callous disregard for the welfare of the overwhelming majority, a fear of change and an almost manic determination to maintain their power, had succeeded in reducing Russia to a seething mass

Fig. 4.17 Members of the Russian nobility dressed for a ball in seventeenth century court costume (top) and workers' quarters in St Petersburg at the turn of the century (bottom). Although there were many causes of the 1905 Revolution, the social and economic conditions of the peasantry and industrial workers cannot be underestimated, especially when compared with the conspicuous wealth of the aristocracy.

of discontent at all levels, barely controlled through the denial of political rights and the systematic implementaton of brute force. The 1905 Revolution can be seen therefore as the by-product of a morally bankrupt regime, and despite its ultimate failure, in the context of subsequent history, it was revealed to be the first great step in the collapse of Tsarist Russia.

Father Gapon and 'Bloody Sunday'

SOCIAL PROTEST

In January 1905, a strike broke out in the Putilov Munitions Works in St Petersburg and spread to other factories in Russia. In the context of this, on Sunday 22 January, Father Georgei Gapon, the organiser of a police-sponsored union, led over 150,000 peaceful, unarmed marchers through the snow to the Winter Palace in the same city. These men, women and children took with them petitions asking for reforms, aimed at achieving a better system for the distribution of food and

*Fig. 4.18 **Burlaki** (bargemen) on the River Volga. These men pulled loads of timber upstream by day; by night they slept in sacks on their barges. This photo is testament to the oppressive living and working conditions of millions of Russian peasants and the poor communications systems.*

employment opportunities. In what was really a social protest, many marchers carried religious icons and pictures of Nicholas II. By and large, the intention of the organisers and the sentiment of the marchers were not political.

At the approaches to the palace, police and militia ordered the procession to halt. Not surprisingly for a march of this size, this could not be carried out quickly. But the officers at the gates to the palace (at which the Tsar himself was not present) panicked and gave the order to shoot. A bloody massacre ensued — estimates for the number of dead range between 100 and 1000, with many thousands injured. The massacre convinced many of the people that the Tsar, the so-called 'Little Father', was a murderer — 'Bloody Nicholas' could do nothing to prevent the outbreak of a revolution which started as a

GOVERNMENT BRUTALITY

Fig. 4.19 The Rise and Fall of Father Gapon. These illustrations show the rapid change in fortune of Father Gapon. On the left he is shown at the head of the Bloody Sunday march. Although the revolution ultimately failed, Gapon became a cause celebre in Russia and Europe for a brief while. His support was sought by all the leading political and radical groups and he was feted throughout Europe as the symbol of freedom in Russia. However, his loyalties were always questionable. Almost certainly an agent of the Okhrana, he was abandoned by them when he began to preach the message of bloody revolution. They betrayed his activities to the SRs, whose revenge was merciless—on the right he is shown dead, lynched on a clothesline in 1906.

social protest, but soon, fuelled by the outrage of lower classes developed into wide-ranging economic and political action. It should be noted that few of these actions were co-ordinated, and that their instigators and participants came from every section of the Russian population.

> **Father Georgei Gapon:** Less of a priest and more of a hard-drinking, gambling popular leader who seemed to have a genuine desire to help the people. He founded a police-authorised union in St Petersburg, with an agenda of social reform but political conservatism, discouraging Jewish and socialist membership. The organiser of the protest which led to Bloody Sunday, his name became a byword for the revolutionary sentiment of 1905, and due to his massive popular appeal, his support was claimed (usually spuriously) by most of the different revolutionary factions. He escaped Russia during 1905, toured Europe as a celebrity, wrote *The Story of My Life*, joined the Social Revolutionaries, but in 1906 was hanged by them for maintaining his police contacts. His legacy was the lesson he taught to the Bolsheviks about the need for popular leadership.

The Events of the Revolution

The initial chronology of events included:

JANUARY 1905

An immediate strike in St Petersburg following Bloody Sunday and protests throughout the Empire — peasants in Kursk openly rebelled against landlords seizing their land.

FEBRUARY 1905

The assassination of Grand Duke Sergei by Socialist Revolutionaries.

JUNE 1905:

Mutiny on board the battleship, *Potemkin* — defeats in Far East had revealed inadequacies of the Russian navy — brutal treatment, poor food and conditions of ordinary seamen — and resentment ran high among the crews of other ships — little could be done to regain control over the *Potemkin* — it cruised close to the fleet and bombarded Odessa, eventually finding safe haven in a Rumanian port.

JUNE–JULY 1905

Although the government appeared to have lost complete control it still refused to make concessions — trade unions and political organisations were established and professionals came together in coordinating a body of 'Union of Unions' — the bourgeois Union of Liberation and zemstva group amalgamated to found the Constitutional Democratic Party (Kadets) which demanded an elected assembly or parliament.

AUGUST 1905

Nicholas II promised a consultative assembly (Duma), elected on the basis of high property qualifications — this was rejected by most liberals and the rest of the population.

Striking printing workers and railwaymen started a general strike which brought the whole country to a standstill — thus a crucial part in the Revolution had been played by a minority of the industrial proletariat — the so-called St Petersburg Council (Soviet) of Workers' Deputies was formed at the spontaneous initiative of workers and it attempted to co-ordinate strikes and activities of various factories. Soon similar soviets or workers' councils were established in other cities to the extent where, briefly, soviets operated as a form of local government and by October, the St Petersburg Soviet exercised more power than the city government.

SEPTEMBER-OCTOBER 1905

The Marxists and revolutionaries were barely visible during the events of 1905. Most remained in exile or were more interested in trouble in rural areas far away from towns and cities. Few fully understood or exploited the potential presented by the collapse of government authority. By the time Marxists such as Lenin arrived at the cities, it was too late — either the Revolution had been crushed or other movements were in control.

ROLE OF MARXISTS

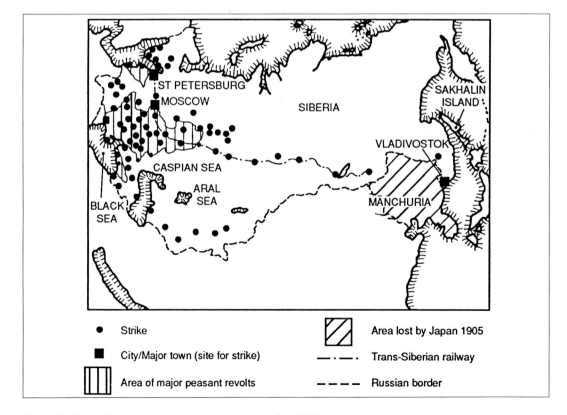

Fig. 4.20 *Map showing mutinies and peasant revolts 1905.*

The October Manifesto

Nicholas II abandoned earlier plans for a military dictatorship and appointed Witte as Prime Minister. Reluctantly consenting to Witte's advice to introduce a constitution as the only means of restoring order, in October, Nicholas issued an Imperial Manifesto which promised:

- fundamental civil liberties
- the franchise to all classes
- that all future laws would require the approval of the State Duma.

Financial Relief for the Peasantry

The government's attempts to lighten the economic burden of the peasants in 1902, had been largely unsuccessful and dilatory. However in late 1905, in response to the support of the peasants for the Revolution, through the *Peasants' Manifesto*, the Tsar authorised laws which gave the peasants genuine land reform, and seemed both to eliminate the debts owed by the rural workers as a result of the mir system and to sweep away the barriers to full individual peasant ownership of land created by the 1861 Emancipation Edict. These laws largely returned the support of the peasants to the Tsar, at least temporarily. The main effects of the laws were to:

- abolish the collective responsibility of the mir for the tax payments of all of its members, thus making each peasant landholder responsible for their own land and removing the financial control of the mir over the individual's means of living
- cancel all pre-existing tax debts
- outlaw corporal punishment
- cancel from 1 January 1907 all redemption payments.

Fig. 4.21 Strikers outside the Putilov iron and steel works January 1905.

Fig. 4.22 Russian workers reading of the announcement of the October Manifesto 1905.

The End of the Revolution

Witte's task was to pacify the Russian people. Having gained the Tsar's support for constitutional and financal reform, he then needed to ensure the loyalty of the army. Mutinies within sections of army were brutally suppressed by Cossack troops loyal to Nicholas II. Following this, the army was used to hunt down and hang hundreds and thousands of rebels and other suspects.

Nicholas II appealed to loyal Russians and counter revolutionary groups like the Black Hundred who waged horrible pogroms on the Jews. In December 1905, a general strike in Moscow was crushed with the death of over 1000 people. It took nearly a full year, but eventually, the Tsarist government managed to suppress all revolutionary activity through the use of the army.

Reasons for the Failure of the Revolution

Most soldiers had remained loyal to the Tsar. Foreign governments, terrified of the impact that a popular revolution in Russia might have on their own populations, advanced loans to support the crisis-ridden Russian economy. The revolution was not planned and lacked effective leadership — most of the leaders of the revolutionary parties were in exile at the start of the Revolution and could not return in time to take charge of the passionate but disparate activities. The Liberals failed to support the Revolution once Nicholas II announced reform in the October Manifesto and failed to object to the December strikebreaking, thus splitting the brief coalition between the Liberals and the St Petersburg Soviet.

ARMY OF LIBERALS

Without the support of the Liberals, and given the support of many of the lower classes for the financial reforms introduced by the government, the

REPRESSION OF SOVIETS

soviets lost too much support. On 3 December, the St Petersburg Soviet was closed by government troops, marking the decline of all the soviets. Finally, acts of terrorism by the lower class movements unnerved the middle classes who were afraid of a complete breakdown of law and order.

Fig. 4.23 Home life for the peasant. This photograph shows a peasant family in their one-room khata. The woman on the left is sleeping on top of the stove.

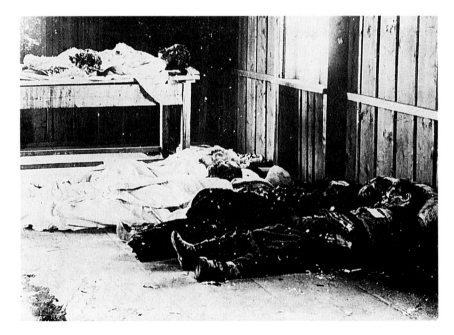

Fig. 4.24 Mortally wounded victims of a pogrom.

Fig. 4.25 Troops firing on protesters in 1905. Ultimately it was army loyalty which saved the regime.

Experiments with Constitutionalism

1905-1914

Establishment of the Dumas

LIBERALS

Between 12 and 18 October 1905, the left wing liberals formed the Constitutional Democratic Party (Kadets) under PN Milyukov (1859–1943). The party denounced the October Manifesto and favoured elected constitutionalism but supported the reforms as a starting point. On 4 December 1905, moderate liberals formed the Octobrist Party under Guchkov — its supporters were mainly nobles, landowners, officials and capitalists. Until 1911, the Octobrists were a source of support for Nicholas II.

Fig. 4.26 Nicholas II opening the First Duma. The members of the State Council are on the left and the members of the Duma are on the right.

Octobrist Party: This party of the political middle ground was formed to provide a liberal voice less radical than the Kadets. Officially its approval of the October Manifesto gave it support among the conservative middle classes and by the time of the Third and Fourth Dumas it was the majority party. However, this was largely a result of the gerrymander, and the Octobrists were quickly identified as an impotent group, whose calls for gentle reform were immediately ignored by the Tsar and later by the people, who wanted action.

As revolutionary violence began to recede, Nicholas II regained the initiative in political matters. To prepare for the opening of the Duma in May 1906, he issued the Fundamental Laws, which provided the basis for what was apparently a form of constitutional government, with an elected Duma with legislative powers. However, beginning with a preamble specifically affirming the Tsar's belief in autocracy, it contradicted the October Manifesto in several important ways. It stated that Tsar's ministers could not be appointed by and were not responsible to the Duma, thus denying representative and responsible government at the executive level. The conduct of foreign affairs remained the exclusive responsibility of the Tsar, ensuring that, at an international level, the image of Russia was still that of a Royal autocracy. Finally, under Article 87 of the Fundamental Laws, the Tsar could legislate by decree during emergencies and the Duma could not pass laws without the agreement of Tsar and Imperial Council.

FUNDAMENTAL LAWS

Nicholas II wrote 'I have a constitution in my head, but as to my heart, I spit on it'. As soon as he could (July 1906), he dismissed Witte, the architect of constitutional reform and the man most directly responsible for saving the Russian government in 1905, but whom Nicholas had never liked. This showed that his personal feelings for his ministers remained more important to him than their ability. Witte's successor was I.L. Goremykin who was replaced by Peter Stolypin in 1906.

PRIME MINISTERS

Fig. 4.27 Voting for the First Duma.

*Fig. 4.28
Members of the
First Duma
representing
ethnic groups.*

I.L. Goremykin (1839–1917): Prime Minister in 1906 and then again from 1914-1916, Goremykin was a weak politician who was prepared to pander to the wishes of the Tsar. He was unpopular with the political groups and according to Witte, his only distinction was his whiskers!

Trudoviki: Supporters of the Social Revolutionaries, this party became the political wing of the SRs, who never officially sanctioned participation in the Dumas, believing them to be the by-product of a bourgeois constitution, but were nonetheless quite willing to have a voice for their policies. The most popular group in the Second Duma, they were hampered by Stolypin's gerrymander for the Third and Fourth Dumas, but were forcibly led by Karensky.

History of the Dumas

FIRST DUMA

Between 1906 and 1916 the quasi-parliamentary Dumas met four times. They were constantly undermined, denied an effective role in government through the Tsar's cynical use of Article 87 and his refusal to sign legislation if he did not approve of it on ideological grounds. Outspoken deputies were arrested. The Duma became little more than an impotent debating society. Elections for the First Duma, which opened in July 1906, returned a significant bloc of moderate socialists and both liberal parties who demanded further reforms — it was dissolved within ten weeks.

The Second Duma in February 1907 lasted three months and resulted in the election of many Trudoviki (supporters of the Social Revolutionaries), Social Democrats, Octobrists and Kadets who became thenceforth the leading political parties in Dumas — its last law passed was engineered by Stolypin and gave greater electoral value to the vote of the rich, thus undermining the democratic nature of the franchise.

SECOND DUMA

Between 1907 and 1912, the Octobrist-dominated Third Duma ran its course but was hampered by the assassination of Stolypin and increased reactionary policies of the Tsar and his Imperial Council. By the time of the Fourth Duma of 1912-17, little scope remained for legislative actions by its members, especially once Russia became involved in the First World War and it became really only a means for limited criticism of the Tsar's regime. It was also a period notable for the splintering of the different political parties which had sprung up out of the 1905 Revolution; clearly both in the eyes of the people and the party members themselves, most of these parties were unable to deliver the reforms they demanded of the Tsar and promised their supporters.

THIRD AND FOURTH DUMAS 1907–1917

Primary Extracts and Questions — Middle Class and Peasant Reactions to the Events of 1905-1906

Executions by firing squads and other forms of capital punishment, now being applied by military courts-martial and so-called 'penal expeditions', do not represent the punishment of the guilty, but crimes on the part of government organs.

FROM A RESOLUTION OF ST PETERSBURG LAWYERS — FEBRUARY 1906

(a) What does this extract reveal about the way in which the civil liberties promised in the October Manifesto were being ignored by the government in 1905-1906?

The Tersk Branch of the Russian Engineering Society examined the question of the industrial development in our country and came to the conclusion that this requires, above all, a market for the sale of production. This market depends on the purchasing power of the population; however the purchasing power of the population is at an exceedingly low level. The people are exhausted and enervated by taxation and the government's misguided policies. The peasantry does not have enough land, earns no profit for its work, and has been reduced to penury.

FROM A STATEMENT OF THE MIDDLE CLASS TERSK ENGINEERS' UNION TO THE DUMA — MAY 1906

The first fundamental measure needed for the development of industry is an improvement in the economic well-being of the people.

In this respect, the first task is to grant supplementary land to the land-hungry peasants and to improve the position of the working class.

(b) How does this extract show that the concerns of the middle class for the welfare of the peasants were motivated by their own economic needs?

Taking into account:
- that a fundamental reform of the state system (for which the entire country has fought for an entire year) cannot be achieved by the State Duma that has been assembled;
- that the State Duma, given its composition and competence, cannot be called a truly popular representative organ; and
- that the attainment of political freedom and realization of labor and agrarian reform can be the business only of a constituent assembly, which embodies all

FROM A RESOLUTION OF THE MIDDLE CLASS NATIONAL ENGINEERS' UNION — APRIL 1906

the fullness of constituent, legislative, judicial and executive power —
the union insists upon the basic demands of its political platform:
1. convocation of a constituent assembly on the basis of a universal, equal, direct and secret electoral law; and as a precondition for the preceding
2. immediate political and religious amnesty
3. elimination of martial law and emergency security measures
4. establishment of freedom of assembly, union, strikes, and real freedom of press and speech.

(c) In your own words, identify the problems Russia faced in 1906 according to the extract.
(d) In your own words, identify the solutions proposed in the extract.
(e) To what extent does the extract address the problem of the social and economic conditions of the people?
(f) To what extent can the extract be seen as a representation of middle class, liberal values?

FROM A RESOLUTION BY PEASANTS IN ROMASHINKO (SAMARA PROVINCE) — JUNE 1906

We came to the following conclusions [about] our material condition:
1. We should have land and freedom: as a person cannot live without air and water, so too it is impossible for us to live without land.
2. In addition, all monastery, church, crown and private land should be confiscated to form a reserve land fund for the entire toiling class.
3. Grant a complete amnesty to all political [prisoners].
4. Abolish capital punishment and establish a legal court.
5. Furthermore, abolish all indirect taxes and replace these with an income tax.
6. All our village authorities should receive a salary, not from the peasant community, but from the state treasury.
7. Abolish township courts and replace them with peace arbitrators.
8. Universal public education and complete access to all educational institutions for our children to study at state expense.
9. We demand the implementation of all freedoms proclaimed in the Manifesto of 17 October 1905.
10. We find ourselves in a hopeless situation! It is impossible for us to move without trespassing on other people's land! By exploiting our lack of rights and our helplessness, the squires oppress us by squeezing out impossible prices, and out of caprice they [sometimes] do not lease the land for any amount of money. We are doomed to starve to death!

(g) Compare this extract with the previous two extracts. What similarities and differences can you observe?
(h) To what extent does this extract focus on social and economic conditions?
(i) To what extent can this extract be seen as representative of the values of the rural peasantry?

Experiments with Constitutionalism (contd.)

Peter Stolypin

Stolypin was an energetic man who understood better than many of his contemporaries the problems facing Russia. Nonetheless, despite his concessions to reform, he remained a staunch supporter of Tsarist autocracy. At first he ruled by decree to consolidate law and order and strengthen repression — before May 1907, convicted by court martial and ordered the hanging of 1700 people. The hangman's noose ('Stolypin neckties') created great fear and resulted in a sharp drop in the number of terrorist assassinations.

Stolypin's reforms

To a large extent Stolypin's reforms were genuine and helped to improve the life of the peasants. He gave peasants the right to pay for their land to be separated from the mir and oversaw the administration of the dismantling of the

Fig. 4.29 Peter Stolypin.

redemption payment scheme. His own schemes were designed to create a prosperous class of conservative, independent farmers (**kulaks**) able to buy their land from the mir outright. He promoted voluntary migration to Siberia to alleviate land hunger and between 1907 and 1909 over two million people moved eastward. He sold huge tracts of Crown and state land to the Peasant Land Bank for sale to its clients. Other reforms included changes in health insurance and education and measures to stimulate the economy — improvement in terms of trade after 1906 assisted economic recovery and resulted in an annual growth rate of 6 per cent.

Weaknesses of Reforms

However, the reforms did not go far enough — despite some apparent structural developments, the real economic and social structure mostly remained unchanged. One third of the peasants remained landless, while 30,000 landlords were in possession of 76 million hectares of agricultural land. Only 10 per cent of all peasant households were in a position to take up the offer to separate land from the mirs.

Farming methods and equipment were still primitive and farmworkers lacked even basic items such as metal ploughs; one third of farms were without stock. Annual taxes of 400 to 500 million gold roubles were still paid annually to landlords by bankrupt peasants. The pace of industrial progress was slow, although the government and some nobles began to gross larger and larger profits, which were considerably weakened by growing debt.

Assassination

From the outset Stolypin was a marked man. He was hated by the left who foresaw that successful agricultural reforms would lose them support among peasants and he was equally detested by the right and by the royal family who believed that his reforms went too far along the path of modernisation. In September 1911, Stolypin was shot dead at a Kiev theatrical performance, the victim of a confused socialist revolutionary who also happened to be a police agent. Some reports suggest that Nicholas II cared little about Stolypin's death.

Grigori Rasputin (1871-1916) and the Royal Family

PERSONALITY

The famous or infamous 'Mad Monk' monk was apparently a strange mixture of cruelty and kindness. He exercised a rapacious appetite for sexual adventure and had formidable powers of persuasion. Eyewitnesses mentioned his unkempt appearance and strong body odour and his drinking bouts frequently ended in orgies and rapes of noble women. Despite his reputation, Rasputin was sought after as an unusual and intriguing companion.

As Rasputin was coming to prominence in St Petersburg circles, Nicholas II was withdrawing more and more from court and public life. Nicholas did not use the October Manifesto to rally support for the monarchy and seemed unaware of the seriousness of his position. After 1905, he came to rely on a succession of unsavoury characters and adventurers for advice almost as if he were trying to block the unwelcome solutions to his political problems being sug-

INITIAL CONTACT WITH THE ROMANOVS

Fig. 4.30 Rasputin, the 'mad monk' described by a contemporary ballerina as having the eyes of a maniac in a peasant face.

gested by people such as Witte and demanded by the revolutionaries. The birth of a son, Alexei, a haemophiliac, added another dimension to Nicholas's problems and increased Tsarina Alexandra's emotional instability. (Haemophilia is a hereditary disease causing impaired blood coagulation, so that even a minor scratch can lead to excessive bleeding.) The Romanovs began a desperate search for remedies for the boy — Rasputin with his reputation for mystical healing soon came to their attention. During numerous crises he was called upon to use his 'powers' to heal the dying boy and seemed to be able to effect temporary cures, as well as encouraging the family's growing reliance on him on a wide range of other matters.

POLITICAL INFLUENCE AND DEATH

After about 1911, Rasputin appears to have developed a political influence over the royal family, especially the Tsarina, Alexandra. Revolutionary groups gleefully distributed suggestive literature and spread rumours that Rasputin and Alexandra, originally a German princess and widely disliked, were sexually involved. The relationship with Rasputin further undermined the reputation of the monarchy, especially after Nicholas proclaimed Alexandra his regent when he assumed direct command of the armies of Russia in 1916. In the same year, the last year of his life, Rasputin was appointed Chief Procurator of the Holy Synod and seemed to be the real force behind the selection of ministers and the formation of domestic and sometimes even military policy. In December 1916 he was assassinated by Prince F.F. Yusupov and V.M. Puriskevitch.

That he ever gained a position of such influence is probably testament not only to Nicholas's increasing detachment from political reality, but also to his dereliction of his responsibility as an autocrat to preserve the state of Russia. Certainly what little confidence the Russian people had in the Tsar was eroded by the rise to power of a figure as controversial as Rasputin.

Foreign Policy

Central Asia

After the conquests and railway building campaigns of his father and grandfather, Nicholas II added no new territory to the Russian Empire and Central Asia. However, colonial rivalry with Britain in this area remained strong and Russia exploited British fears that it still harboured intentions on the British controlled areas in Persia, Afghanistan and India. Eventually in 1907 this tension was eased as a result of the Entente treaty — strictly delineated regions of influence separated by a buffer zone drawn up in 1905 were ratified.

Far East

EARLY POLICY

During this period, Russia's preoccupation with the Far East intensified. As a result of the 1860 Treaty of Peking, which established Manchurian

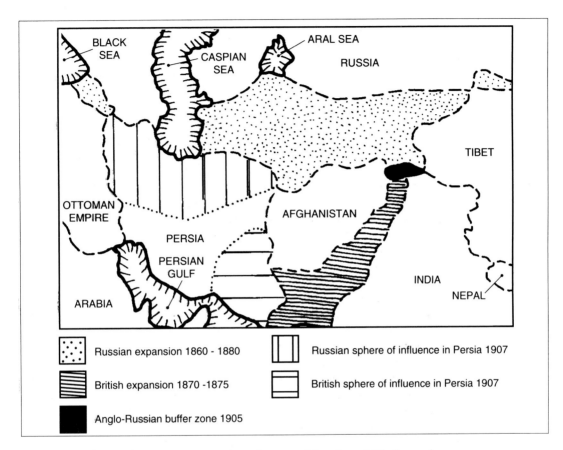

Fig. 4.31 Russian and British activity in Central Asia 1860-1907.

borders which jutted into Russian territory between Irkutsk and Vladivostok, the 1867 sale of Alaska to the United States (approximately two cents an acre) and the 1875 handover of the Kurile Archipelago to Japan in return for Japanese agreement of Russian sovereignty over the island of Sakhalin, Russia's position was stronger than previously. However, Russia was not happy with this state of affairs for several reasons:

- Russia wished to eliminate the Manchurian salient
- Russia had no ice-free port in the Far East — expansion to the Liaotung or Korean Peninsulas was required for this
- Japanese occupation of the Pescadores Islands, Formosa and the Liaotung Peninsula after its victory in the Sino-Japanese War of 1895 seemed to threaten Russian interests in the area.

Over the next ten years Russia took the following actions in order to further its position in the area:

INTRIGUES WITH CHINA AND KOREA

- With German support (in the hope that Russia would not expand further in the Balkans) Russia convinced Japan to leave the Liaotung Peninsula to China.
- Russia loaned China 400 million francs and established the Russo-Chinese Bank in 1895. The next year, as a result of a treaty in which

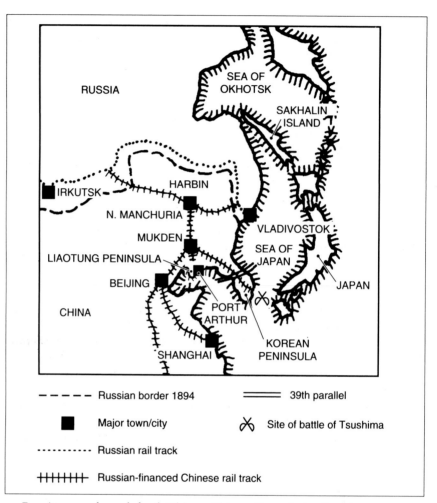

Fig. 4.32 Map
showing Russia
and Japan in the
Far East 1894-
1905.

Russia agreed to defend China, China allowed the Russians to com-
mence the building of the Chinese Eastern Railway across Manchuria. This
work was undertaken by Russian navvies under the protection of
Russian soldiers.

- In 1898, Russia demanded compensation for Germany's annexation of
  Kiao-Chow. Probably through bribes, Russia gained a 25 year lease of the
  Liaotung Peninsula, a railway extension from Harbin in Manchuria to
  Darin on the peninsula and, most importantly, the ice-free Port Arthur.
- Over the next three years, ignoring Japanese requests for recognition of its
  sovereignty in Korea in return for Russian sovereignty in Manchuria,
  Russia negotiated the recognition of Korean neutrality through the
  Nissi-Rosen Convention of 1898 and, in 1902, guarantees of English
  and German neutrality in the Far East.

- In 1900, using the pretext of security risks as a result of the Boxer Rebellion, Russia occupied all the major cities of Northern Manchuria and increased its troop numbers there.
- Nicholas II, began to investigate and exploit resources in Manchuria and even Northern Korea.

WAR 1904–5

The Japanese quickly became angered by Russia's refusal to agree to its interests in Korea and Russia's unsubtle domination of Manchuria and forays into Korea. Russia persistently ignored Japan's requests over Korea while flaunting its interests in Manchuria. Eventually this proved too much, and on 8 February 1904 Japan attacked Port Arthur. Russia's response was to escalate this into full-scale warfare. In the years after the Russo-Japanese War, the two parties signed official treaties recognising their mutual fishing rights and unofficial protocols recognising Japanese interests in Korea and Southern Manchuria and Russian interests in Mongolia and Northern Manchuria.

European Alliances

GERMANY

As a result of the clash of interests between Austria and Russia (and therefore Germany and Russia) in the Balkans, Russia found itself without European allies in 1890. Russia was keen to extend its influence over Bulgaria and Serbia, although the latter was a client state of Austria, to the rest of the Balkans. This can be attributed to both territorial ambition and a reaffirmation of Pan-Slavic principles. In addition, Russia saw the Ottoman Empire as a threat to its Southern provinces. Turkey's control of the straits of Constantinople meant that it could deny access through them to the Black Sea fleet — this threat was realised during the Russo-Japanese War. Thirdly, Germany was denying its banks approval to finance Russian loans.

Fig. 4.33 Contemporary Russian cartoon commenting on Russia's interests in the Far East. Russia is shown here as a benevolent protector of the Japanese and Chinese aggesion in Korea.

FRANCE AND THE DUAL ENTENTE

At around the same time, through diplomatic links in Paris, Russia began to cultivate a friendship with the French. In 1889 and again in 1890, French banks provided 4 per cent loans to Russia. Britain, through its Mediterranean agreements with Austria and Italy, seemed to favour the triple alliance. It seemed only natural that Russia and France should turn to each other for support. After three years of negotiations an Entente was ratified in January 1894, guaranteeing mutual support in event of Alliance attack. State visits and continued French loans cemented the relationship during the 1890s.

BRITAIN AND THE TRIPLE ENTENTE

The status of Britain still vexed the governments of Europe. Russia was keen to guarantee German support against Britain — the Central Asian question was as yet unresolved. Nicholas went as far as signing the Treaty of Björko secretly with Kaiser Wilhelm in July 1905, guaranteeing full support in the event of war. However, this clearly clashed with Russia's alliance with France and neither the Russian, German or French politicians approved of it when they found out about it three months later. France in particular remained extremely disaffected with Germany over Morocco. The treaty was never ratified. Austria's increasingly heavy hand in the Balkans and Britain's growing naval competition with Germany, caused the two sides to gravitate towards each other. With the signing of the convention of 1907, establishing the spheres of influence in Central Asia, the way was open to convert the Franco-Russian Entente and the Anglo-French Entente of 1904 into a Triple Entente whose interests directly opposed the Triple Alliance.

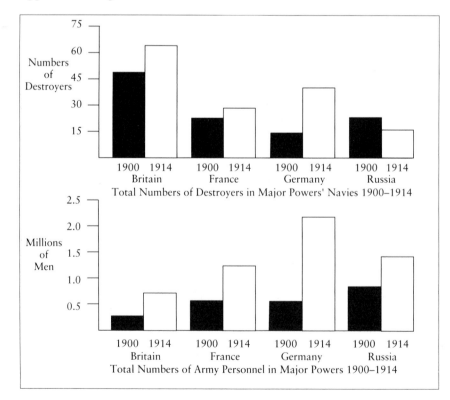

Fig. 4.34 Chart showing European great powers destroyer and army increases 1900-1914.

A. Navy Spending

	Russia	France	Germany	Britain
1890	4.4	8.8	4.6	13.8
1900	8.4	14.6	7.4	29.2
1910	9.4	14.8	20.6	40.4
1914	23.6	18.0	22.4	47.7

B. Military Spending

	Russia	France	Germany	Britain
1890	24.6	28.4	24.2	17.6
1900	32.1	27.8	33.6	21.4
1910	53.4	37.6	40.8	27.6
1914	64.8	39.4	88.4	29.4

Fig. 4.35
European great
power expenditure
on defence
1890–1914 in
millions of pounds
sterling.

The Balkans and World War I

BALKAN CRISES TO 1913

Due to Russia's preoccupation in the Far East and Austria's domestic problems, the Balkans were quiet in the 1890s. However, through diplomatic and religious links, Russia gained a military agreement with Serbia by 1902, and remained influential in Bulgaria. By the time of the Bosnian crisis of 1908 though, Austria had gained the upper hand and was able to annex Bosnia unchallenged by a Russia which feared German reprisal. Between 1908 and 1912, Russia encouraged the development of a Bulgarian and Serbian bloc to counter Austria. But when in 1912-13 Serbia and Bulgaria used this to attack Turkey and then to attack the Austrian-sponsored state of Albania, Austria and Germany demanded a Serb back down. The consequent Treaty of London in 1913 saw a compromise whereby Serbia's Adriatic ambitions were frustrated and Russia, which had kept 400,000 troops on alert during this time was thus indirectly rebuffed.

RUSSIA AND WAR

Austria's subsequent political, judicial and military demands on Serbia as a result of the assassination crisis of June–July 1914 left Russia, and more particularly Tsar Nicholas, thoroughly cornered. Nicholas, as yet unable to fulfil the Romanov tradition of adding to the Empire, and seemingly defeated diplomatically on all previous attempts to secure Russia's century-old ambitions in the Balkans, felt that he had little choice. He backed Serbia completely on 24 July in the full knowledge that Austria was acting with the reassurance of Germany's blank cheque. On 25 July he decided to mobilise if Serbia was attacked and on 30 July a full mobilisation ensued. He had intended to mobilise against Austria-Hungary and Germany initially, but although he changed his mind and wanted mobilisation against Austria alone, his plans were so inflexible that he could not implement this change. On 31 July, Germany demanded Russia's backdown but this was no longer possible within the twelve-hour time frame set by Germany and on 1 August 1914, Russia found itself at war in Europe.

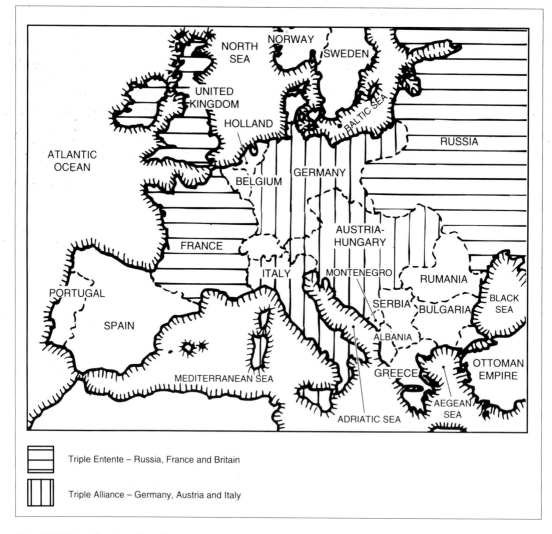

Triple Entente – Russia, France and Britain

Triple Alliance – Germany, Austria and Italy

Fig. 4.36 Map showing the alliance system in Europe 1914.

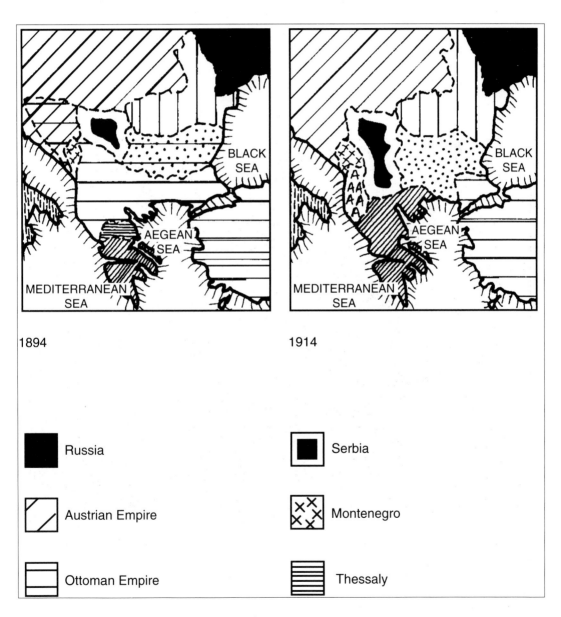

Fig. 4.37 Maps showing the Balkans 1894 and 1914.

Fig. 4.38 *The young lions: graduates of the Corps du Pages in the uniforms of the Imperial Guard. Although they loooked splendid, their technical education was poor and their understanding of tactics even weaker.*

Fig. 4.39 The autocrat at the declaration of war. Nicholas is standing alone on the balcony of the Winter Palace, while a huge crowd cheers the announcement that Russia was at war. Although whipped up by nationalistic fervour at first, the peasants and industrial workers soon became disillusioned by the war, which stretched Russian social, political and economic systems to breaking point and beyond by 1917.

Social and Economic Development

Process of Development

The industrial boom of the 1890s was closely linked to Sergei Witte (1849-1915), who was Minister of Finance from 1892-1903. Witte understood that without an aggressive strategy for industrial growth, Russia would remain a nation of agricultural peasants and that having no industrial infrastructure made it a relatively inferior military power. When the world depression of the 1890s temporarily halted activity, Witte decided to intervene more directly in economic affairs. Under the Witte System, industrialisation of Russia became a primary objective. He borrowed the ideas of the German economist, Friedrich List, raising tariffs to raise revenue and to protect infant domestic industries. During the 1890s, tariffs accounted for one third of the value of all exports.

WITTE SYSTEM

Witte also encouraged the investment of foreign capital but this was only possible if the rouble was convertible to gold. In turn, convertibility was only possible if Russia achieved a positive balance of payments. This favourable balance of payments was achieved by the export of agricultural products, especially grain, even when world grain prices fluctuated frequently and dramatically. Having attained a positive balance of payments, the

CURRENCY

Fig. 4.40 Sergei Witte.

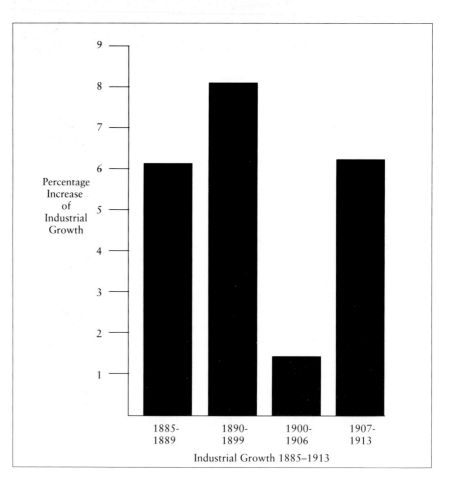

Fig. 4.41 Rate of industrial growth in Russia 1885-1913.

Fig. 4.42 Grain storage at the port of Odessa. By 1900, Odessa was Russia's main grain exporting port, yet at the same time, many Russians were starving.

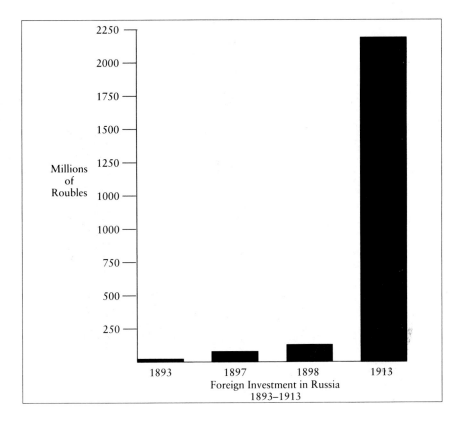

Foreign Investment in Russia 1893–1913

Fig. 4.43 Foreign investment in Russia 1893-1913.

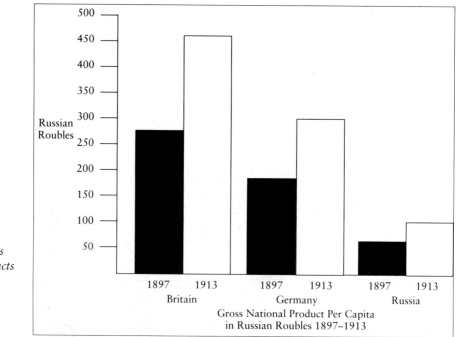

Russian
Roubles

1897 1913 1897 1913 1897 1913
Britain Germany Russia

Gross National Product Per Capita
in Russian Roubles 1897–1913

Fig. 4.44 Gross national products of Britain, Germany and Russia, 1897-1913.

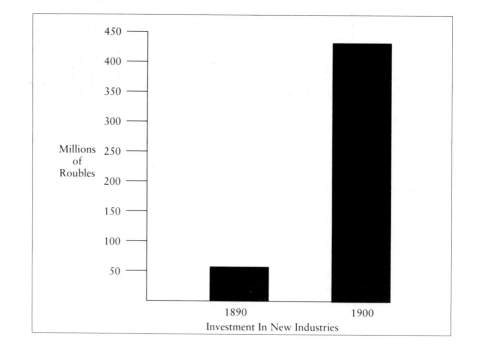

Millions
of
Roubles

1890 1900
Investment In New Industries

Fig. 4.45 Increases in investment in new Russian industry 1890-1900

Russian currency was able to be placed on the gold standard in 1897 and
achieved greater stability.

As a result, between 1890 and 1915 capital (mainly French, Belgian,
and British) invested in Russian industry rose from 26 per cent to 41 per cent
of total capital invested. This permitted doubling of budgets for investment in economic projects such as railway construction. Witte proposed to
use foreign currency earnings and gold reserves to conduct trade and
attract and repay foreign loans — whilst Finance Minister he was able to do
this quite successfully.

INVESTMENT

*Fig. 4.46 An
engineering
works. Notice the
lack of powered
machinery and
also of protective
shields on the
equipment.*

Later Finance

Between 1900 and 1912, there was a significant increase in bank deposits from
1,165 million roubles to 3,952 million roubles — the value of deposits in
savings banks rose from 860 million roubles in 1903 to 1,594 million
roubles in 1912. In 1910 there were 31 joint stock banks in Russia — by 1914
there were 47 joint stock banks with 743 branches throughout the Empire.

FINANCIAL BOOM

However, despite this pattern of increased savings and Witte's initial
success at balancing the budget and attracting foreign investment and
loans, the rate of growth was perhaps too high for Russia's primitive technology and communications systems. With inefficient practices and an
increasing reliance on foreign loans to compensate for this inefficiency, as well
as the exhaustive drain on the Imperial Treasury caused by the successive disasters of the famines of the early 1900s, the Russo-Japanese War, the

STRUCTURAL WEAKNESS

1905 Revolution and the First World War, the structure of the Russian economy could not cope with the enormous strains placed upon it.

DEBT

With spiralling debt and an incapacity to meet it, the Tsarist government found itself unable to pay its way — most importantly, it could not afford to pay or support its soldiers on the Eastern Front adequately, and their increasing frustration severely affected their tenuous loyalty in the lead-up to the 1917 Revolutions.

Industry and Modernisation

INDUSTRY

The Industrial Revolution in Russia followed the common pattern of exploitation in other European countries — low wages and appalling conditions for workers in the new cities. By 1900 three million workers were employed in industry and transport. After 1900, industrial strikes and lockouts increased bankruptcies and decreased production in heavy industry. Despite the disruption of the 1905 Revolution, economic recovery commenced in 1906. Improvement in the terms of trade for agricultural products increased peasant prosperity, as did the Stolypin land reforms.

INEFFICIENCY AND FOREIGN COMPETITION

However, inefficient agricultural methods and outdated equipment proved to be a significant burden for the Russian economy and hampered industrial growth. In 1913, the last year of European peace, Russia lagged far behind the Western powers in terms of production: Russia's coal production was 10 per cent of Britain's and oil production was 30 per cent of the USA's. Russia produced only half as much steel as Britain and 25 per cent as much cotton textile. However, unlike her agricultural processes, Russia's highly concentrated and mechanised industry was one of the most technologically

Fig. 4.47 Industrial production in Russia in millions of puds 1860-1913. (Note: 1 pud = 16.38 kg)

	1860	1876	1900	1909	1913
Coal	7.3	111.3	1003	1591	2214
Pig Iron	18.2	25.2	177	175	283
Steel	0.1	1.1	163	163	246
Petroleum	0.6	10.9	632	563	561

Fig. 4.48 World industrial production in millions of tons 1914.

	Russia	France	Germany	Britain	Russian World Ranking
Coal	36	40	190	292	5
Pig Iron	4.6	5.2	16.8	10.4	5
Steel	4.8	4.6	18.3	7.8	4

advanced in the world and encouraged bigger foreign investment.

But, despite technological competence compared to most nations, the scale of Russian industry was insufficient to compete on the world market with the great powers, Britian, France, Germany and the United States.

Primary Extracts and Questions — Industrialisation

The owners of a cotton-spinning mill in Egorev (Riazan Province), the Khludov brothers (both with the rank of honoured citizen), while accepting a total ban on child labour at night in their factories in the summer, hold that minors (from age 11) should be allowed to work up to thirteen hours at night in the winter (dividing the work with one hour for lunch and one hour for breakfast). In the Khludovs' opinion, this would not be onerous for the children, since they perform the lightest work in a cotton-spinning factory. As for the ban on night labour by children in the winter, the Khludovs find this rule exceedingly restrictive, since the elimination of child labour will cause adult workers to lose their jobs. 'Thus the children, having been deprived of wages from the factories, will not bring their parents any material assistance, will resort to idleness (which is harmful for their age), and shatter their health, for they will not be in the light, healthy surroundings of the factory, but in the stuffy atmosphere of their hut.'

A BOURGEOISIE OPINION ON CHILD LABOUR — 1861

(a) What does this extract reveal of conditions of child labour in Russian factories in the mid-nineteenth century?
(b) What does this extract reveal of middle-class attitudes to child labour?

Sanitary conditions at the workers' settlement of Yuzovka are highly conducive to the contraction and spread of disease. The market place and streets are full of filth. The air is rotten with the stench from factory smoke, coal and lime dust, and the filth in gutters and organic wastes on streets and squares. The interiors of most workers' living quarters are just as unhygienic . . . Petty clerks and some skilled workers live in shacks. These are long buildings divided into several large and small sections. Inside they are extremely dirty and crowded with tenants. The majority of workers live in so-called cabins built in the outskirts of the settlement . . . These cabins are simply low, ugly mud huts. The roofs are made of earth and rubbish. Some of them are so close to the ground that at first sight they are nearly unnoticeable. The walls are covered with wood planks or overlaid with stones which easily let in the dampness. The floors are made of earth. These huts are entered by going deep down into the ground along earthen stairs. The interiors are dark and close, and the air is damp, still, and foul-smelling. The cabins are untidy, and far more unsightly than the shacks. The furnishings are completely unhygienic, although frequently the workers live here with their families and infant children . . .

In the majority of [Moscow] factories there are no special quarters for the workers. This applies to workers in paper, wool and silk finishing . . . Skilled hand craftsmen . . . sleep on or under their looms, for lack of anything else . . .

The mines I visited are themselves structurally defective. There are frequent cave-ins, which make the inadequate ventilation even worse. The air becomes so thick in the underground passages that the lamps go out — or as the miners say, 'the sun stops shining' . . . The lateral tunnels, or 'stoves', branch off from the main tunnels. The width of the stoves varies from three and a half to four and a half feet. Thus the miners must always be stooped over . . . The miners must lie on their

FROM A REPORT ON THE CONDITIONS OF INDUSTRIAL WORKERS IN PROVINCIAL TOWNS AND THE LARGE CITIES IN THE 1880s

sides, and prop themselves on their elbows to face the coal-rock wall . . .

Work in a [steel] mill never stops, day or night. There are two twelve-hour shifts a day, which begin at 6.00 am and 6.00 pm. The men have a half-hour for breakfast (8.30-9.00) and one hour for dinner (1.00-2.00) . . .

In the cloth factory No. 48, which was typical of such establishments, 'the air in the dye-house was so saturated with steam I suspected that it was impossible to see anything. I groped my way about the dyeing room as if blindfolded — evidently there was no ventilation at all. The machines were very crowded together, and belts criss-crossed in all directions. Moving around the machines is extremely hazardous, and accidents could easily happen to even the soberest and most careful workers' . . .

The very worst, most unhealthy conditions I saw were in the tobacco factories . . . The shops where tobacco is chopped and dried are so filled with caustic dust and nicotine fumes that each time I entered one of these rooms I had spasms in my throat and my eyes watered . . . though I am a smoker myself. Yet even women sometimes work in this atmosphere . . . Children work in these factories as wrappers, baggers (making the little paper tobacco bags), and packers. There were even children under twelve working there . . .

According to my observations of 181 industrial establishments, only 71 pay their workers regularly . . . This leaves over one hundred factories . . . in which wages are not fixed, and depend completely on the will and the financial position of the owner or manager.

(c) What does this extract reveal of industrial conditions for the working classes in the nineteenth century? Structure your answer in a chart under the following column headings:

Type of Workplace   **Working and Living Conditions**

(d) What would have been the likely effects of these types of conditions on proletariat support for the government?

(e) From your own knowledge, how did conditions such as these help the spread of Marxism?

(f) From your own knowledge, what measures were taken by the government to change these conditions? When were these measures introduced? How effective were they?

FROM SERGEI WITTE'S SECRET MEMORANDUM ON INDUSTRIAL DEVELOPMENT — 1899

The economic relations of Russia with western Europe are fully comparable to the relations of colonial countries with their metropolises. The latter consider their colonies as advantageous markets in which they can sell the products of their labour and of their industry and from which they can draw with a powerful hand the raw materials necessary for them . . . Russia was, and to a considerable extent still is, such a hospitable colony for all industrially developed states, generously providing them with the cheap products of her soil and buying dearly the products of their labour. But there is a radical difference between Russia and a colony; Russia is an independent and strong power. She has the right and the strength not to want to be the eternal handmaiden of states which are more developed economically.

(g) From the extract, what was Witte's primary motivation for industrial development?

(h) What are the likely reasons why Witte made no mention of the conditions of the workers in his plan?

(i) In what way was this typical of government attitudes to the conditions of the workers?

Social and Economic Development
(contd.)

Railway Building

In the 1890s railway industry accounted for over one third of all output. Yet despite enormous growth to 1900 (53,000 km of track), the railway system was still inadequate to meet the demands of Russia's widespread population and the need for rail to carry goods to markets. The economic impact of railway construction was profound: transport costs were reduced; bulk haulage of grain to markets and ports became feasible; and the iron and coal industries of Ukraine were stimulated — by 1900 there was an annual output of pig iron of 3.43 million tonnes, and of coal 18 million tonnes.

EUROPEAN RUSSIA

In 1891 the government started the Trans-Siberian railway, to link Moscow with the the Pacific coast; it was largely completed in 1904. By 1914 the government owned and operated two-thirds of Russian railways. The effect of this railway link was very significant. The urbanisation begun during the 1890s not only increased the urban economy of Russia, but also spread the poor social and economic conditions of the proletariat. The government used the rail link to encourage many of the starving peasants of European Russia, afflicted by the many famines of the 1890s, to move east. But there they found little more than they had left. It is hardly surprising that most of the strike action which occurred in 1905 outside European Russia happened along the Trans-Siberian track.

TRANS-SIBERIAN RAILWAY

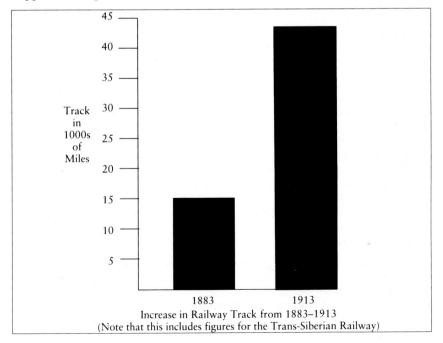

Track in 1000s of Miles

Increase in Railway Track from 1883–1913
(Note that this includes figures for the Trans-Siberian Railway)

Fig. 4.49 Chart showing increases in Russian rail track 1883-1913.

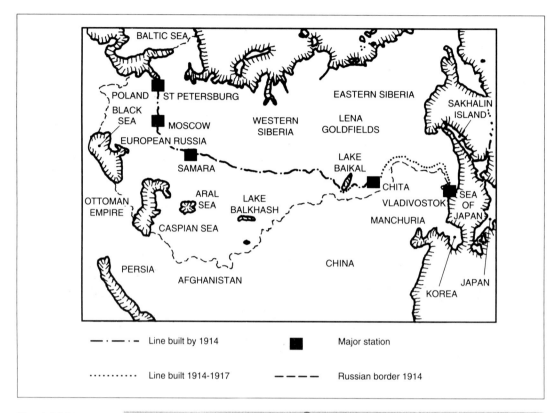

— · — · — Line built by 1914	■	Major station
·········· Line built 1914-1917	— — — —	Russian border 1914

Fig. 4.50 Map showing the development of the Trans-Siberian railway.

Fig. 4.51 The completion of a bridge on the Trans-Siberian railway.

Results of Industrialisation

Few of the personal comforts that eventually accompanied progress in the West came to the bulk of the Russian population — consumer goods were continually in short supply, real wages rose slowly for industrial workers, and working and living conditions were possibly worse than before. The spread of liberal ideas and growth of an independent bourgeoisie were hampered by the state. Little could be done to improve the general conditions of the new urban proletariat or rural peasantry. There were few moderate ideas in politics — opinion increasingly polarised into those who advocated violent revolution to overthrow the old order and those who

Fig. 4.52 Map showing the major centres of European Russian industry before World War I.

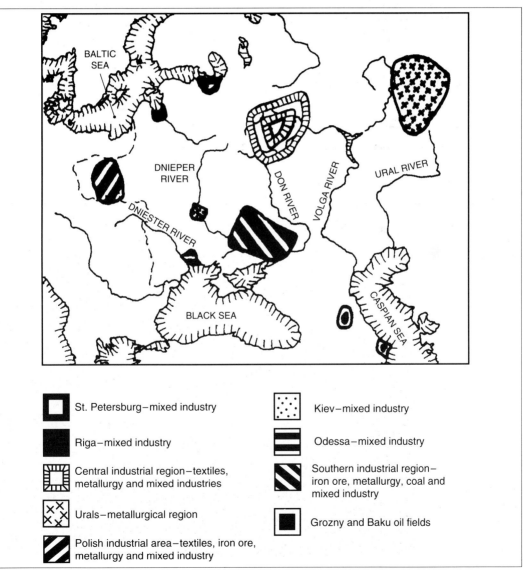

St. Petersburg—mixed industry

Riga—mixed industry

Central industrial region—textiles, metallurgy and mixed industries

Urals—metallurgical region

Polish industrial area—textiles, iron ore, metallurgy and mixed industry

Kiev—mixed industry

Odessa—mixed industry

Southern industrial region— iron ore, metallurgy, coal and mixed industry

Grozny and Baku oil fields

Fig. 4.53 A female peasant working at harvest time, c 1900. Notice that she is working without the aid of machinery.

believed that change could be introduced peacefully by supporting the autocracy.

Foreign Debt

One of the consequences of foreign investment in Russian industry was increasing debt. Between 1894 and 1903, annual payments to foreign creditors rose from 300 to 400 million roubles each year. By 1904, the total state debt amounted to 6.5 thousand million gold roubles. With over half of this owed to creditors in France, Britain and Belgium, there was little prospect of overcoming this debt. The state was increasingly prepared to accept larger budget deficits to compensate for the absence of a ready supply of private capital. Witte's right wing critics feared that excessive dependence upon foreign bankers endangered Russia's sovereign status, while left wing critics believed further agrarian reforms would encourage prosperous peasantry and increase their revenue-yielding capacity.

Taxation and the Peasantry

PEASANT TAXATION AND CONDITIONS

Successive economic policies left the peasantry financially poorer — during Witte's term of office, state revenue was doubled to help pay for industrial development. By 1903, a quarter of total government receipts came from its monopoly on spirits — a situation which did nothing to encourage the government to take steps to address Russia'a culture of alcoholism. The high tax on sugar beet production also undermined the peasants' standard of living.

By 1900, the misery of the agricultural peasants was growing — most lived in leaking huts, were clothed in rags and malnourished. Many working adult Russians owed huge sums of money in tax arrears and lacked adequate credit facilities to buy additional lands. Sales of grain were forced in order to pay for taxes and created a buyer's market which usually depressed grain prices. All members of a mir were held collectively responsible for the mir's payment of tax until 1905. Mass whippings were inflicted to force peasants to hand over taxes.

Rural unrest was widespread and openly encouraged by revolutionary groups. The abolition of tax debts and redemption payments in 1905

RURAL UNREST

Fig. 4.54
An itinerant
musician.

assisted the Tsar in removing a substantial, immediate burden from the peasants and thus temporarily diverted much of their support away from the revolutionary movements. What support there had been was very disorganised and it would not be until after the 1917 Revolutions that the left wing could bring the peasantry firmly under their wing.

Shortage of Land and the Nobility

LAND HUNGER

The shortage of cultivable land close to commercial outlets worsened the plight of peasants. Between 1860 and 1900 there was a decrease in the average size of peasant allotments, mainly due to a sharp rise in the pop-

Fig. 4.55 A village scene. A father and son standing in the main street of their village. Notice the duck-boards laid down for the spring and autumnal mud. Paved roads in the provinces were hardly a consideration for the government in St Petersburg, although much of their revenue was gained from taxation of the villages.

ulation (1858 to 1914: from 74 million to 155 million). Together with the lack of livestock to work and fertilise the land, this threatened rural life and its benefits. The 1891 famine in particular was devastating, prompting the government into adopting relief measures, although as 1905 shows, these measures were like most Russian reforms in the nineteenth century — too little, too late.

Although Stolypin's land reforms did not create a large kulak class by 1914, it is significant that by this time, four times as much land was in the hands of the peasantry as was in the hands of the lower gentry and the old land-owning nobility. Most of the wealthy families of the nineteenth century had been sent broke by their own extravagance and their failure to modernise their methods of production.

By 1914, the land-owning nobility was a spent force. They were no longer able to give the Tsar the support that their predecessors had given. The bureaucratic nobility (the Chinovniks) had almost entirely replaced the gentry as a source of economic, social and political influence in Russia.

Population Shift and Rural Poverty

Many peasants unable to meet redemption payments in the western provinces, emigrated to the virgin lands of Asiatic Russia. By 1904, nearly one million settlers had crossed the Urals. Government schemes encouraged more than two million more peasants between 1907 and 1909 to migrate to West Siberia, an area which soon became important for grain and dairy products. Some of the emigrés became seasonal labourers on large estates of nobility in Ukraine — however, many more moved to find work in industrial towns and factories.

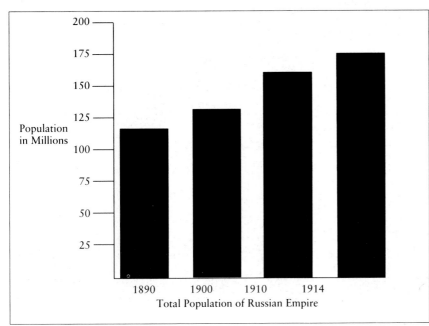

Fig. 4.56 Chart showing total population statistics for Russia 1890-1914.

Urban Proletariat and the Growth of a Middle Class

WORKING CONDITIONS

Country people seeking work in the cities found themselves in an unfamiliar world — the conditions made them even more unhappy than before. Working conditions were unrestricted until 1897 when the working day for men was limited to 11.5 hours 6 days a week. However, few restrictions were placed on the employment of women and children who made up over half of the urban workforce. From 1904, each factory with more than 100 employees was supposed to have medical services, though this was often restricted to crude ambulance facilities and a nurse. Government factory inspections, established in 1899, were ineffectual.

PROLETARIAT DISSENT

The constant influx of rural unemployed meant that wages remained low. More than half of Russia's industrial workers worked in large factories employing more than 500 persons. Thus the industrial proletariat evolved a high degree of organisation and strike power. Urban discontent simmered as living and working conditions continued to deteriorate.

BOURGEOISIE GROWTH

However, the level of industry was sufficient to maintain the growth of a new urban middle class in the major centres. Numbering around 7 per cent of the population by 1914, they fulfilled the function of a professional class — doctors, engineers, lawyers and small business proprietors. Due to the government monopoly over most heavy industry, most of these businesses were limited to shops and small factories. But their growth only served to emphasise liberal demands for economic freedom and to sharpen the visible differences between rich and poor.

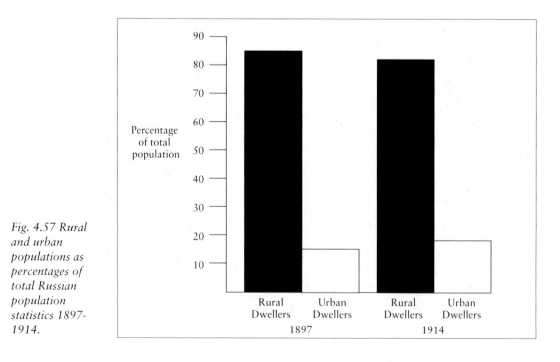

Fig. 4.57 Rural and urban populations as percentages of total Russian population statistics 1897-1914.

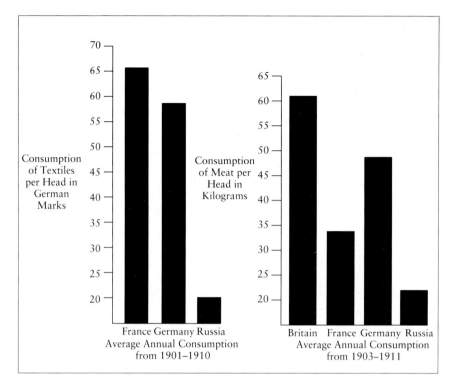

Consumption of Textiles per Head in German Marks

France Germany Russia
Average Annual Consumption
from 1901–1910

Consumption of Meat per Head in Kilograms

Britain France Germany Russia
Average Annual Consumption
from 1903–1911

Fig. 4.58 Russian per capita consumption of meat 1903-1911 and textiles 1901-1910 compared to Western powers.

Fig. 4.59 Burzhui (bourgeoisie) from Moscow 1910.

Political Impact of Industrialisation

INCREASED DISSENT

Despite the impetus of economic change, Russia was still a backward nation on the eve of World War I. This conflict was to expose the system to its utmost — industrial backwardness was soon to be translated into military weakness and to the collapse of the Tsarist state.

From 1900 on, revolution was always likely. A few of the more independent and enterprising industrial workers founded artels, workers' co-operatives, but these were very much the minority of work places. Certainly from 1912-1914, the increase in the number of strikes among the urban workers disaffected by their conditions, led many of the Bolsheviks to believe that revolution was imminent. The socialist groups had declined in popularity between 1907 and 1912, due to the promise of reform from the Tsar and Stolypin. However, by 1911, it was clear that the reforms, both constitutional and agrarian, had not achieved the wide-ranging effects demanded by the poor conditions of the workers.

LENA 1912

Perhaps the most important single event in ending worker support for the Tsarist state was the Lena goldfield strike/massacre of 1912 (described in the document study on page 200). The callous treatment of the strikers convinced many that the old regime was never going to help their plight and the socialists gained many members and supporters. It was only the brief period of nationalistic euphoria brought on by the start of the First World War I that brought the people back to the Tsar.

WORLD WAR I

However, the conditions of the soldiers and the home front, the failure of the armies, the apparent incompetence of the administration, and the appalling winter of 1916-1917 meant that by March 1917, Nicholas could no longer preserve his position of power. The Romanov dynasty was swept away by a wave of revolutionary dissent that had been brewing for hundreds of years — ultimately, the failure of the Tsars to provide substantial social, economic and political justice for their subjects proved to be their undoing.

Primary Extracts and Questions — Working Class Dissent on the Eve of World War One

LENIN ON THE FAILURE OF STOLYPIN'S LAND REFORMS — 1911

This is the failure of Tsarism on this last road — the last conceivable road for Tsarism.

(a) What did Lenin mean by 'the last conceivable road for Tsarism'?
(b) From your own knowledge, suggest reasons why the failure of the reforms meant the failure of Tsarism.

GRAHAM, ENGLISH WRITER, COMMENTS ON MIASS AND THE RED TIDE — 1913

Miass is in the electoral division of Troitsk, and during the whole of the summer of 1912 the Russian General Election was proceeding. No one would have thought it from the political atmosphere of Miass. There were no posters, voting cards, public meetings, or private canvasses. Indeed I am assured not two people in the whole population exercised their right of suffrage. No one would take the two hundred mile journey to choose between a score of strangers for a rep-

Fig. 4.60 St Petersburg 1914. The Ball of the Coloured Wigs and a soup kitchen for the unemployed on Vasilevsky Island. The contrasts between the lifestyles of the urban rich and the urban poor were dramatic — and obvious to both the people and the revolutionaries. Yet few of the wealthy were able to understand the implications of these striking distinctions.

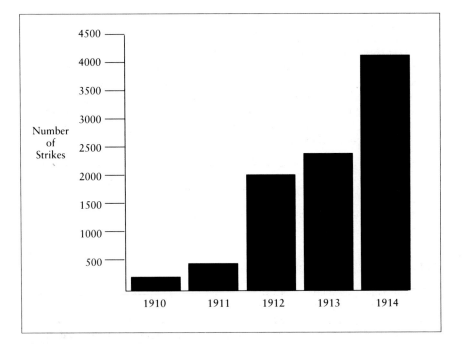

Fig. 4.61 Chart
showing
numbers of
strikes in Russia
1910-July 1914.

resentative. Miass will only become alive electorally when it has an electric
tram to its railway station and cheap polling day excursions to its electoral
centre, or when a Socialist member sends motor cars for the people, or when Miass
becomes a town and has a member for itself and its district. As it is, its population
would almost unanimously vote for the left candidate, the Radical. But it is
outside the contest altogether. What is true of Miass is true also of Kishtim and
hundreds of other villages on the Urals — all these gold-mining centres are
undeveloped Socialist power. They will be brought in later, and will swell the red
tide which must rise in Russia . . .

(c) From the extract, explain why the Russian electoral system was biased
against the rural workers.
(d) From your own knowledge, suggest other shortcomings of the system.
(e) From the extract, suggest reasons for the anticipated transformation of the villages
into part of 'the Red tide'.

**RUSSIAN LABOUR AND
FOREIGN CAPITAL — A
WORKER, QUOTED BY
GRAHAM, COMMENTS ON THE
LENA GOLDFIELD STRIKE —
1913**

One workman began to talk of the strike on the Lena gold-washings; the case was
just the same as theirs — an English company who paid their men just the rate of
wages prevalent in the country district when they started working.
The men formed a union, just as we are forming, and they demanded a higher
wage. 'We are digging out millions weekly,' said they, 'and you are giving us
barely enough to get drunk on.' The English company said, 'We've had
enough of strikes in other concerns; we are not going to have any nonsense here.
This is not England, it is not even Russia, it is Siberia — and what are you? Convicts, sons of convicts, nothing more; dogs, not men. No! You work for what you
get, and do it quickly, or else . . .' Or else they would set the soldiers on them. You
know the story. The factory had a guard of gendarmes to prevent looting and keep
order; the captain of the gendarmes was ready to do the dirty work and teach the

men an example. It happened just as at St Petersburg on Black Sunday . . . The captain cried out to the men that they were forbidden to move beyond a certain gate; the workmen paid no attention, and the consequence was that the captain called on his men to fire. They sent volley after volley into the peaceful crowd of workmen, and four hundred of them fell dead or wounded. That is your English company . . . The news soon found its way to Russia. It appeared in all the papers and even made the 'black hundreders' indignant . . . We held sympathetic strikes. We gained over to our side, we labour Socialists, many who had up to then been only lukewarm.

(f) From the extract, explain why, by 1912, workers felt that little had changed since 1905.
(g) How does this extract show the way that socialist groups gained support in the period 1912-1914?
(h) Why would even the members of the Black Hundreds have disapproved of the Lena incident?

Historians' Opinions

- the major problems facing the Marxists were organisational — they spent most of their energy at this time sorting them out   **CHRISTIAN**
- the liberals were concerned mainly with political and legal issues, the socialists were concerned mainly with economic and social issues — this reflected the different desires of the different classes in 1905 — the middle class wanted legal and political reform, the workers wanted more money and better living and working conditions
- in the short term the 1905 reforms were able to shore up the autocracy — however, the long term failure of agrarian reforms meant a failure to create a conservative agrarian peasantry and a failure to consolidate a political alliance with nobility and capitalists — by 1914 Nicholas II was left with only the support of the army and the bureaucracy

- the most surprising aspect of the 1905 revolution was that the government survived and the Tsar retained his power   **WOLFSON**
- the lessons provided by the 1905 revolution included educating the Bolsheviks about timing, tactics and organisation, showing the liberals the process of parliament and revealing to the Tsar's government that something had to be done to relieve the pressure on the agricultural workers

- historians looking for something good to say about Nicholas habitually point out that he was a good husband. This he was, but family happiness has never yet saved a dynasty   **WESTWOOD**
- the death of Alexander III raised the hopes of the liberals for new, real constitutional reform — Nicholas II's coronation speech in which he professed to reaffirm the autocracy of his father and the failure to grant further power to the zemstva made traditional liberalism seem futile and many turned instead to more radical solutions
- the decline of Populism after the death of Alexander II was due largely to exhaustion, repression, a sense of failure and the attraction of revolutionary movements — so great was the alienation of the people from the state that Marx's theories about the decay of the capitalist state were capable of being

made to seem more attractive to the people — due to its breadth of ideas, Marxism was capable of gaining a very wide base of support

- Witte's policy of encouraging foreign investment and obtaining foreign loans for Russian capitalists and the government to expand industry meant that in the short term the economy expanded and local industry was given an enormous boost — however the level of foreign debt was so high by 1912 that although the economy was growing, it could not cope with the repayment of the foreign debt and a serious balance of trade problem emerged just before World War I
- in real terms the economic and social position of both rural workers and women did not change significantly after 1861
- the introduction of social insurance laws in 1905-12 and growth of trade unions and thus the increased level of strike action meant that the living and working conditions of workers in the cities did improve after 1905 but still not enough to cope with the rapid changes in urbanisation — however the harsh methods used by the government to deal with strikers increased the tension
- Witte's policy of taxing the peasants hard and Stolypin's policy of favouring rich kulak peasants meant that many of the poorer agrarian workers were squeezed off the land and into the rapidly more crowded and uncomfortable life of an urban worker — it seemed as though the Marxist theory of the proletariat was coming true — those who stayed on the land were becoming increasingly frustrated by the favourable treatment of the kulaks

Problems and Issues

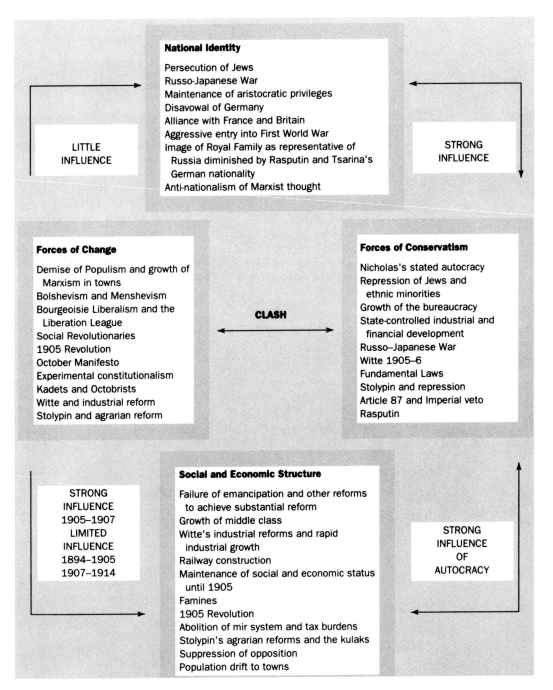

National Identity

Persecution of Jews
Russo-Japanese War
Maintenance of aristocratic privileges
Disavowal of Germany
Alliance with France and Britain
Aggressive entry into First World War
Image of Royal Family as representative of
  Russia diminished by Rasputin and Tsarina's
  German nationality
Anti-nationalism of Marxist thought

LITTLE
INFLUENCE

STRONG
INFLUENCE

Forces of Change

Demise of Populism and growth of
  Marxism in towns
Bolshevism and Menshevism
Bourgeoisie Liberalism and the
  Liberation League
Social Revolutionaries
1905 Revolution
October Manifesto
Experimental constitutionalism
Kadets and Octobrists
Witte and industrial reform
Stolypin and agrarian reform

CLASH

Forces of Conservatism

Nicholas's stated autocracy
Repression of Jews and
  ethnic minorities
Growth of the bureaucracy
State-controlled industrial and
  financial development
Russo–Japanese War
Witte 1905–6
Fundamental Laws
Stolypin and repression
Article 87 and Imperial veto
Rasputin

STRONG
INFLUENCE
1905–1907
LIMITED
INFLUENCE
1894–1905
1907–1914

Social and Economic Structure

Failure of emancipation and other reforms
  to achieve substantial reform
Growth of middle class
Witte's industrial reforms and rapid
  industrial growth
Railway construction
Maintenance of social and economic status
  until 1905
Famines
1905 Revolution
Abolition of mir system and tax burdens
Stolypin's agrarian reforms and the kulaks
Suppression of opposition
Population drift to towns

STRONG
INFLUENCE
OF
AUTOCRACY

Fig. 4.62 Problems and Issues—Nicholas II.

EXERCISE AND SKILLS REVISION

1. Research and write a brief biography (no more than 250 words) of ONE PERSON from each of the following lists: to what extent did this person attempt to support or undermine the Tsarist autocracy?

Witte	Nicholas II	Lenin	Gapon
Stolypin	Alexandra	Trotsky	Martov

Include both primary and secondary sources in your account **and confine yourself to the period 1894-1914.**

2. Write properly structured paragraph responses for each of the following questions:
a. Why were liberals frustrated by Nicholas II's coronation speech?
b. How did Witte control the industrial growth of Russia to 1905?
c. Why was there social and economic distress in the rural areas prior to 1905?
d. Why was there social and economic distress in the urban areas prior to 1905?
e. Why did Russia enter the Russo-Japanese War?
f. What were the effects of the Russo-Japanese War on Russia?
g. What social, economic and constitutional reforms were granted by Nicholas II?
h. Why were these reforms inadequate?
i. What influence did Stolypin have on Russia?
j. Why did the image of the Royal Family suffer in the period 1894-1914?
k. Why did Russia ally itself with France and Britain, not Germany?

3. a. Construct a mind map to explain the foreign policy of Nicholas II.
b. Construct a second mind map to show the development of liberal, Marxist and socialist groups in Russia 1894-1914.

4. Write three part structured responses on the following topics:
(i) Autocracy
a. What were the main reasons for the outbreak of the 1905 Revolution?

(6 marks)

b. How did the Tsarist autocracy survive this threat to its position?

(12 marks)

c. To what extent was Nicholas II in control of his country in 1914?

(12 marks)

(ii) Social and Economic Changes
a. What were the major problems facing Russia's agricultural economy between 1890 and 1905? *(6 marks)*

b. How did Russia attempt to industrialise from 1890 to 1914?

(12 marks)

c. Why was Russia's economy weak, despite apparent growth, by 1914?

(12 marks)

Essay topics
5. a. Write an essay of at least 1000 words in response to the following:
The [October] Manifesto marked the formal end of autocratic government; for the first time the Tsar was forced to share his law-making powers. (Christian)
To what extent do you agree with Christian's statement?
b. Using all the evidence available to you on Russia from 1800 to 1914, write an essay of at least 2000 words in response to the following:
What were the major changes that occurred in Russian society and its economy between 1800 and 1914 and why did they occur?

The following may help you to answer the essay questions:
Consider carefully each of the following key areas:

- Causes, Course and Results of 1905 Revolution
- Radicals and Revolutionaries 1894-1905
- Radicals and Revolutionaries 1905-1914
- Constitutional Reform and The Dumas
- Foreign Policy
- Nationalism and Minorities
- Industrial and Financial Reform
- Agrarian Reform
- Russia on the Eve of the First World War

Consider the following statement made by Nicholas II in his first formal speech as Tsar:

'Let all know that . . . I shall preserve the principle of autocracy as firmly and undeviatingly as did my father.'

Consider the following extract from the *The October Manifesto*, 1905:

We lay upon the Government the execution of Our unchangeable will....
3. To establish as an unbreakable rule that no law shall go into force without its confirmation by the State Duma and that persons elected by the people shall have the opportunity for actual participation in supervising the legality of the acts of authorities appointed to Us.

Consider the following extract from a telegram sent from the Saratov Townsmen to the Holy Synod on 15 November 1905:

The government announced on 17 October that no law will come to pass without the Duma, but on 3 November it issued a decree on proclamations, with the demand that the government implement this in several days. This is anarchy.

Consider the following extract from the *The Fundamental Laws of the Russian Empire*, 1906:

4. The supreme autocratic power is vested in the Tsar of All the Russias. It is God's command that his authority should be obeyed not only through fear but for conscience's sake ...
7. The Tsar exercises the legislative power in conjunction with the Council of the Empire and the Imperial Duma.
8. The initiative in all branches of legislation belongs to the Tsar. Solely on his initiative may the Fundamental Laws of the Empire be subjected to a revision in the Council of the Empire and the Imperial Duma.
9. The Tsar approves of the laws, and without his approval, no law can come into existence.
10. All governmental powers are in their widest extent throughout the Russian Empire vested in the Tsar ...
11. The Tsar appoints and dismisses the President of the Council, the ministers themselves, and the heads of the chief departments of administration, as well as all

other officials where the law does not provide for another method of appointment and dismissal ...

80. No new law shall go into force without the sanction of both the Council of the Empire and the Duma and the ratification of the Tsar.

Consider the following statement made by Trotsky about the Dumas and the Fundamental Laws:

All is given, and nothing is given . . . A constitution is given, but the autocracy remains.

Consider the following extract from Kochan and Abrahams, *The Making of Modern Russia* on the Electoral Laws of 1907:

The Coup of 3 June 1907 illegally narrowed the franchise to secure the elimination of the voice of the poorer peasants and most of the border nationalities from subsequent Dumas.

New Skills and Exercises

Document Studies

You need to address three broad issues when analysing historical sources:
- What information does the source give me?
- How reliable is the source?
- How useful is the source?

ANALYSING HISTORICAL
SOURCES

- **What information does the source give me?**
  - author/producer of source?
  - date of production?
  - place of production?
  - historical context of (background events to) source?
  - for what purpose was the source produced?
  - what was the intended audience of the source — public, private, limited?
  - What views and ideas are expressed in the source?
  - What evidence is offered in support of these views?
  - Are there any other details that the source gives me?

- **How reliable is the source?**
  With the information you gain from answering these questions, you then need to denote how reliable the source is. For this, assess:
  - *objectivity:* even-handed, and fair treatment which considers a range of views in a balanced fashion and attempts to gain the truth by examining the facts, not to prove a particular point of view.
  - *comprehensive coverage:* whether or not a source has covered all of the relevant detail and factual material necessary to provide the background information for forming a balanced view.

– Use the following as a useful guide:
- Do you believe that the source is accurate in the way it relates facts?
- Has the source covered all the necessary facts in its topic area?
- How has the author's purpose affected the objectivity of the source?
- Have the author's opinions interfered with an objective coverage of the facts?
- How do the author's views/ideas affect the objectivity of the source?
- What likely effects have the geographical origins, date of publication and historical context had on the production of the source?
- Will the identity of the author be likely to affect the objectivity of the source?
- Do you trust the source?
- In what particular areas is the source reliable to be used to support an argument or to provide an example?

- **How useful is the source?**
  Every source has some use to the historian, even if only as an example of an unreliable source! Its usefulness can be determined by the following questions:
  – Of what is the source an example?
  – How reliable is the source?
  – For what purposes is the source reliable?
  – Which arguments can the source be used to support or refute?

GENERAL POINTS

- **Degree:** don't be absolute in your opinions. Generally speaking, most sources have some elements of both reliability and usefulness. Therefore you should be subtle in the way that you refer to these issues — sources are generally *more* or *less* reliable or useful for a *particular purpose*.
- **Bias:** a bias is a leaning towards a particular opinion or point of view. Every statement or opinion is biased towards any number of views. *Therefore it is pointless to say simply that a source is biased* — you would have to indicate the extent of the bias and the point of view towards which the source is biased. However, rather than using the word 'biased', it is better to refer to 'reliability', the reasons for which a source may or not be reliable and the way that your use of the source will affect its reliability.
- **Captions and Headings:** you can tell a lot about a source from its caption or heading, including the name of the author/producer, the date and place of production, the title, the purpose or object of the source and its historical context. Make sure to read it closely before going on to analyse the source and/or answer a question on it.

ANSWERING DOCUMENT STUDY QUESTIONS

There are four broad types of questions which you may be given in a document study, which will normally contain three to four sources. *You should allocate your time very strictly according to the total number of marks for each question.* Students too often comment at unnecessary length on the questions of less value and thus jeopardise their overall mark for the document study.

- **Detail Questions**

  These questions require short answers and normally come at the beginning of a document study and there may be up to four of them. Answer the question by giving a small piece of detail which you can find in the source supplied. Be specific in your answer and refer to the source where appropriate. These questions are normally worth one or two marks each for a total of around four marks out of twenty-five.

- **Explanation of a Term Question**

  This type of question normally comes second in a document study and usually you will only be asked one of them. It requires a properly structured paragraph answer. Answer the question by explaining in your own words the meaning or importance of a particular term or factor identified from one of the sources supplied. Use the source as part of the evidence for your answer and thus refer to it directly, but also draw on your own knowledge of historical forces and events. These questions are usually worth five or six marks out of twenty-five.

- **Historiography Questions**

  These questions usually come third in a document study and usually you will only be asked one of them. They require an answer of two to three properly structured paragraphs. Answer the question by explaining in your own words either the *reliability* and/or the *usefulness* to a historian of certain historical sources. To do this successfully, go through each source in order according to the question and identify all the relevant information that you can gain from it, and then decide on its reliability and/or usefulness. Use the source analysis process shown on page 206 when doing this. Refer to the sources directly as well as the information they contain. These questions are usually worth between six to eight marks out of twenty-five.

- **Interpretation Questions**

  These usually come last in a document study and you will probably only be asked one of them. They require an answer of at least three to four properly structured paragraphs. The question will ask you to refer to a certain number of the sources in the document study and your own knowledge in attempting to answer a question on the interpretation of the events surrounding the sources. For example 'why', 'how', 'how important', 'to what extent' and so on. Make sure to refer to all the sources specified by the question; your own knowledge of the events referred to and other sources not contained in the document study.

  In your answer, structure the order of the paragraphs in a way that explains the question logically. Build your references to the sources into these paragraphs, rather than just structuring the answer around the sources themselves. Write a conclusion that summarises your argument in relation to the question. These questions are usually worth between eight to ten marks out of twenty-five.

EXERCISE—DOCUMENT STUDY

Social and Economic Conditions and the Origins of the 1905 Revolution

Instructions:
- Allow 45 minutes for the completion of this task.
- Use the mark allocations as an indication of the length and detail required in each answer.
- Ensure that your answers, where appropriate for the individual questions, include close reference to Sources A, B, C and/or D, and/or your own knowledge.

Source A: Ralph Sawyer, *Modern World History*, 1988

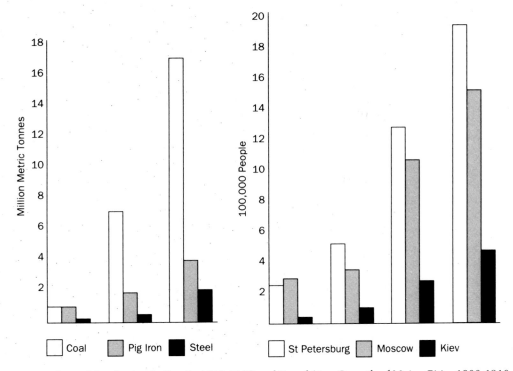

Fig. 4.63 Industrial Production in Russia 1880-1900 and Population Growth of Major Cities 1800-1910.

Source B: Father Georgei Gapon, *The Story of My Life*, 1906

> The normal working day . . . is eleven and a half hours of work, exclusive of meal times. But . . . manufacturers have received permission to work overtime, so that the average day is longer than nominally allowed by law — fourteen or fifteen hours. I often watch crowds of poorly clad and emaciated figures of men and girls returning from the mills. It was a heart-rending sight. The grey faces seemed dead,

or relieved only by eyes blazing with the rage of desperate revolt. Why do they agree to work overtime? They have to do so because they are paid by the piece and the rate is very low. Returning home exhausted and resentful after his long day's labour, the workman sees the sad faces of his wife and hungry children in their squalid corner where they are packed like herrings. What wonder that . . . he carries off some of his small earnings to the public house and spends them on vodka!

Source C: S.M. Kravchinsky, *The Russian Peasantry*, London 1894.

Emancipation has utterly failed to realise the ardent expectations of its advocates and promoters. The great benefit of the measure was purely moral. It has failed to improve the material conditions of the former serfs, who are on the whole worse off than they were before Emancipation. The bulk of the peasantry is in a condition not far removed from starvation . . . The frightful and continually increasing misery of the toiling millions of our country is the most terrible indictment against the Russian government . . . A whole third of our peasantry has become landless rural proletarians in modern Russia.

Source D: Map of Russian Imperial Railways and Events of 1905

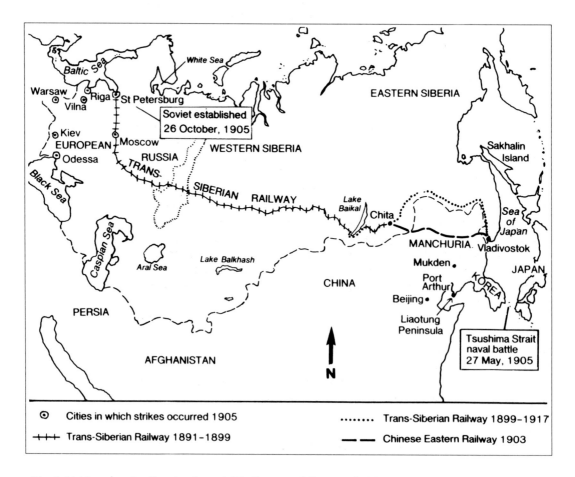

Fig. 4.64 Map showing Russian Imperial Railways and Events of 1905.

1. a. According to Source A, which was the most populous city in Russia in 1800? *(1 mark)*

   b. According to Source A, which was the most populous city in Russia in 1900? *(1 mark)*

   c. According to Source A, of which commodity did Russia produce the most in 1900? *(1 mark)*

   d. According to Source A, of which commodity did Russia produce the least in 1900? *(1 mark)*

2. From your own knowledge, explain why the Emancipation Edict mentioned in Source C failed to relieve social and economic distress to 1905. *(5 marks)*

3. How useful would a historian find both Sources B and C in attempting to understand the nature of social and economic conditions in Russia 1894-1905?
   (You must refer to the origins, motives and audiences of the sources as well their contents.) *(6 Marks)*

4. Using each of the sources and your own knowledge, explain the importance of social and economic conditions in Russia to the outbreak of the 1905 Revolution. *(10 Marks)*

Glossary

Alexandra Feodorovna Tsarina: born Princess Alix of Hesse-Darmstadt (granddaughter of Queen Victoria of Britain), she became Nicholas II's wife and Empress of Russia. By all accounts, she was a narrow-minded and hysterical woman who exercised a considerable influence over her husband, drawing him away from state matters to those of their family. Responsible for transferring her beliefs in Rasputin to Nicholas, her German ancestry also made her very unpopular with her Russian subjects.

Black Hundreds: this was an organisation of conservative forces, created to unite nationalist and anti-semitic feeling. It organised pro-Tsarist propaganda and pogroms and counted Nicholas II among its members. In 1905, it formed the Union of Russian Peoples, perhaps the first true fascist organisation in Europe.

Bolsheviks: under Lenin's leadership this more radical faction of the RSDWP called for a 'dictatorship of the proletariat' to be brought about by an elitist party of professional revolutionaries, and disavowed membership of any constitutional body. Formed as a separate party in 1912, they never achieved widespread popularity except among urban workers, but this and their dynamic leadership cadre eventually saw them emerge victorious in 1917.

Bund: see page 147

Constitutional Democratic Party (Kadets): the Kadets were formed through the amalgamation of the Union of Liberation and the zemstva group. They became the first leading party of the Dumas, attracting much of the liberal vote. Despite their official disapproval of the October Manifesto and the Fundamental Laws, they claimed to participate in the parliamentary system in order to win greater freedoms for the people, mainly in the areas of constitutional and civil liberties reform. After the dissolution of the First Duma, the leaders of the Kadets issued the Vyborg Manifesto, denouncing the Tsar's use of Article 87, and after Stolypin's arrests of many of them for sedition, the Kadets dropped to second party in the Second Duma and then third in the Third and Fourth Dumas. Their voice was loud and leadership positive until and during the Revolution of 1917 but their ability to act was limited, due to the popularity of the socialist groups.

Gapon Father Georgei: see page 158

Goremykin I.L.: see page 166

Kadets: see Constitutional Democrats

kulaks: a wealthy sub-class of peasants created by Stolypin. Kulaks could afford to buy their land from the mir outright, but were resented by the vast majority of poorer peasants who could not afford to do so.

Lenin aka Vladimir Ilyich Ulyanov: Lenin became a revolutionary in 1887 after the execution of his elder brother for his participation in revolutionary activities. Expelled from the Kazan University for revolutionary activities in December 1887, he passed his law exams by studying at home and practised as a lawyer in St Petersburg. In 1895 he was gaoled for 15 months and then exiled for three years in Siberia. Released in 1900 he went to London, Munich and Geneva where he tried to rebuild the RSDWP. He helped to publish a newspaper called *Iskra* (*The Spark*) which was smuggled into Russia and he wrote *What is to be Done?* in 1902 which became the blueprint for the future Bolshevik party and Marxist-Leninism. Subsequently the leader of the Bolshevik faction of the RSWDP from 1905-1907 and then 1912 onwards, he lived abroad until the 1917, when he returned to orchestrate and successfully lead the second revolution of that year, founding the Bolshevik/Communist state.

Liberation League: a specifically bourgeois liberal group formed in 1903 which sought to reconcile the middle class and their anti-revolutionary sentiment. They sought reform through legal means and concentrated on the zemstva for their demands for constitutional and civil liberties reform and attracted the support of members of the gentry, senior ranking military and bourgeoisie. For those liberals for whom this organisation proved to be too radical, a delegation of zemstva members formed a less radical forum for liberal thought, and were even allowed by Plehve to meet, although only in private.

Martov aka Julius Ossipovich Zederbaum: Martov was one of the early leaders of the Marxist movement in the 1880s. His concentration on helping the workers to improve their conditions, rather than explaining to them the principles of Marxist class consciousness, won the Marxists their initial support in the towns. Sent to Siberia for his part in the 1895 St

Petersburg strikes, he returned in 1900, but split with his one-time friend and supporter, Lenin, over the issues of elitism and the *Iskra* board. Martov was a supporter of Economism, a belief that strict Marxism seemed not to be working and that more effort should be spent on working with the people to improve conditions and in supporting the liberal desire for a constitution. He became the leader of the Menshevik faction of the RSDWP.

Mensheviks: this more peaceful faction of the RSDWP wanted a less radical socialist party, were regarded as 'legal Marxists' and wanted to await the evolution of capitalism and a proletariat prior to the incitement to revolution. They were led by Martov, Plekhanov and at first Trotsky, although he later joined with the Bolsheviks. They gradually became a prominent group in the Dumas, but despite some success in manipulating the events of the first revolution of 1917, they proved to be incapable of establishing long term power in Russia.

Octobrist Party: this party of the political middle ground was formed to provide a liberal voice less radical than the Kadets. Officially its approval of the October Manifesto gave it support among the conservative middle classes and by the time of the Third and Fourth Dumas it was the majority party. However, this was largely a result of the gerrymander, and the Octobrists were quickly identified as an impotent group, whose calls for gentle reform were immediately ignored by the Tsar and later by the people, who wanted action.

Plehve Vyacheslav: see page 144.

Rasputin Grigory: the Russian monk, who through his dynamic personality and seeming mystic ability to help with Tsarevich Alexei's haemophilia won his way through to the confidence of the Royal Family, despite reputation for debauchery. This influence, especially during World War I, where it seemed that he was controlling Alexandra the Regent's actions, and his appointment as Chief Procurator of the Holy Synod in 1916 sapped the people's confidence in the Romanovs. Rasputin was assassinated in 1916 by Prince F.F. Yusupov and V.M. Puriskevitch, who were alleged to be former lovers of his.

Russian Social Democratic Workers' Party (RSDWP): founded in 1898 at a secret congress in Minsk the Russian Social Democratic Workers' Party aimed to unite Marxists. However, a dangerous rift soon developed in the party with emergence of 'economism'. In 1899, the party was infiltrated by the police and disbanded. Its failure provoked a bitter dispute among Russian Marxists as to whether size and worker participation or party organisation and policy were the crucial issues. Within five years disagreements over nature of the party led to the division of the RSDWP into two factions, the Bolsheviks and the Mensheviks.

Socialist Revolutionary Party: founded in 1901 by Victor Chernov (1876-1952) and B.V. Savinkov (1879-1925), the Socialist Revolutionaries (SRs) became the largest party of the left in the first 15 years of the century. They attracted those who believed that peasants not industrial workers held the key to precipitating a successful revolution. The SRs had their disagreements about political strategies and lacked the tight discipline of the Social Democrats but were particularly feared by authorities for their terrorist activities. Despite their boycott of the Duma elections, their sympathisers, the 'Labourists', did stand and became the second most popular party in the first Duma and then the most popular in the Second Duma. Despite a significant loss of seats in the right-wing gerrymandered Third and Fourth Dumas, through their new leader, Karensky, the SRs remained a powerful influence until the Bolshevik revolution in 1917.

St Petersburg Council (Soviet) of Workers: this Workers Council, formed in 1905 to co-ordinate revolutionary activity among the proletariat, became the means of worker protest and attracted delegates from all the socialist parties and groups. Despite its initial success in attracting support from the people and running local governmental affairs, and despite the valiant but only moderately successful efforts of Trotsky as an orator and popular leader, the Soviet proved unable to match the troops sent by Witte to close it down in November 1905. The Soviet provided a rude shock for leaders such as Lenin, who came to realise that revolution could be a spontaneous action of the people and that to be successful it needed more than just a well organised party elite — it also needed the support of workers bodies such as the Soviet.

Stolypin Peter: prime minister from 1906-1911, Stolypin understood quite well the problems facing Russia, but was nonetheless a firm supporter of Tsarist autocracy. His ruthless application of the hangman's noose to crush revolutionary uprisings and conspiracies won it the soubriquet of 'Stolypin's necklace'. His program of economic reform included agrarian change, with the creation of the kulak class, the sale of Crown and State land for peasant purchase and the encouragement of migration to Siberia. Education, health insurance and finacial reform also ensued, but his assassination in 1911 by a socialist revolutionary with police contacts was largely the result of his alienation from all the political groups and the Royal Family.

Trotsky Leon: see page 148.

Trudoviki (Labourists): see page 166.

Union of Unions: the third and most radical of the liberal groups founded in the first five years of the twentieth century, this body was formed by professionals in 1905 to coordinate their activities during the revolution, but disspiated due to the formation of the Kadets.

Witte Sergei: never particularly liked by Nicholas II, nonetheless, Witte was perhaps the most able of all the Tsar's ministers. He came from German ancestors and was the son of an official. After university, he joined a railway company and came to the attention of Alexander III by warning him that the Imperial train's timetables were too breakneck in speed — a derailment in 1888 where Alexander emerged shocked but unhurt seemed to prove Witte's worth. Appointed Minister of Transport in 1892 and then Minister of Finance in the same year, Witte used the policies of expansionist Bunge — high taxation on the peasantry, large-scale railway construction, attraction of foreign capital, protectionist tariffs and entering the rouble onto the gold standard. Dismissed by the untrusting Nicholas in 1903, he was appointed Prime Minister from 1905-6 as a recognition of his ability to deal with the crisis. However, he was dismissed as soon as he had regained control for the Tsar. His great legacy for Russia was its modernisation, although living standards were kept low to preserve capital for further expansion.

Zionism: the political movement formed internationally in the 1890s with the express purpose of returning the Jewish people to a Jewish homeland in Palestine.

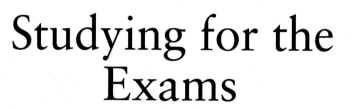

Studying for the Exams

New Skill

History Exam Techniques

Here are a few suggestions on how to approach studying and writing answers for your History Exams.

DOCUMENT QUESTIONS

You will be given a series of documents you have not seen before and asked a series of questions on them. It is not really possible for you to study for these particular documents, but prepare by learning all the information on the topic the document study will be based on. In this way, you will be able to place the documents in their contexts. But remember the following points about how to answer the document questions in the exam:

1. What are the instructions? What form do your answers have to take?
2. Make sure to use *full sentences* where they are required — note that for Question 1, short answers will do.
3. Make sure to support your answers by including references to the documents which support your answers. Accurate referencing will be the best evidence that you can offer for your ideas and will probably mean better marks too.
4. Where a question requires you to provide an answer based on the documents and your own knowledge, be sure to refer to information and sources from both the documents provided *and* your own knowledge.
5. Pay attention to the mark allocation and allocate your time accordingly.

ESSAY QUESTIONS AND THREE PART STRUCTURED RESPONSE QUESTIONS

1. Remember, when you are writing your responses in the exam, you are *answering a question*. You are not just writing a story about a piece of history, but you are showing how the evidence and facts relate to your answer to the question. If you are vague in your answer, you will lose marks.

2. The first thing to do is draw up a set of notes covering all the topics for essays you have to be able to write. If you have been efficient, you will already have done this when you made your notes whilst studying the topics.

3. Once you have made your notes and learnt them, it is time to start practising your essay writing. If you are lucky, you will have a list of the possible essay questions for the exam. If not, then you will have to think very carefully about each topic and work out what the main ideas are and the sorts of questions that may be asked about them. If you are not sure, ask your teacher, who may not tell you what the questions will be, but may give you a few hints! Wherever possible, use past papers as a guide.

4. For each topic, write out a plan for the way that you are going to write the essay. Remember to plan them around the structure of Introduction, Body and Conclusion.

5. Write out a full version for the first essay topic with your plan in front of you. When you have finished it, take out a red pen and mark it. Fix up any corrections and rewrite it. Do the same for each essay topic.

6. When you are happy with each essay, show it to a friend or family member and see what they have to say about it. If you have time, show it to your teacher.

7. When you study from these essays, pay more attention to the order in which you discuss points than the precise words you use. Do not simply learn essays by heart—you may end up with a rigid approach making it difficult to answer unusually worded questions. You could lose many marks for answering with a prepared response.

Both essays and structured response questions require longer answers with a particular structure. Essays should have the following parts:

ESSAYS

- **Introduction:** answer the question, outline the main points in support of your argument and provide definitions of any complex terms.
- **Body:** a series of properly structured paragraphs, each with a key sentence, body and conclusion relating the paragraph back to your answer to the question. The body provides the evidence for your answer and each paragraph should be confined to discussing *one* major point. The order of the paragraphs in the body should follow the order of the points you made in the introduction.
- **Conclusion:** summarise your argument and re-answer the question.

Three Part Structured Responses should have the following parts; each part is marked independently:

THREE PART STRUCTURED RESPONSES

- **Part A:** provide about five pieces of information either in paragraph or list form in answer to a narrative question (eg What?). This part is worth six marks.
- **Part B:** provide a short essay response to a methodology question (eg How?, In what way?). Write a body of at least three to four properly structured paragraphs, each paragraph dealing with one major point and a con-

clusion in which you summarise your argument. This part is worth twelve marks.

- **Part C:** provide a short essay response to an interpretative question (eg Why?, To what extent?). Write a body of at least three to four properly structured paragraphs, with each paragraph dealing with one major point and a conclusion in which you summarise your argument. This part is worth twelve marks.

When you write either an Essay or a Structured Response, always allow about five minutes to think about the question and to plan your response before you start writing.

GENERAL HINTS

1. Don't leave it all until the last night! If you do that, you will have almost no chance of learning everything and your mark will reflect this.
2. Don't leave it all until the last moment: allow yourself at least 4 weeks to start your intensive exam study. Make sure that you allow time every night during this period before the exam to do some study. And don't be surprised when you find that it is going to take a lot longer to get everything done than you expected.
3. When you get into the exam, **make sure to read the instructions first!** Plan how much time you will need to spend on each part or section of the exam and stick to those time limits.
4. If you finish before time is up, go back over your work and check it for accuracy and spelling.
5. Make sure that you get a good night's sleep before the exam—assuming you have studied properly in the days and weeks beforehand!
6. Remember that your performance in an exam reflects how well you have prepared for it. The most important keys to exam success are:

LEARN THE FACTS

LEARN YOUR SOURCES

KNOW THE EXAM FORMAT

PRACTISE RESPONSES

Exercises—Preparing for Your Exam

Learning the facts

Use the following list of points as a basis for your study notes on Russia 1800-1914. When have prepared your notes, you can use this list to test your knowledge.

1. Russia in 1800
   - Geography
   - Social System and Serfism
   - Economic Structure
   - Political System and Institutions
   - Role of Church

2. Alexander I
   - Limited Reforms to 1812
   - Influence of Speransky and Golitsyn
   - Interest in Constitutionalism
   - Threat of Napoleon
   - Holy Alliance and Metternich
   - Arakcheyev and Repression

3. Nicholas I
   - Decembrist Revolt
   - Nicholas System and Growth of Bureaucracy
   - Orthodoxy, Autocracy and Nationality
   - Peasants — Revolts and Repression
   - Superfluous Men and Intellectual Suppression
   - Pan-Slavism and Westernisation
   - Limited Economic Reform
   - Middle Class
   - Crimean War

4. Alexander II
   - Reasons for Reform
   - Emancipation
   - Financial and Tax Reform
   - Zemstva and Judicial Reform
   - Education, Military and Other Reform
   - Reactionary Policies 1866-1881
   - Radicals and Revolutionaries
   - Early Industrialisation and Urbanisation
   - Territorial Expansion and Poland

5. Alexander III
   - Character and Beliefs
   - Influence of Pobodonostsev
   - Russification
   - Treatment of Minorities
   - Return to Orthodoxy
   - Financial Reform
   - Witte and Industrialisation
   - Urbanisation

6. Nicholas II and the 1905 Revolution
- Character and Beliefs of Nicholas II
- Autocracy Affirmed
- Witte and Industrialisation
- Marxism in the Towns
- Liberal Resurgence
- Social Revolutionaries
- Famine and Agricultural Crisis
- Social and Industrial Unrest
- Russo-Japanese War
- Causes of the Revolution
- Events of 1905
- Reasons for the Failure of the Revolution
- October Manifesto

7. Nicholas II 1905-1914
- October Manifesto and Fundamental Laws
- The Dumas
- Kadets and Octobrists
- Trudoviki
- Bolsheviks and Mensheviks
- Stolypin —Repression and Reform
- Industry and Debt
- Renewed Unrest
- Foreign Policy and World War I
- Rasputin and the Royal Family

Remember that once you have learnt your facts, it is then appropriate to consider how they fit into the problems and issues studied. The questions you will receive will be designed to look at the facts *as they are relevant to the problems and issues*. It is useful to construct a series of mind maps, looking at developments within the problems and issues over the whole period. The mind maps in Chapters 2, 3 and 4 will prove helpful for this. Look at them in terms of the four broader themes of:

NATIONAL IDENTITY

FORCES OF CHANGE

FORCES OF
CONSERVATISM

SOCIAL AND
ECONOMIC
STRUCTURE

Learning your sources

The next step is to prepare a list of sources to support the facts you have learnt. This is vital for exam success because responses that use, acknowledge and discuss sources in support of an argument are rewarded more favourably than those that do not. Prepare a list of both primary (written at the time of the event) and secondary (written after the time of the event) sources and you will need sources that:

- refer to specific events
- refer to the general situation in Russia during the seven specific time periods shown above
- refer to the change or lack of change in historical trends in Russia over the whole period 1800-1914

These sources may be direct quotes from the text of authors, or a paraphrase of the author's meaning into your own words.

Build these quotes or sources into your notes and memorise them. Keep them to about two to three lines long—this will make the job of learning them easier. Remember, you are supposed to be displaying knowledge of sources and using them to support your arguments, not rewriting great slabs of other books.

How many quotes you should learn depends on your ability to memorise them! However, try to include at least one source for each paragraph of the body in an essay or in parts b and c of a three part structured response.

Practice Exam Questions

Since the HSC Option for Russia in the Nineteenth Century is examined with a three part structured response, the following questions are all set out in this way. However, if you wish to practice normal essays, then any of the parts b or c are suitable.

(a) What major social problems were created as a result of the Industrial Revolution?
(6 marks)
(b) What attempts were made by Russian governments up to 1914 to improve the conditions of the working classes? *(12 marks)*
(c) How far were the improvements in Russian workers' conditions the result of trade unions gaining rights and benefits for their members? *(12 marks)*

(a) Briefly explain the political repression that existed in Russia under Nicholas I and Alexander II. *(6 marks)*
(b) What were the reforms introduced by Alexander II? *(12 marks)*
(c) How effective were they in reducing discontent in the period up to 1905? *(12 marks)*

(a) What do you understand by the term "liberalism" as used in relation to Russia in the nineteenth century? *(6 marks)*
(b) What forces acted against liberalism in Russia in the nineteenth century? *(12 marks)*

(c) To what extent was liberalism successful in Russia by the end of the nineteenth century? *(12 marks)*

(a) Briefly describe Russian society following the emancipation of the serfs. *(6 marks)*

(b) What impact did rapid industrialisation have on Russian society by 1905? *(12 marks)*

(c) How effective were the measures adopted after 1905 in preserving the Tsarist govenment? *(12 marks)*

(a) What were some of the main reasons for the development of revolutionary political movements in nineteenth century Russia? *(6 marks)*

(b) What were the main aims of revolutionaries? Discuss *one* particular revolutionary movement *only*. *(12 marks)*

(c) Why were revolutionary movements generally unsuccessful in Russia in the period 1800-1900? *(12 marks)*

(a) Describe the main features of Russia's economy in the late nineteenth century. *(6 marks)*

(b) What did the Russian government consider to be the costs and benefits of industrialisation? *(12 marks)*

(c) How significant was industrial growth in undermining support for the government in the period up to 1905? *(12 marks)*

(a) Outline the ways in which the Russian governments used political repression during the period from 1815 to 1914. *(6 marks)*

(b) How did individuals or groups resist this repression? *(12 marks)*

(c) To what extent did governments become less repressive by 1914? *(12 marks)*

(a) What social and economic problems existed in Russia in the nineteenth century? *(6 marks)*

(b) How did Tsar Alexander II attempt to solve these problems? *(12 marks)*

(c) Why did revolutionary groups develop in Russia, despite the reforms which were made? *(12 marks)*

(a) What were the main features of economic development between 1848 and 1871? *(6 marks)*

(b) In what ways did economic development affect political change in the second half of the nineteenth century? *(12 marks)*

(c) How important was industrialisation as a force of change in the nineteenth century? *(12 marks)*

(a) What were the main features of political reform prior to the late 1860s? *(6 marks)*

(b) In what ways did economic developments affect political reform in the second half of the nineteenth century? *(12 marks)*

(c) How important was industrialisation as a force of political and social change in the nineteenth century? *(12 marks)*

(a) What were the major changes introduced by the Emancipation Edicts of the 1860s? *(6 marks)*

(b) How far did the changes introduced into Russia in the second half of the nineteenth century produce real social, economic and political change? *(12 marks)*

(c) Why was there a revolution in Russia in 1905? *(12 marks)*